Ernst Logar (ed.)

REFLECTING OIL

DE GRUYTER

—

Contents

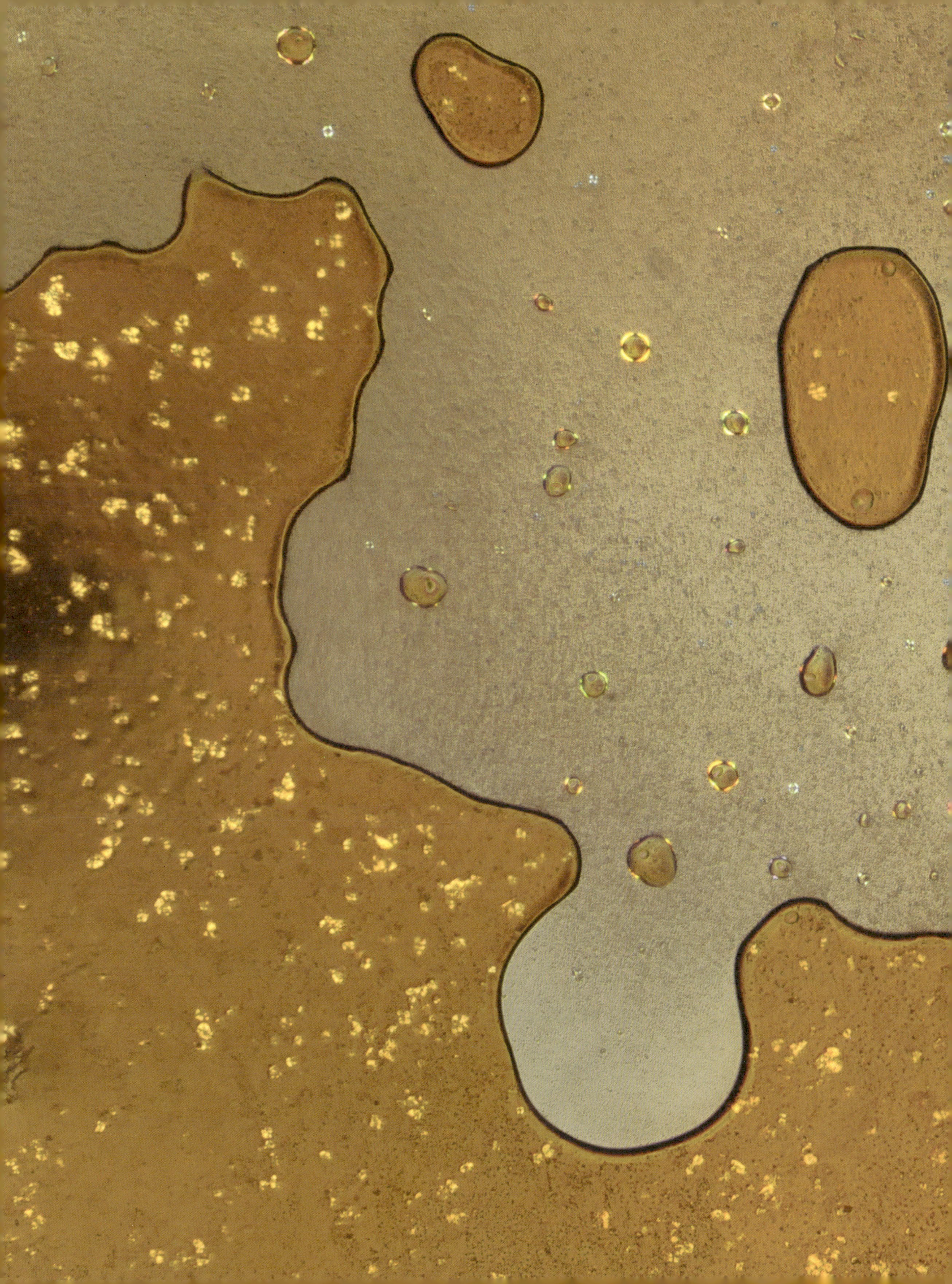

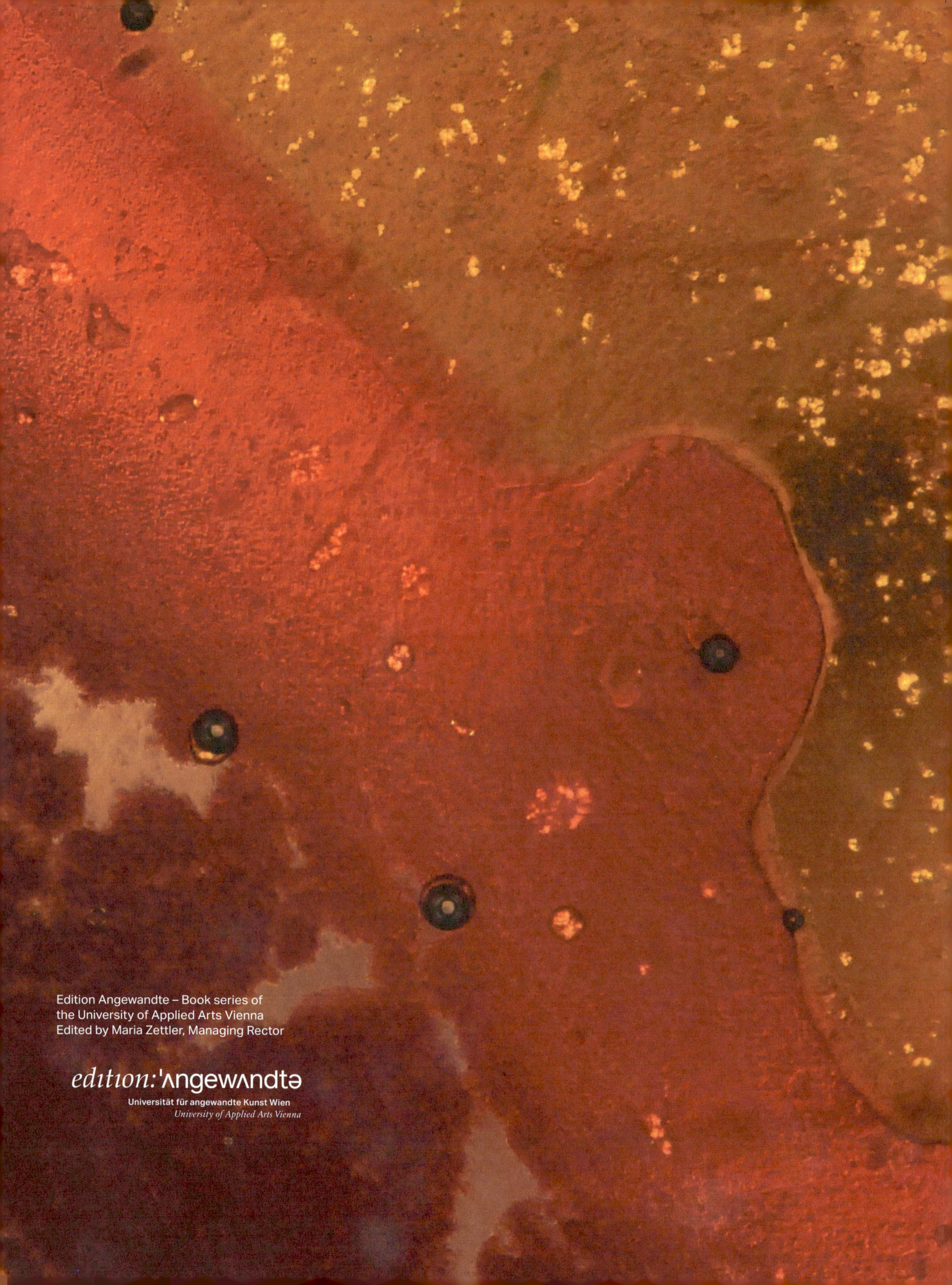

Edition Angewandte – Book series of
the University of Applied Arts Vienna
Edited by Maria Zettler, Managing Rector

edition:'ʌngewʌndtə
Universität für angewandte Kunst Wien
University of Applied Arts Vienna

Editorial

Ernst Logar

artistic research
crude oil
energy transition

As our contemporary society slowly shifts away from fossil fuels as an energy source, there is still an urgent need to reduce CO2 emissions, which are contributing to global warming and climate change. In order to better achieve the transition towards sustainable energy sources, it is essential to understand how energy sources shape a society and its culture. Even though modern life is primarily built upon an omnipresent culture of oil (petroculture) and the resource's wide range of applications and uses, there is very little public knowledge or awareness about it.

The interdisciplinary artistic research project *Reflecting Oil: Arts-Based Research on Oil Transitionings* (2019–2024) sheds light on this important topic and offers an innovative and multiperspectival reflection on crude oil. It approaches the substance from a holistic perspective, giving rise to new representations and narratives about oil that should bring about a radical change in public perception and new visions of a sustainable future without oil.

To give readers an overview of the book's content right from the start, I would like to briefly guide you through the various chapters. This publication captures the artistic research project in all its facets, organized into four chapters that correspond with the structure of the project and its research formats and methodologies.

After the preface by Alexander Damianisch and his introduction to the concept of "cognitive resonance," Chapter 1 consists of introductory statements by the three cooperation partners. My essay as the project leader outlines the basic ideas of the research process; Holger Ott, as our domestic cooperation partner (Department Geoenergy, Montanuniversität Leoben, Austria[1]), presents the project from the perspective of a petroleum engineer; and the text by Imre Szeman, our international research partner (Petrocultures Research Group, University of Alberta, Canada), looks at petroculture and crude oil against the backdrop of the term "experiment."

The second chapter features an exemplary selection of artistic crude oil experiments based on innovative approaches to the perception of the substance, whose findings provide new knowledge and creative incentives for future investigations.

The *Reflecting Oil Colloquium*, held at the University of Applied Arts Vienna from June 9 to 12, 2022, is documented in Chapter 3: the book structure follows the workshop formats of the three working groups. Working group 1 takes an experimental approach to crude oil in the chemistry laboratory; group 2 deals with the in/visibility of the substance on the levels of image and text; group 3, in turn, speculates about a potential transformation process towards the post-fossil age in the form of a graphic novel. The sequence of the colloquium contributions is aligned with their thematic focus, spanning from the geological formation of crude oil to its actual visibility and geopolitical impacts.

The fourth and final chapter is dedicated to my artistic works inspired by the experiences and knowledge obtained in the overall interdisciplinary research process, which were presented as part of the exhibition *Reflecting Oil—Petroculture in Transformation* at the Angewandte Interdisciplinary Lab (AIL) from October 2 to November 15, 2024. My works and the contributions by participants of the *Reflecting Oil Colloquium* are documented, reflected upon, and contextualized by art historian Raphaelle Occhietti.

This book features a broad spectrum of perspectives on and perceptions of crude oil, which overlap, intersect, and refer to one another in their contents. To reveal these connections, a system of keywords has been integrated into the layout, exhibiting the interdisciplinary and collaborative nature of the research process and the true complexity of this subject.

Hoping that this project and publication can contribute to a much needed step in the transition towards a sustainable future, I wish you an inspiring and insightful read.

1 In the book, Montanuniversität Leoben is referred to as the University of Leoben. In 2024, the Department Petroleum Engineering was renamed the Department Geoenergy.

Preface

Alexander Damianisch

cognitive resonance
artistic research
crude oil
alchemy

First let me introduce the concept of cognitive resonance,[1] it is about understanding that emerges when incompatibilities are reconciled, and my belief is, that artistic research is an important key practice for its fruition—and the *Reflecting Oil* project is an outstanding example.

Indeed, in our imaginations, it was once possible to turn water into wine and iron into gold, and to even turn research into art and art into research, with the welcome fact that the latter metamorphosis actually works. It is always interesting to ask how such a material and conceptual transformation manifests concretely, and what remains, with a dash of fantasy, of the so-called trans-substantive hope? One example is Ernst Logar's artistic research, which epitomizes such a capacity for change, its deployment and critique. He and his team have succeeded by emphatically directing our attention to a very specific and extremely bitter substance: crude oil.

Artistic research is framed here as a modern variant of alchemy, and new materialism also comes into play, whereby art is tuned, as it were, as a vessel for the intangible and as an instrument for the elusive with no small responsibility and potential. In the history of science and epistemology, both are original and valid, and both resonate vibrantly in *Reflecting Oil*. It is wonderful that Ernst Logar and his team come quite close to us in their joint research—and this is precisely where the special appeal of the project lies. It is their approach to the found material, but also how they handle the very artistic results. The project space is at once a studio and a laboratory, working on reality, models, and ideas, alternative perspectives and idiosyncrasies. These are results unfolding within each individual dedicated to this and similar research. Once more, it is the viewers who are transformed; in this sense, too, this research comes very close, confronting us with its relevance: the project demonstrates that thinking oil can be turned into gold is a short-sighted misconception. When some believed this to be the case, things went wrong—especially when organic material once alive simply goes up in smoke, burns away. Many a dream shattered in its fulfillment. This is what we are currently experiencing, sinking deeper and deeper into the mess; what remains is evidence of failure and our fundamental responsibility.

"The materiality of oil as a substance," reads the project description, "is the basis of our research project *Reflecting Oil*," which investigates "the role of oil in geopolitical conflicts, as a cause of environmental pollution, and also as a socio-cultural object of desire," making it visible in a new way. This formulation alone encapsulates the tangents between the dirty, the raw, and the dangers of what is valuable to us. Should we speak of the danger of valuable things or of the value of danger, or even both? How was it again with water and wine, iron and gold? How can it be continued with oil...?

This book is a new attempt to explore such relationships with the means of art and to unearth perspectives that have gone undiscovered until now. Once again, art transforms the everyday—iron, water, stone, or in this case, oil—and helps us to see the unexpected in a way that no one has ever seen before, scrutinizing our perception.

Sustainability entails envisioning and cultivating what is essential, and then being prepared to give up what once seemed possible but was not really essential. *Reflecting Oil* teaches us anew that we are well advised to not only feel but also perceive and reflect with all our senses. To allow the connections to come close, to grasp them in a cognitively resonant way. It is not enough to simply say "hindsight is always wiser." It is crucial to recognize that being wise also means, as Ernst Logar and his team do, to enthusiastically and ingeniously wrest new aspects from the dirt that previously went unrecognized. Perhaps this also gives rise to something like hope—we will read about it. Because, as we all know, hope dies last... Let's embrace our responsibility, and this research is an excellent source of inspiration.

In short: let's start taking our cognitive resonance seriously.

1 Cognitive resonance refers to the dynamic process of the continuously evolving combination of perception, understanding, reflection, and creation in a constant state of critical openness and transformation towards an interest (object) as well as the interest (subject) itself.

—01

—01/01

Shattering the Oil Mirror: A Holistic Understanding of Crude Oil

Ernst Logar

artistic research
science
crude oil
senses
experiments
holistic understanding
Invisible Oil
petro-subjectivity
petrocultures
energy transition

Standing in a dark room, you look into a wood-framed Plexiglas box filled to the brim with crude oil, its odor pervades the entire room. To the quiet hum of a running pump, you gradually make out the reflection of your own face, your own identity, peering back through the circulating oil. The installation *Reflecting Oil* was first presented at the Peacock Visual Arts Centre in Aberdeen, Scotland, in 2008. For me, it encapsulates our petroleum-driven civilization in a haunting way, and this work has had significant bearing on my artistic practice in recent years.

As of late, I have been particularly interested in the term "petro-subjectivity," which was coined by the American artist Brett Bloom, who describes it as follows: "Petro-subjectivity is something that each of us experiences constantly. It is a sense of self and the world that shapes who we are and how we think. It stems in part from the fact that the use of oil is present in everything we do. It has shaped the concepts that govern our thinking. Our use of language and the basic concepts that structure our existence are breathed through the logic of oil relationships and form the metaphoric universe we bathe ourselves in when we speak to one another about who we are, what we do and what the world around us consists of."[1]

In Titusville, Pennsylvania, in 1859, Edwin L. Drake was the first entrepreneur to commercially extract crude oil, which officially marked the beginning of oil production. At that time, crude oil, in its refined form as petroleum, was initially used to

Invisible Oil exhibition view
Peacock Visual Arts Centre, 2008

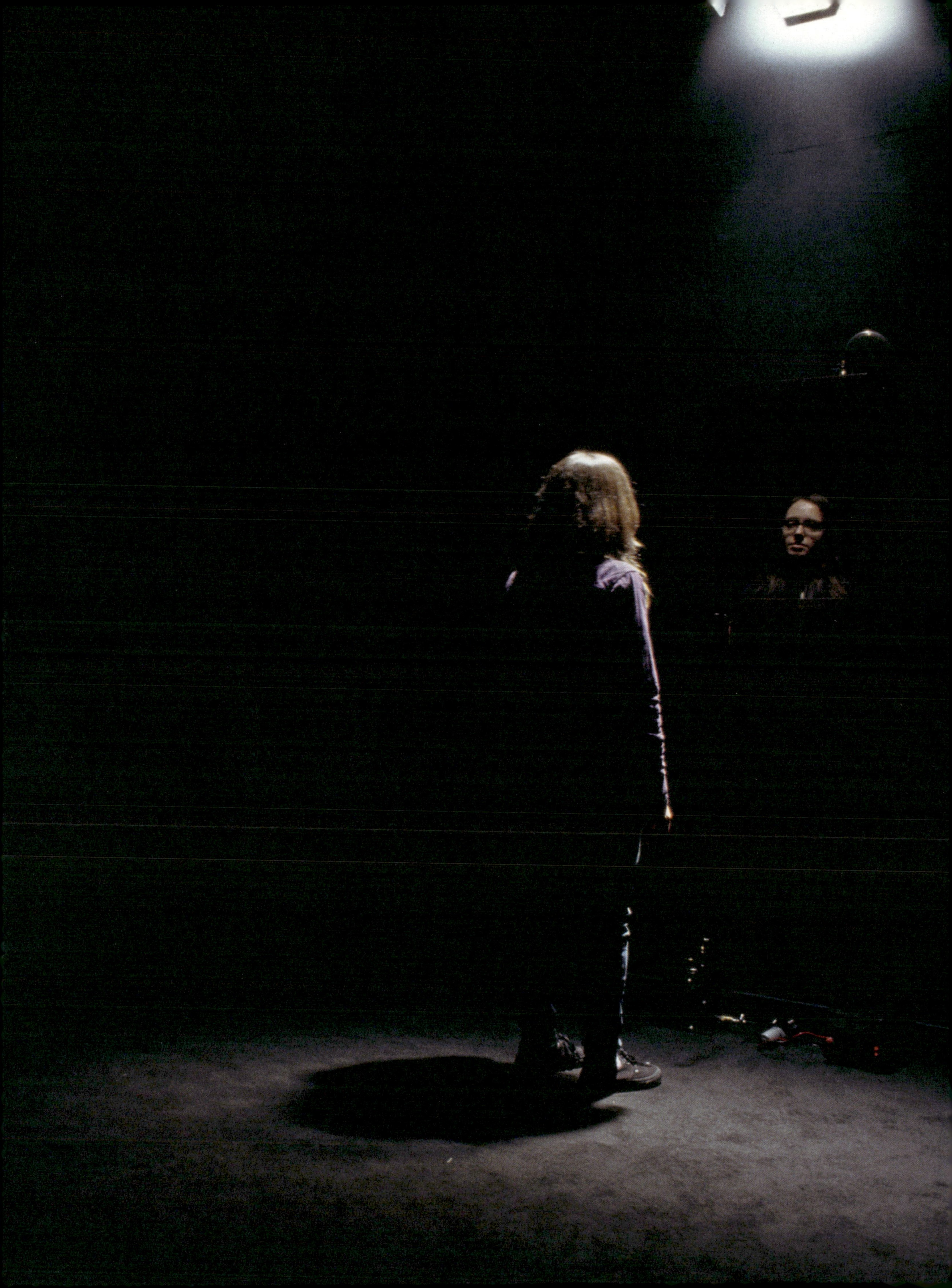

fuel lamps and replaced the widely available whale oil. It was not until the invention of the internal combustion engine and the serial production of automobiles at the end of the nineteenth century that the extraction of crude oil began on a massive scale. The two world wars of the twentieth century, in which oil played a key role on the battlefield, contributed to the rapid development of oil production and crude oil refining. The 1950s ushered in the Great Acceleration: crude oil served as a fuel for the unbounded mobility of people and goods and, thanks to advances in petrochemicals, as a primary substance for shaping the material world, thus paving the way towards our ubiquitous petrocultures.

In addition to its role as an energy source, crude oil today is a highly versatile, transformable substance, which, in its processed form, governs many spheres of our everyday world, from food production, medical care, and housing to the globally networked work world—as such, it permeates our present at all levels and in very complex ways.

The idea for *Reflecting Oil* came to me on a research trip for the exhibition project *Invisible Oil* in Aberdeen. Fish processing, shipbuilding, and the textile industry were once the most important economic factors for the city, long before it experienced an unexpected oil boom at the end of the 1960s, which earned Aberdeen the title "Oil Capital of Europe." However, with the progressive decline of the North Sea oil reserves, the city's self-designation shifted to become the "Energy Capital of Europe" in 2005.

The intensive exploration of Aberdeen and its petroleum industry marked a turning point in my artistic career. It drew my attention to the cultural and economic significance of oil, a resource that has had a momentous impact on modern society. As Brotherstone and Manson noted in 2007: "The product serves its purpose largely unseen, finding its way into internal combustion engines, or the energy market more generally, with little perceived connection to its origins or the process that developed it. […] Nor has cultural production been such as to draw public consciousness towards the industry, its ways of working, and its broader significance."[2]

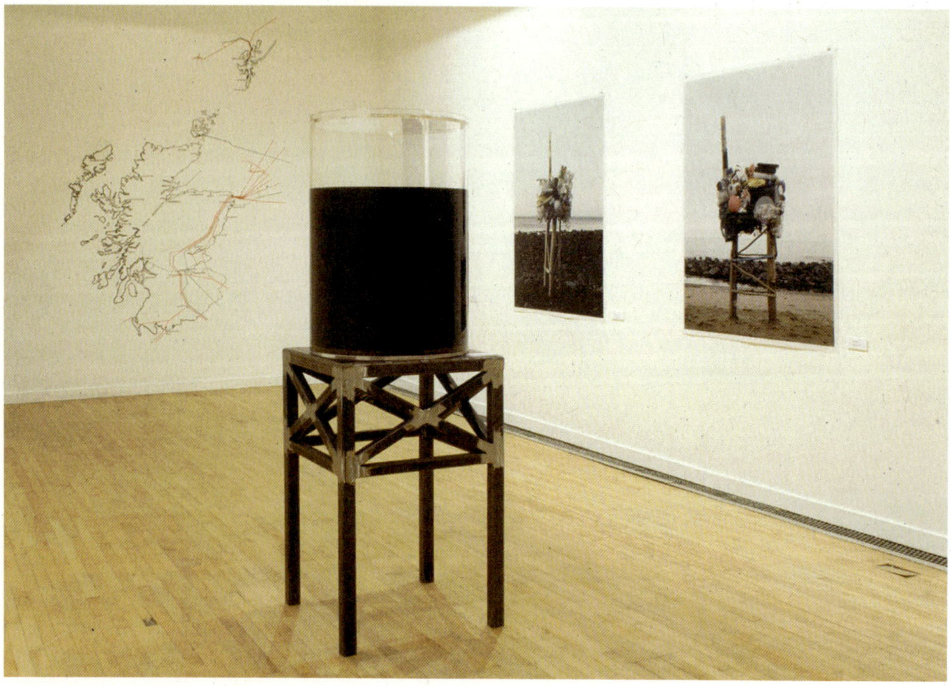

Invisible Oil exhibition view
Peacock Visual Arts Centre, 2008

For most people, oil is an abstract concept that is primarily perceived in its monetary representation as US$ per barrel. Unlike tangible objects, substances such as crude oil are often relegated to a subordinate role in everyday culture. This is due to the particular physical and chemical properties of crude oil, but also to the prevailing visual bias in contemporary society. An automobile, for example, has a high cultural value, while the fuel that powers it is rarely seen as an independent element.

This distorted awareness of crude oil is the subject of my sculptural work *158.987294928 Litres*. It conveys a physical and sensual manifestation of a barrel of crude oil: sensual as the viewer is confronted with the specific smell of crude oil that pervades the gallery space from the open cap of the transparent oil barrel. Visual perception is supplemented on an olfactory level.

Oil is an omnipresent substance that we rarely encounter tangibly with our senses, yet it has profound repercussions on our existence. This ambivalent relationship obscures our actions and gives rise to detrimental effects for our planet and livelihood, as Ross Barrett and Daniel Worden, among others, have pointed out: "Oil culture, we argue, has helped to establish oil as a deeply entrenched way of life in North America and Europe by tying petroleum use to fundamental sociopolitical assumptions and aspirations, inventing and promoting new forms of social practice premised on cheap energy, refiguring petroconsumption as a self-evidently natural and unassailable category of modern existence, and forestalling critical reconsiderations of oil's social and ecological cost."[3]

Our belief in the apparent infinite availability of oil was shaken, at the latest, by the energy crisis in the wake of the Ukraine war in 2022. Since then, the global dependence on fossil fuels and the associated risks have been the subject of heated public debate. Among the grave consequences of our sustained use of fossil fuels and upholding the status quo are human-made global warming, the massive decimation of biodiversity, and the escalation of political tensions and armed conflicts. The solution to this dilemma calls for a holistic understanding of our world—in its complexity, vulnerability, and natural limitations. Scientific knowledge production forms the basis of our modern civilization. However, as a result of its mechanistic approach, science has paid too little attention to the complex networks of life and their interrelationships. The consequences of this one-dimensional perspective on the interwoven aspects and entangled processes of life are now clearly evident on a global scale.

Just a few centuries ago, science was still considered part of the arts, but as it evolved it continuously specialized and abandoned a holistic perception of the world, as Fritjof Capra explains: "Galileo's strategy of directing the scientist's attention to the quantifiable properties of matter proved extremely successful in physics, but it also exacted a heavy toll. During the centuries after Galileo, the focus on quantities was extended from the study of matter to all natural and social phenomena within the framework of the mechanistic worldview of Cartesian-Newtonian science. By excluding colors, sound, taste, touch, and smell—let alone more complex qualities, such as beauty, health, or ethical sensibility—the emphasis on quantification prevented scientists for several centuries from understanding many essential properties of life."[4]

"As such, scientific work is governed by strict methodological rules, yielding a conceptually categorizable type of knowledge: [...] academics are supposed to view their subject matter from an objective distance. Rather than grasping an issue, academics shed light on it. Rather than taking a stand, they have a point of view. The use of such visual metaphors for the pursuit of knowledge discourages an active involvement with the subject matter and promotes a science-based model of detached observation."[5]

Art, by contrast, attempts to grasp the world with all the senses, to fathom it with artistic means, and to reveal new perspectives while doing so. Artistic research is not only based on sensory perception but also a critical process of reflecting on what has been perceived, supported by frameworks of conceptual order. In this way, it strives for a holistic understanding of the world in all its complexity and diversity.

In 1969, German artist Hans Haacke already pointed to a broader perspective in the context of real-time systems with his work *Circulation*, an approach that Fritjof Capra sums up in *The Systems View of Life: A Unifying Vision*: "The first, and most general, characteristic of systems thinking is the shift of perspective from parts to the whole. Living systems are integrated wholes whose properties cannot be reduced to those of smaller parts."[6] Following this path, artistic research can lead to a new understanding of the world and life, open up unexpected perspectives, and generate valuable knowledge for society.

The ambition of the project *Reflecting Oil: Arts-Based Research on Oil Transitionings*[7] was to take a holistic view of crude oil in order to understand the substance in all of its facets. The University of Applied Arts Vienna (Department of Site-Specific Art) served as a research center in cooperation with partners from the University of Leoben, Department Geoenergy (DGE, formerly Department Petroleum Engineering), Austria, and the Petrocultures Research Group at the University of Alberta, Canada. The project involved conducting interdisciplinary workshops and crude oil experiments.

Drawing on an intertwined collaboration between art and science, such interdisciplinary investigations into crude oil as the basis of our petromodernity can be vital for the necessary shift towards sustainable energy cultures. A more comprehensive understanding and awareness of how oil and fossil fuels shape our lives can stimulate the necessary cultural, social, and technological transformations towards a sustainable and holistic future, as the Petrocultures Research Group notes: "To image a society after oil means first understanding what oil is to us—how it shapes current desire, identity, and practice, comfort and pain, consumption and penury."[8]

Reflections on crude oil in the petroleum sciences and humanities typically take place without direct physical experience of the substance. This lack of contact is logical in view of its specific properties (viscosity, lubricity, unusual odor, toxicity, etc.), but the question arises as to why this connection to the material properties and its sensual qualities is not explicitly sought after in the aforementioned sciences.

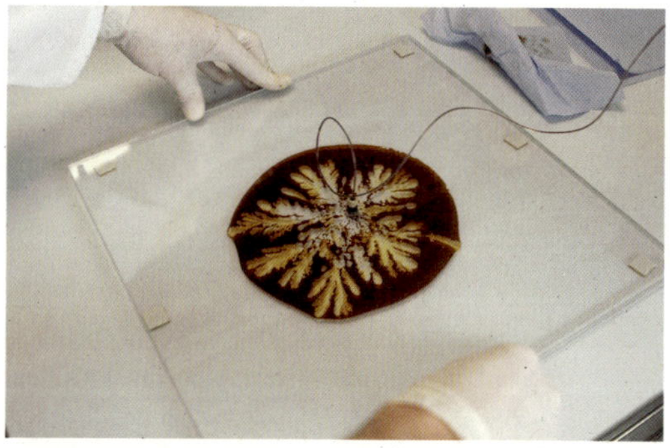

Hele-Shaw experiment
Department Petroleum Engineering (DPE) laboratory
University of Leoben, 2020

"The senses, in fact, are not just one more field of study, alongside, say, gender, colonialism or material culture. The senses are the media through which we experience and make sense of gender, colonialism and material culture. And, in McLuhan's words, the medium is the message."[9]

A direct engagement with the unpleasant properties of crude oil can help to critically analyze the perceived negative aspects of the substance. Crude oil is a complex mixture of a multitude of volatile hydrocarbons and diverse contaminants. To work artistically with the substance in its original geological state is a challenging process and a laborious endeavor. In the *Reflecting Oil* project, the artistic research process entailed practical handling and observation of the raw substance. This mode of research focused on sensory perception—such as the differentiation of colors and smells, tactile perception, and aesthetic and symbolic interpretation—and provided findings on the levels of multi-sensory and practical knowledge.

The investigations into the physical and chemical properties of crude oil with an eye on its cultural significance were carried out in the laboratories at the University of Leoben together with DGE petroleum scientists and invited experts from various disciplines. At the beginning of the project, we conducted standardized crude oil experiments with a more scientific approach; in the subsequent stages, the experiments were modified artistically in an attempt to incorporate symbolic and cultural aspects and introduce other contextual questions. Viewing the experiments and results from a wide variety of perspectives throughout the project period unfolded an extensive scope for interpretation.

"At the heart of this newfound awareness of oil's importance to our sensibilities and social expectations—our belief, for example, that sociality is of necessity narrated by perpetual growth, ceaseless mobility, and the expanded personal capacities and possibilities associated with the past century's new flood of energy into our lives—is our recognition that over the course of our current century we will need to extract ourselves from our dependence on oil and make the transition to new energy sources and new ways of living."[10]

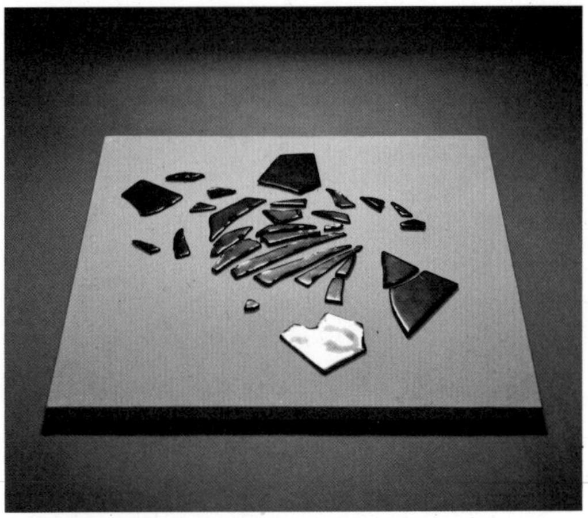

Ernst Logar
Smashed, 2024
Bitumen, sandstone

The project was structured into different sections and ran through the following phases: in 2020, petroleum and petroculture experts from different disciplines were invited to online workshops to share and discuss the role of crude oil from their respective fields of expertise. Parallel, the Vienna team (based at the University of Applied Arts Vienna, led by Ernst Logar) performed crude oil experiments together with the Leoben team (based at the DGE, led by Holger Ott) in the laboratories of the University of Leoben. Throughout the cooperation, there were regular online meetings between the two teams to discuss and reflect upon the workshops and experiments. We analyzed the interdisciplinary work process, the different approaches in art and science, and the divergent forms of knowledge production in great depth.

At the interim of the project in June 2022, the *Reflecting Oil Colloquium* was organized at the University of Applied Arts Vienna. Based on the previous workshops and experimental processes, three working groups were formed to address different topics relating to crude oil. Employing coordinated work methods and a variety of different tools, the interdisciplinary working processes spurred numerous artistic and scientific works (texts, photographs, videos, objects, and narratives). In the second half of the project, the experiences gained in the colloquium brought forth new crude oil experiments with the Leoben team. Once again, scientific experiments were undertaken and enhanced with artistic strategies focused on the sensory properties of the substance. These olfactory and tactile examinations were limited due to the toxic properties of crude oil. The sense of taste, which is an important parameter in the sensory evaluation of substances, was excluded for safety reasons.

The complete range of knowledge transfer and practical formats—from the online workshops and crude oil experiments to the *Reflecting Oil Colloquium* and corresponding collective reflections—paved the way for the final project exhibition *Reflecting Oil—Petroculture in Transformation*, which was open to the public from October 3 to November 15, 2024, at the Angewandte Interdisciplinary Lab in the Otto Wagner Postsparkasse (Austrian Postal Savings Bank). The artistic and scientific works by the project participants were curated and presented according to the collective and interdisciplinary research processes and juxtaposed with my own works created as project leader and artist.

The publication before you now summarizes the artistic research project in all its facets and conveys the numerous conclusions and findings in an experimental and open format. The publication in itself is an artistic object that attempts to expand our understanding of crude oil and its accompanying realities. At the same time, I hope that it will encourage us, as subjects of the Oil Age, to make the leap to a more sustainable and holistic energy future.

"Faced with the uncertain and precarious future, our faltering petrocultures are able to do little more than cycle through the hopes, dreams and nightmares of the past. [...] The true adventures lie ahead."[11]

1 Brett Bloom, *Petro-Subjectivity. De-Industrializing Our Sense of Self* (Ft. Wayne, IN: Breakdown Break Down Press, 2015), 4.

2 Terry Brotherstone and Hugo Manson, "North Sea Oil, its Narratives and its History: An Archive of Oral Documentation and the Making of Contemporary Britain," in *Northern Scotland* 27, no. 1 (May 2007), 32.

3 Ross Barrett and Daniel Worden, "Introduction," in: *Oil Culture*, eds. Barrett and Worden (Minneapolis: University of Minnesota Press, 2014), XXIV.

4 Fritjof Capra and Pier Luigi Luisi, *The Systems View of Life: A Unifying Vision* (Cambridge: Cambridge University Press, 2014), 8.

5 Constance Classen (ed.), *The Book of Touch* (Oxford: Berg, 2005), 5.

6 Capra and Luisi, 80.

7 The project is supported by the Program for Arts-Based Research (PEEK) of the Austrian Science Fund (FWF- AR547), www.reflectingoil.info.

8 Petrocultures Research Group, *After Oil* (Edmonton: University of Alberta, 2016), 14.

9 David Howes, *Empire of the Senses. The Sensual Culture Reader* (Oxford: Berg, 2005), 4.

10 Sheena Wilson, Imre Szeman and Adam Carlson, "On Petrocultures: Or, Why We Need to Understand Oil to Understand Everything Else," in: *Petrocultures: Oil, Politics, Culture*, eds. Wilson, Carlson, and Szeman (Montreal: McGill-Queen's University Press, 2017), 3.

11 Simon Orpana, *Gasoline Dreams: Waking up from Petroculture* (New York: Fordham University Press, 2021), 238.

—01/02

Towards Petro-Objectivity: The Scientist's View

Holger Ott

experiments
petroleum engineering
crude oil
Hele-Shaw cell
tipping point
pore space
distillation
petro-objectivity
energy transition

The climate crisis causes society to rethink. We are questioning our lifestyles and energy consumption. We are aware—at least in part—of the consequences of our actions and our climate targets are becoming more ambitious. But despite all these good intentions, our climate footprint is, unfortunately, not changing, or only insufficiently, and we are unable to reduce our dependence on fossil resources—why is that? Perhaps we need to start with an analysis.

Technology: Technologies to help with the energy transition are constantly being developed and refined. Technical prerequisites are necessary to achieve the energy and climate transition, but alone they are not sufficient. We have enough mature technologies at hand for a rethink and to switch to a sustainable energy supply, so this is not about our technological maturity, it is about our maturity as a society. The question we need to ask ourselves is: how long will it take to rebuild our existing infrastructure into something capable of supplying society with enough energy and all kinds of goods, while also maintaining our prosperity and protecting the climate? In other words, what is required for such a reorganization? Or, is the transformation of our "energy-hungry" society into a sustainable version of itself realistic? Probably not!

Attempting to deal with the substance of oil is important because, despite all our efforts to reduce our dependency on them, fossil fuels will likely remain with us for some time to come.[1] Social change is slow for many reasons, including a lack of available alternatives, raw materials, investment funds, labor, etc. All socio-economic energy and climate scenarios point in the same direction.[2] Consequently, this means that not only must we move away from fossil fuels, we must also learn to deal with them and their proxy—crude oil. And this involves rethinking many aspects of our lives, from increasing energy efficiency to controlling emissions and reviewing our high-energy lifestyles.

Figure 1
Hele-Shaw experiment where crude oil is displaced by milk. The complex pattern is a result of instable displacement.

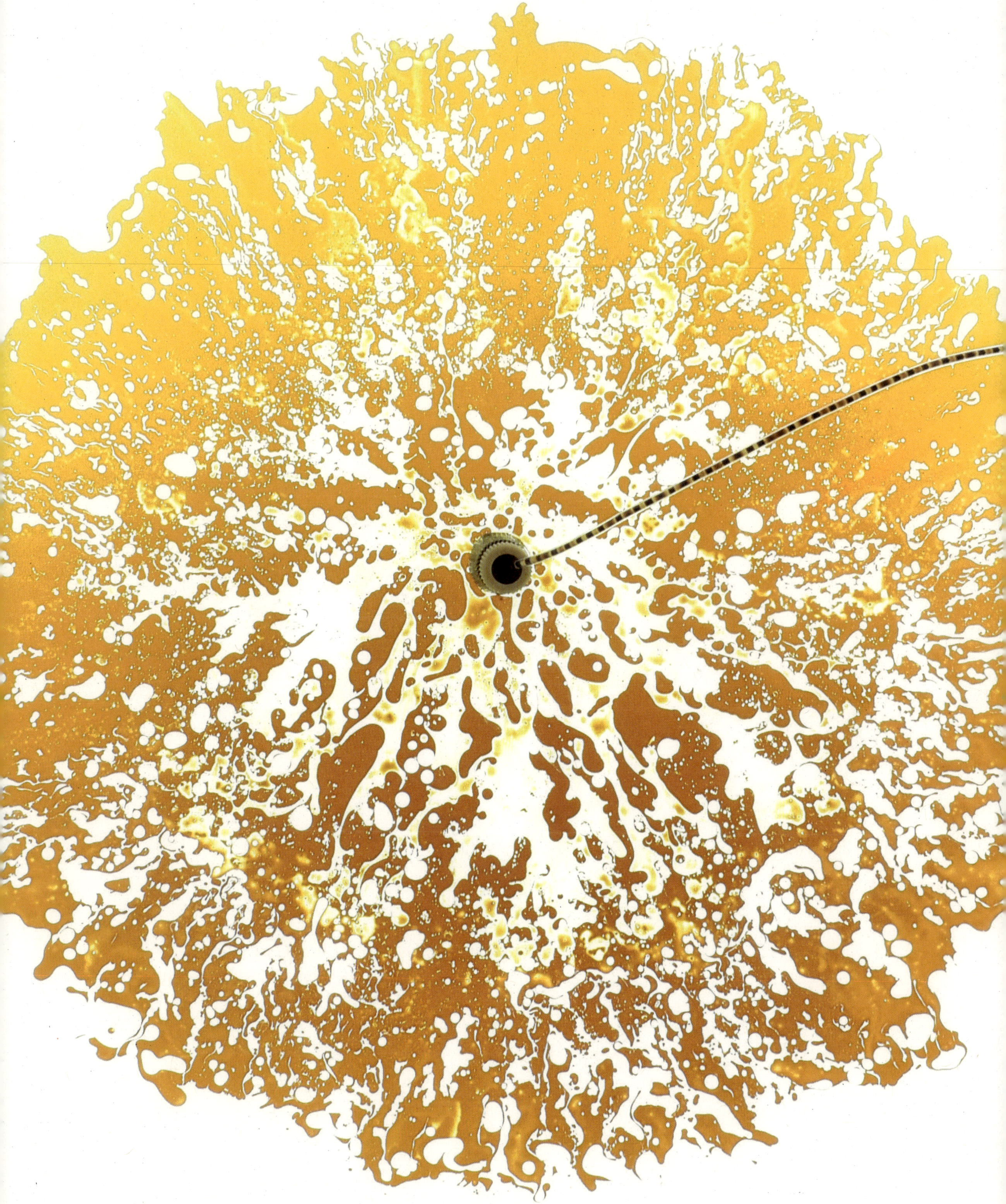

Culture: The energy transition is, therefore, not just about technological change; socio-economic and cultural aspects also need to be taken into account—this is where *Reflecting Oil* comes into play. The *Reflecting Oil* project takes a science-based arts approach whereby a multidisciplinary team is tasked with looking at and reflecting on crude oil—one of the most important fossil resources in modern society—from different perspectives. The focus is on experiments that provide an intuitive, rather than a quantitative, approach to the substance and its materiality. The aim is to try to understand crude oil both in itself and in relation to the materiality of other more familiar substances that are part of our daily lives. By building a relationship with the otherwise abstract substance of petroleum, we can find ways to handle it more effectively for as long as is necessary as well as find a way out of our dependency. To give the reader an impression of what this endeavor has involved, I would like to describe a few of the experiments/installations that were carried out as part of the project. As a scientist, I find technical approaches far more intuitive; however, *Reflecting Oil* is less about quantitative analyses than about experiencing the properties of crude oil and interpreting them in the context of personal behaviors, energy, and the climate.

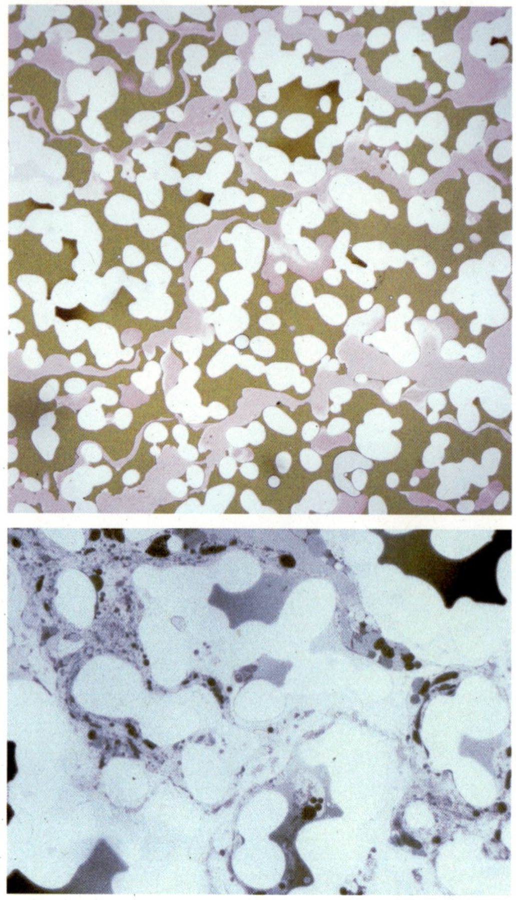

Figure 2
Microfluidic experiments showing the mixing of relevant cultural substances during the displacement of crude oil. The different magnification levels are chosen to show the typical structure formation. Upper image: While human blood (light red) emulsifies oil (light brown) with an immiscible percolation pattern, milk (lower image), which is itself a stable emulsion, is able to emulsify crude oil to a certain extent; microscopic structures form, which are partially resolved by optical imaging.

Science-based Arts—An Experimental Approach

It is the meeting of two worlds, two ways of thinking, and two approaches—one scientific and technical, the other artistic. Both come together and utilize each other, resulting in a symbiosis. The experiments carried out for the project are partly based on scientific approaches that, in a certain way, share the same goal of "experiencing" oil. Nonetheless, this experience is slightly different in that it is not about quantifying the chemical and physical properties of oil, but about experiencing them through the senses. Because this sensory experience is a personal and individual one, it requires references in order to provide it with attributes. The comparison to reference substances we are all familiar with allows crude oil to be categorized in a personal coordinate system. These reference substances, also referred to as cultural substances, could include water, honey, milk, blood, etc.—things that have certain personal associations and allow for a common understanding. The quantity of substances, their properties, and the experimental possibilities they offer open up a rich, multidimensional space of experience.

The experiments that were carried out for the project are extremely diverse and, for me, some were also very expressive. For example, the Hele-Shaw experiments[3] (explained below) express both predictability and loss of control. The future cannot be predicted and depends on critical parameters in analogy to the mobility of oil. It is not necessarily the interpretation of experiments that differentiates artistic approaches from scientific ones, but rather the personal, cultural, geopolitical associations that are made. The experiments themselves are really only a vehicle for understanding. Actual insights come from very different people with diverse backgrounds coming together to reflect in groups, which always brings new and surprising aspects to light.

Hele-Shaw experiments: In these experiments, various liquids such as oil and water are injected into a narrow gap between two glass plates, displacing the liquid already present in the gap. Technically speaking, this process is very similar to the displacement of oil in reservoirs by water injection, a common method of oil production. This displacement process can lead to instabilities,[4] the occurrence of which is predictable but very difficult to control. As there are ways to avoid these instabilities, they are not symptomatic of oil recovery, but are metaphorical for fossil fuels that are provided in abundance and the consequences that develop as a result of their use. Technically, such flow instabilities occur at a "tipping point"[5] when the mobility ratio of injected and displaced fluids becomes greater than one.[6] Once this tipping point is reached, we can say with certainty that instabilities will occur, but it is difficult to predict the exact extent—this is quite comparable to tipping points and instabilities in climate physics or metaphorically for conflicts and wars in the context of access to oil. Repeating such an experiment, or variations of it, results in patterns that are structurally similar but different in detail, highlighting the unpredictability of the exact outcome. This serves as a reminder of the different potential paths our future may take, which may follow certain broad patterns but remain inherently unpredictable in their specific details.[7]

Mixing and dynamics: Contact between fluids can result in miscible or immiscible mixing, depending on their interfacial tension. Water and oil are naturally in contact in the subsurface as a result of hydrocarbon formation and migration processes. They are typically immiscible and coexist in the pore space of the reservoir rock. In petroleum engineering, fluids are injected into oil reservoirs to displace and recover the crude oil. Interfacial tension, wettability (the affinity of fluids to wet the rock-forming minerals), and fluid viscosities are classical design parameters that can be modified for efficient oil recovery.[8] These effects can be studied visually in microfluidic chips that mimic the pore structure of porous rocks. Fluids can be injected into and recovered from the chip, and the displacement process in the pore space can be observed using optical microscopy.

In the course of several experimental sessions, known cultural substances were brought in contact with crude oil. Typically, the individual fluids are filled into test tubes and mixed through shaking before being left to stand for a period of time so as to allow the fluids to separate by gravity into new and thermodynamically stable fluid phases. This mixing is turbulent. In microfluidics or porous media, the flow is laminar, and this mixing has been observed in detail.[9]

In these experiments, crude oil was brought into contact with substances that are very familiar to us: honey, milk, and Coca-Cola. They mixed with the crude oil in different ways, resulting in new optically homogeneous or heterogeneous liquid phases of different colors and structures. The observations can be explained by miscible or immiscible behavior. Depending on how compatible or different the liquid is from crude oil, the liquids mix, ignore each other, or form emulsions which have been observed optically.[10] In microfluidics, the liquids appear almost transparent or very light, which is due to the very thin pore space of the chip used. Coca-Cola and oil were found to be immiscible and separated from the remaining oil phase in a percolating cola phase. Milk, on the other hand, has a certain fat content and is itself a stable emulsion: upon contact with crude oil, both liquids formed emulsion-like structures in the pore space. This indicates an exchange of substances between crude oil and milk and a certain affinity between them.

In these experiments, the properties of crude oil can be understood through cultural substances that are known to us. It turns out that the behavior of these substances during mixing corresponds to our everyday experience of bringing oily and watery substances into contact and possibly emulsifying them with more complex substances such as surfactants.[11] Examples include the homogenization of milk, or the stabilizing of vinegar and olive oil to form a homogeneous salad dressing. Thus, we are actually very familiar with the behavior and interactions of crude oil from ordinary household substances.

Distillation, smell, and appearance experiments: In petroleum engineering, the appearance (color) and smell of crude oil do play a role in characterizing it, but only a minor one. Gaining an intuitive understanding of the appearance and smell of oil requires appealing to two of our most important senses. In a series of experiments, we investigated the smell and appearance of crude oil. We focused not only on crude oil as a whole, but also on its coarse components. Although crude oil is a homogeneous substance, its chemical composition is very complex and individual. This complexity is difficult, if not impossible, to characterize or visualize. A simple approach to differentiation is distillation, in which light fractions of the crude oil are evaporated at gradually increasing temperatures and liquefied again by condensation elsewhere. This separates different fractions with increasing boiling points. Distillation is a fundamental industrial process that starts with crude oil to create other products or fuels. We carried out this fractionation on a small scale in the laboratory and observed—visually, by smell, or by other means—the different fractions separately. I, however, want to focus on their smell and appearance.

As expected, the lighter fractions are more volatile and less viscous. Still, what was surprising, though not unanticipated, was that we obtained a transparent and colorless liquid phase as the light fraction, which is completely counterintuitive when you actually see it happen—to extract a transparent liquid, a type of naphtha, from deep dark crude oil is an experience in itself. What remains in the flask after several distillation steps can be better described as a deep, dark solid; the type of material used in road construction. Not only does the appearance and viscosity vary greatly from fraction to fraction, but the smell does too. The light fraction developed a very intense and pungent odor. Since these are the most volatile components, the intensity is understandable, as the most volatile components have the lowest vapor pressure and escape easily into the surrounding air. The pungent smell of the distillate, on the other hand, was also somewhat surprising and had nothing in common with the smell of undistilled crude oil, which to the untrained nose smelled a little strange, if not as unpleasant. Although naphtha is a direct distillate of crude oil, the derivatives or fuels that we personally come into contact with are not comparable to crude oil itself, which remains an abstract substance for most people.

But let us go back to the basics of oil for a moment—this project is about crude oil as a cultural yet abstract substance. Is crude oil crude oil? As mentioned above, and as has become clearer to us in the course of the project, crude oil is a very complex substance with a molecular composition that can only be incompletely characterized scientifically. This composition and the associated properties vary not only from reservoir to reservoir, but also within reservoirs, and not just in small ways either; for example, naturally occurring hydrocarbons vary from the gaseous state (natural gas fields) to the solid state (tar sands). Our project has focused primarily on conventional oil. In order to characterize crude oil, various samples from Austria, Norway, Central Asia, and the Middle East were filled into glass bottles and evaluated visually and by their smell. The goal was to develop categories or a coordinate system in which all the oils could be represented. The procedure was similar to a wine tasting, where color, texture, aroma, and flavor are analyzed. While the color of such dark substances could be seen with an appropriate light exposure, varying between greenish and reddish brown and degrees of darkness, their smell was much more subtle and tricky to discern. Overall, the attributes we found varied between, for example, "pungent aggressive" and "creamy soft," and between "herbal" and "wet asphalt." These descriptors were recorded in a jointly developed "olfactory crude oil wheel." As in wine tasting, the differences between the oils were subtle and could only be worked out iteratively.

Team Reflections

The experiments are reflected upon in meetings attended by members of the project's multidisciplinary team: artists, art historians, engineers, and scientists who bring very different perspectives to the discussions and interpretations. In addition, guests from all over the world and different disciplines are invited to participate in workshops or experiments in Leoben and Vienna; the workshops broaden the team's perspective through presentations and discussions on topics ranging from proletarian ecology and game design, to oil and climate change. In this way, the team expands its multi-perspectival view of oil, leading to a comprehensive understanding of its properties and role in society. This approach has made me personally aware of the value of gaining a comprehensive understanding of this

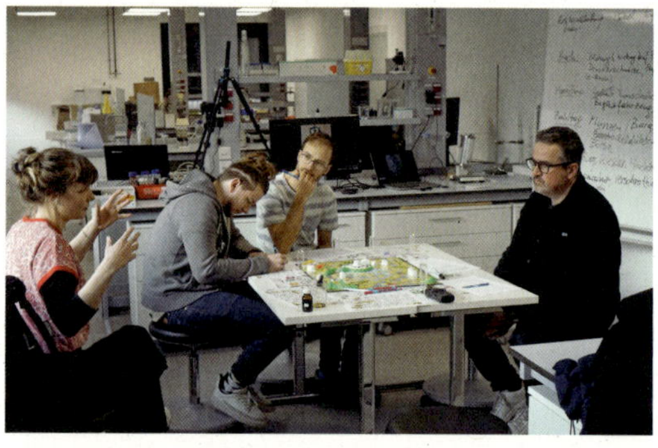

The Revised Game of Life experiment, Department Petroleum Engineering (DPE) laboratory University of Leoben, 2024

substance and our cultural dependence on it, and that a more holistic approach is needed to solve our current problems, one that goes beyond just its technical, economic, or cultural aspects.

Reflecting Oil in Education

A primary goal of the project is to share the team's experience of this "science-based art approach" with students from various disciplines in order to inspire them and raise their awareness of the energy transition. The involvement of students means that the concepts developed during our investigations can be tested all while infusing the project with fresh ideas and creativity. The Petroculture[12] and Energy Transition Seminar, held in Leoben and Vienna, brought together students and faculty members from engineering and the arts to discuss our deep cultural dependence on fossil fuels and possible ways out. The group explored the historical, technical, and cultural aspects of the culture-energy complex and sought solutions. Groups of engineering and art students conducted scientific experiments and produced artworks that demonstrate the role of the science-based art approach in addressing contemporary energy issues. The perspectives developed help bridge the gap between scientific concepts and public awareness, making complex issues more intuitive and accessible to all. In particular, final presentations introducing the students' creative output and joint discussions show that such work is mutually inspiring and that students from different disciplines learn from each other. Critical questions are asked across disciplines and discussions are held outside personal comfort zones. New spaces open up! It turns out that simple truths are not enough and solutions require an interdisciplinary approach. This seminar and other activities are the first steps towards a multidisciplinary education in petroculture.

My Learning and Potential Project Impact

Let us return to the problem. Our planet is home to seven billion people, most of whom are increasingly dependent on energy. Fossil fuels currently provide over 80 percent of this energy.[13] This is an enormous dependency—it is not only a dependency on energy, but also a dependency on specific energy sources and their characteristics (high energy density, cheap to extract, easy to transport). So, our reliance on crude oil is not only technical, but, as I have come to realize in the course of the project, also social and cultural, all of which are closely linked to these characteristics.[14] Therefore, it is not enough to rely on technical solutions alone; a cultural change also needs to take place, starting with me as an individual. A term that captures this problem is "petro-subjectivity" as defined by Brett Bloom.[15] Petro-subjectivity refers to the way our understanding of ourselves and the world around us is shaped by the use of oil.

Mitigating the effects of our petroculture, of which climate change is the most dramatic element, requires us to look not only at ways to turn away from oil but also at how we deal with oil. But this is an ideologically charged issue that polarizes society. This polarization is unhelpful and prevents constructive solutions. For this reason, and now that our goals have been defined, it is also appropriate, necessary even, to look at the problem, and therefore at oil, analytically and perhaps even dispassionately—objectively! Let us try another term: "petro-objectivity," which may refer to the ability to look at oil as a fuel from an objective perspective, without being influenced by personal beliefs or interests. It is important to understand the environmental, economic, and social impacts of oil in order to take the right actions to reduce our dependence on fossil fuels. An objective view of oil can help inform policy decisions based on facts and data, rather than personal beliefs or interests. In the *Reflecting Oil* project, we try to grasp the materiality of the substance with our senses, which is a subjective approach. On the other hand, we also strive for a shared and interdisciplinary understanding of the material, which means objectivity in the best sense of the word. This is why I believe that *Reflecting Oil*, with its shared understanding of the material, can grow beyond previous approaches.

1 Intergovernmental Panel on Climate Change (IPCC), *Climate Change 2022* (Cambridge, UK and New York, USA: Cambridge University Press, 2023). Detlef P. van Vuuren et al., "The Representative Concentration Pathways: An Overview" in *Climatic Change* 109, 5 (2011). Nico Bauer et al., "Shared Socio-Economic Pathways of the Energy Sector—Quantifying the Narratives" in *Global Environmental Change* 42 (2017), 316 – 330.

2 Ibid.

3 Henry Selby Hele-Shaw (1854–1941) was an English mechanical and automobile engineer. Hele-Shaw experiments are used to study fluid mechanical effects and displacements in confined spaces by observing the flow of fluids between two closely spaced parallel glass plates. These experiments are widely used to visualize and quantify fluid-displacement instabilities.

4 Larry Lake et al., *Fundamentals of Enhanced Oil Recovery* (Society of Petroleum Engineers, 2014).

5 The term "tipping point" commonly refers to a critical threshold at which a tiny perturbation leads to a significant and often irreversible effect: Timothy M. Lenton et al., "Tipping Elements in the Earth's Climate System" in *Proc. Natl. Acad. Sci. U. S. A.* 105, 6 (2008), 1786–1793.

6 G. M. Homsy, "Viscous Fingering in Porous Media" in *Annual Review of Fluid Mechanics* 19 (1987), 271–311. Steffen Berg & Holger Ott, "Stability of CO2-Brine Immiscible Displacement in *International Journal of Greenhouse Gas Control* 11 (2012), 188–203.

7 François Gallaire and P. T. Brun, "Fluid Dynamic Instabilities: Theory and Application to Pattern Forming in Complex Media", in *Philosophical Transactions of the Royal Society A* 375, 2093 (2017).

8 Larry Lake et al., *Fundamentals of Enhanced Oil Recovery* (Society of Petroleum Engineers, 2014).

9 Alimohammad Anbari et al., "Microfluidic Model Porous Media: Fabrication and Applications in *Small* 14, 18 (2018). Ahmad Kharrat et al., "Development of Foam-Like Emulsion Phases in Porous Media Flow" in *Journal of Colloid and Interface Science* 608, 1 (2022): 1064–1073. Holger Ott et al., "Fluid-Phase Topology of Complex Displacements," in Porous Media in *Phys. Rev. Research* 2 (2020).

10 Ibid.

11 Ibid.

12 Petrocultures Research Group, After Oil (Edmonton, Alberta: Petrocultures Research Group, 2016), 11.

13 Statistical Review of World Energy. Nico Bauer et al., "Shared Socio-Economic Pathways of the Energy Sector—Quantifying the Narratives," in *Global Environmental Change* 42 (2017), 316–330.

14 Ibid.

15 Brett Bloom, *Petro-Subjectivity. De-Industrializing Our Sense of Self* (Ft. Wayne, IN: Breakdown Break Down Press, 2015).

—01/03

Experimenting with Oil

Imre Szeman

experiments
oil modernity
crude oil
Alberta oil sands
fossil fuels
energy transition

Experiment #1: Oil Modernity

There have been all manner of experiments conducted on and in relation to oil. Yet the level of ongoing technological innovation and invention required to drag the stuff out of the ground is still not readily apparent. In the broad cultural imaginary, oil comes gushing from the earth when old-hat local know-how is combined with the brute muscular energy of roughnecks—the stuff of nineteenth-century black-and-white photos or Hollywood films like *The Treasure of the Sierra Madre* (1948), *Giant* (1956), or *There Will Be Blood* (2007).[1] This vision of oil's origin—as marked by bodily toil and cries of "Eureka!"—has been as effective in moving it out of sight and out of mind as has the complex technological network that transmutes liquid into something without substance: energy. After all, what could the muck and grease accumulating in the soil below oil derricks possibly have to do with the energy that appears from neat white sockets located conveniently in walls and gives life to the shiny computers plugged into them? If there have been oil experiments, we believe they are—they must be—a thing of the past. Technology has moved on, and so, too, has the energy which brings it to life.

The reality of things is of course quite different. Oil remains essential to the daily operations of contemporary life, despite the planetwide growth in renewable energy, and continues to be a way for wealthy companies and countries to retain and further expand their wealth. The ever-growing difficulty of accessing fossil fuels has necessitated endless mechanical and scientific experimentation to keep it flowing at current levels of demand—over 102 million barrels per day.[2] After a century and a half of petromodernity, producers have been forced to hunt for oil in more and more remote locales. Giant sea-bound oil derricks housing hundreds of workers can be found off the coastlines of almost every continent. In the Arctic tundra, oil flows out of drill sites made possible by advanced equipment designed to withstand the extreme cold. Fracking, a process of injecting a sophisticated chemical stew into the ground at high pressures, has been invented to free natural gas from shale rock. Perhaps the most significant of all these experiments is the extraordinary system of pipelines encircling the planet, moving petroleum and gas across rivers, plains, and mountains to markets, where another transmutation takes place—not liquid into energy, but black into gold.

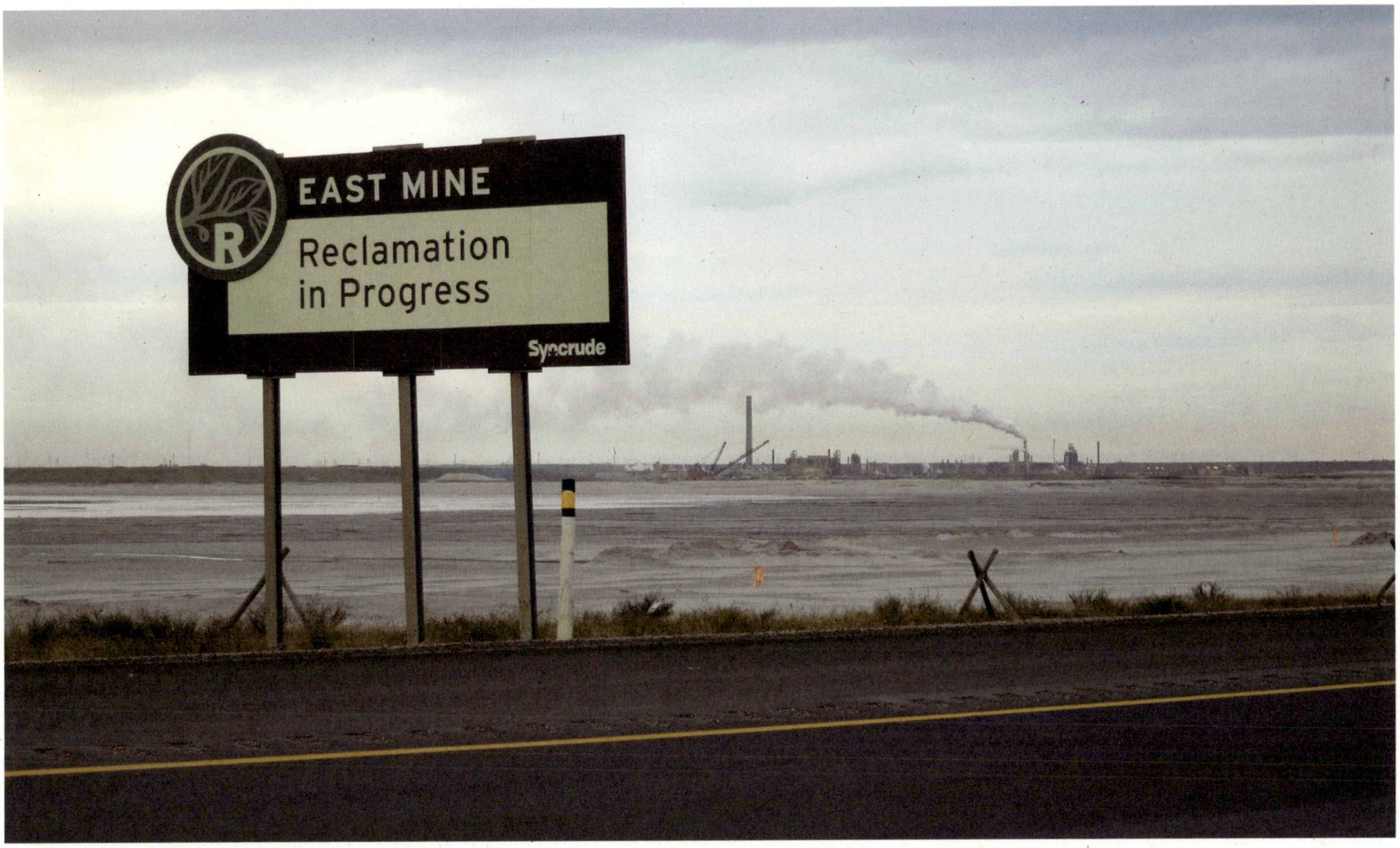

Alberta oil sands, Highway 63, 2015

These contemporary experiments, deliberately hidden from view and increasingly difficult to visualize, have become a key element of the enormous technocratic apparatus that sustains modern existence—a global, material system most of us neither fully understand nor want to know about. As ever, the rule of the modern citizen-subject in the Global North holds true: out of sight, out of mind, especially when it comes to the traumas being daily inflicted on the planet.[3]

The necessity of experimenting with oil is especially evident in the vast landscape of the Alberta oil sands. The challenge of freeing usable oil from the sand to which it is bound has led to radical and extreme technological experiments. The systems of trucks and conveyors used in the oil sands are of an unimaginable scale; the pipes and towers of the processing facilities are not far behind. It has been argued that, taken as a whole, the oil sands constitute the largest capital project on the planet at present—indeed, perhaps of all time, having already consumed US $200 billion on an extraction site the size of Florida. The sheer cost of surface mining—the process still being used in the oil sands—has necessitated that companies experiment with new ways to get at the precious black stuff, such as steam assisted gravity drainage (SAGD), or the invention of new, increasingly toxic chemical solvents to separate sand from oil. The physical space of the oil sands is viscous and dirty, a canyon of extraction as deep as any ever cut into the earth by human beings. The oil produced in Alberta is made, enabled, and kept alive by satellites and computers, with AI-assisted oil extraction likely just around the corner.

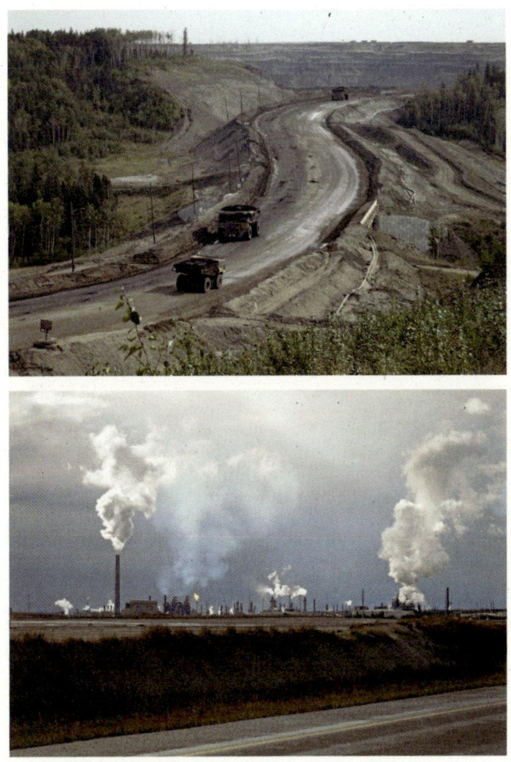

Alberta oil sands, Suncore mining site and the Syncrude plant, 2015

These are only the most recent experiments on the oil sands. In the 1950s, geologist Manley Naitland invented a way of getting oil from the sands that, he hoped, would have allowed companies to sidestep the need for big machinery and chemical magic. Naitland imagined a post-WWII technical use for nuclear weapons: oil recovery. Buried underground and used carefully, the intense heat and shockwaves generated by a small nuclear device would boil oil out of sands; the giant cavity created underground by the blast would in turn act as a perfect container within which to collect the oil left behind (and later would be an ideal space for CO2 to be injected into the ground). Naitland's calculations suggested that each blast would create an underground cave holding two million barrels of oil. Such experimentation with oil might seem like pure fantasy. And yet, in July 1959, the governments of Canada and Alberta were ready to approve Project Oil Sands to meet energy demands for an expansive post-war economy. Only the large reserves of recoverable oil that still existed at the time quashed these extreme plans; one suspects that only the environmental consciousness that has developed in the intervening sixty years has pushed extreme experiments such as this one to the back pages of history books.[4]

The extremity of these technological experiments with oil underlies what has constituted the real experiment of oil: modernity itself. It is no exaggeration to suggest that the twentieth and twenty-first centuries would not have been the same without oil—a source of energy with a huge energy output per unit of fuel which is easy to store and transport, and which forms the basis of all manner of other substances without which it is hard to imagine life on the planet today (plastics being only the most well-known of these). Histories of the century alert to the significance of energy inevitably provide a vision of the recent past in which the presence of oil is amongst the central forces shaping human life—if not the single *ur*-force to which all other narratives can be connected. John Robert McNeill's environmental history of the twentieth century, *Something New Under the Sun*, quickly identifies the capacities, technologies, and infrastructures enabled by oil to be the single most significant factor in the massive expansion of population over the century, which in turn has generated larger increases in water consumption, CO2 production, and so on.[5]

The experience of the modern would have been utterly different in the absence of this single commodity; the presence of oil allowed for the creation of modern cities, automobile traffic, global trade, and migration on an unprecedented scale, the agricultural revolution—which is to say: modern life itself. Researchers in the energy humanities have alerted us to just how deep and constitutive the impact of fossil fuels has been, pointing to the manner in which the availability of energy has defined modern notions of labor, gender, family, autonomy, and selfhood, right down to the ontological depths of being.[6] That the modern has been an experiment with oil is only beginning to dawn on us, as we consider what might happen in the absence of our primary energy source—a question for which we have not even developed partial answers, but have chosen to address instead with science fiction imaginings of miraculous new sources of energy (e.g., unobtanium in *Avatar*, spice in *Dune*, fusion energy in real-world physics labs) that will hopefully appear to fuel clean, green, shiny space-age cities.

We know the world is becoming uninhabitable due in part to the use of fossil fuels. Yet we still haven't come to accept that we're oil creatures through and through, to draw a link between the multiple social and cultural commitments we've made to fossil fuels, and the depths of those commitments. The ongoing experiments in fossil fuel extraction have continued to animate the experiment of oil modernity, whatever the consequences. Where does this leave us?

Experiment #2: Abstract to Real

A truly radical experiment in relation to oil would be to envision a new kind of modernity. This would be a modernity imagined sans oil—which is not the same as saying this it would be without energy at all. What would be missing in this

Hele-Shaw experiment
Department Petroleum Engineering
(DPE) laboratory
University of Leoben, 2020

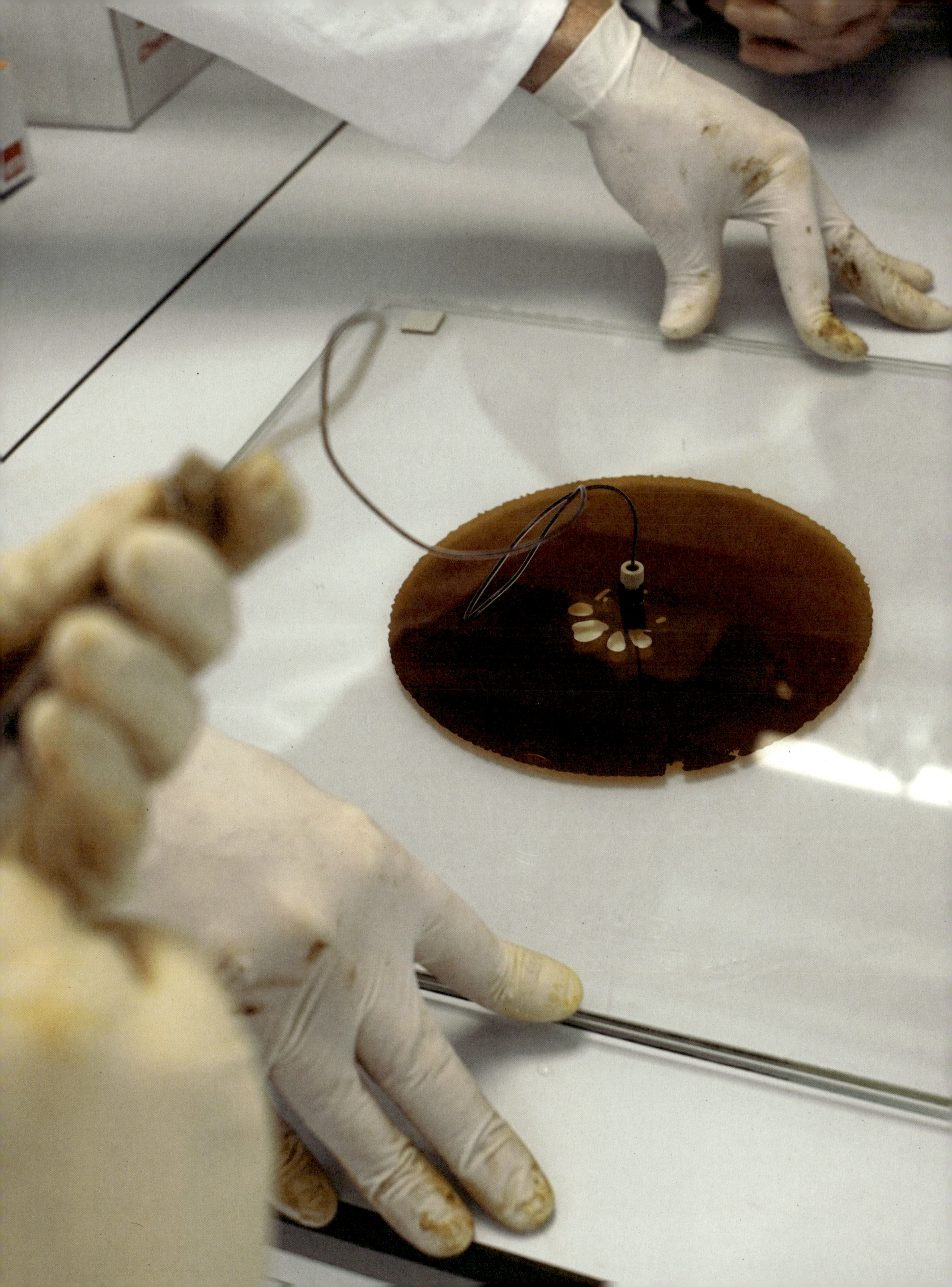

new modernity would (to begin with) likely be some of the specific capacities of oil and the conveniences it affords. Oil can be easily moved and stored and can be used in any weather at any time of year; it is a form of energy that has become co-terminus with daily life itself. If fossil fuels have indeed shaped labor, gender, the family, autonomy, and much more, in a renewable modernity, current ways of living and being will need to be nudged in different directions. We have some hints of what such a modernity might look like. Sociologist Elizabeth Shove has argued that the fluidity and unpredictability of wind and solar energy—sometimes available, sometimes not—means we need to reimagine the social relationship between time and energy, because we need to attune ourselves to the ebb and flow of energy over the course of the day, month, and year.[7] But shifting us from one experiment—modernity as oil—to another social and historical experiment—modernity without it—has proved far more difficult than one might have imagined. We love being creatures of oil and, despite ourselves and our concern for the environment, fear becoming something else.

Artists possess a unique ability to reimagine the mundane and overlooked aspects of our lives, transforming them into sources of insight and inspiration, and providing us with the energies needed to reimagine ourselves. The critical work of artists committed to change is to intervene—aesthetically, conceptually, and politically, or more likely all three at once—to re-narrate imaginaries so that we can abandon the destructive comforts of one experiment for the uncertainties and political possibilities of another. The *Reflecting Oil: Arts-Based Research on Oil Transitionings* project, spearheaded by Ernst Logar, exemplifies this critical, transformative potential. Through a series of innovative projects and interventions, Logar and his team have sought to make the pervasive yet invisible presence of crude oil tangible to the public, employing photography, sculpture, and installation to illuminate the substance's profound significance and ubiquitous influence on modern civilization. *Reflecting Oil* is an experiment designed to challenge the conditions of oil modernity, while simultaneously initiating the energy experiments that we need to do next.

In oil modernity, the fundamental experience of fossil fuels is no experience of it at all. It would be an overstatement to say that no one in the era of oil has ever seen, felt, or smelled the substance. Those living near extraction sites, or who have had to manage the traumatic impact of oil spills on human and non-human communities, know oil intimately, even if they would rather it had remained a mystery. Even so, for most of those on the planet, oil modernity is defined by absence, invisibility, and withdrawal. We don't normally note the presence of oil in our lives, except perhaps in an abstract, intellectual way—as the subject of dinner table discussions about the ubiquity of plastics or the challenges of energy transition. Instead, we treat the presence of fossil fuels in our lives and homes as commonplace, boring, and banal.

Oil modernity is a shell game of epistemology and ontology, of deferred knowledge and experience, of the practice of unseeing a substance to be found everywhere. A glance around the room in which I am writing this essay, for instance, reveals it to be drenched in fossil fuels—in the plastics of my computer keyboard, the mouse on my desk, the stuff filling my desk drawers (pens, rulers, staplers), and the wheels on the desk chair. Fossil fuels lurk about in other, more magical ways, too, which can be much harder to detect. Every one of the objects I've just named made their way in my life by transiting oceans in vessels powered by fossil fuels and crafted in factories more likely than not fueled by coal, gas, or oil. It requires real effort for me to keep fossil fuels "visible" in this way; even as someone who has been thinking about oil for two decades, the only real way of spending my time and living my life—the more intuitive and ready-to-hand way—is in ignorance of the networks of relationships and physical matter that shape my reality. To be truly modern—to

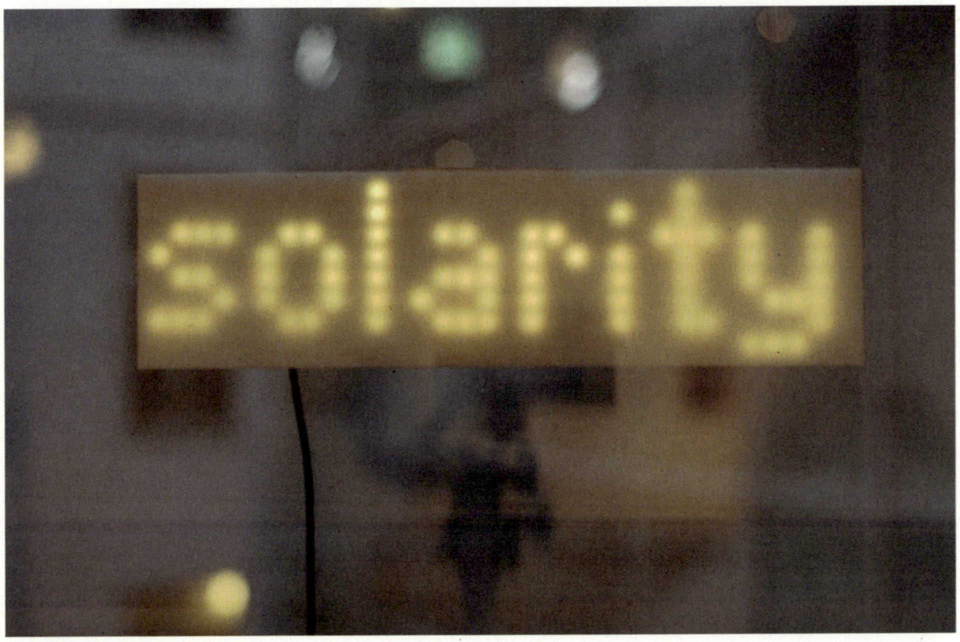

Ernst Logar, *Solarity*, 2024
LED display, electronic parts, solar cells, rechargeable battery

embrace progress, growth, and wealth—means that we (have to) accept we cannot know about oil, because in a very real way the expectation is that we should live as if it doesn't really exist. When oil shows up on beaches and in rivers, spilled out of pipelines or drill sights, it isn't a sign of the normal state of things, i.e., its ubiquity as the blood that keeps the social body alive. It is treated instead as a small error from which we should not draw bigger conclusions. If anything, these exceptions compel us to plod forward as usual, happy in the not-knowing reinforced (in a way one might not have imagined) by these small glimpses into the physical existence of oil.

We depend deeply on the energy generated by fossil fuels. And yet we don't know much (if anything) about its actual substance. It is precisely because oil in modernity is framed as substanceless and made hidden that it can be so powerful to render it into *substance*. Giving oil a physical reality, insisting on its material qualities, on its feel, texture, liquidity, smell, and even taste, constitutes a fundamental challenge to oil modernity. Indeed, there is perhaps no more effective challenge, at once epistemological (the hidden becomes visible), ontological (it transmutes oil back into substance), and political (revealing the lies on which oil modernity has staked itself). I wrote above that the fundamental experience of fossil fuels is no experience of it at all. This is precisely why we need experiments to translate fossil fuels into experience. What connects the varied experiments of *Reflecting Oil* is an acknowledgment of the specific characteristics of oil, the modes of perception required to experience it, and an investigation of its roles in everyday practices, which are deeply embedded in historical and cultural contexts. Logar and his partners insist on perceiving the reality of substance behind and beneath the metaphorical and cultural meaning that accompanies anything physical. The experiments in apprehending and encountering the multisensory forms of substance create a more nuanced understanding of the material beyond its mere chemical properties. The new methodology of substance guiding the investigations in *Reflecting Oil* make it impossible for us to take oil modernity at its word, showing us the limits and problems of the game of material absence on which it so deeply depends.

The collaboration between artists, scientists, and engineers in this project underscores the importance of interdisciplinary approaches in addressing complex global issues, illustrating how art can play a vital role in fostering a deeper understanding of the challenges and opportunities of transitioning away from fossil fuels. Logar's project provides an excellent starting point for the collective experiments we need to undertake to move past the experiment of oil modernity and its consequences for all inhabitants of the planet.

Experiment #3: Revolution?

Reflecting Oil exemplifies the political force of the energy humanities. When it comes down to it, what I have been arguing over the past decade is not that we should use fewer fossil fuels because of their impact on the planet—a familiar argument made by groups and individuals intent on limiting the production of greenhouse gases and damage to the environment. Rather, it's that the liberal-capitalist subject is a subject that has been developed around the use of ever-increasing amounts of energy—and of a specific kind of energy, with specific attributes and capacities. As such, if we are to successfully make a transition to new forms of energy, we will need to create a new kind of subject or hope that such a subject will come into being as a consequence of the implementation of new forms of energy. Without such changes to subjectivity, it is unlikely that a transition to renewable energies will work as hoped, at least not with the intensity demanded by the problem of climate change. We need to create a renewable, sustainable, solar/wind subject, one animated by different goals, expectations, and hopes. We need to re-set our bodies, selves, desires, hopes, and dreams. If it seems like an impossible task, it is. The circumstances we find ourselves in demand nothing less than we take up the challenge of flipping the impossible to the possible and do so with the speed of a revolution.

Who will lead such a revolution? What are the presumptions and imaginaries that guide it? And what steps need to be taken from now into the future to make this revolution come about? These are the questions I've been asking myself in my writing. Through his experiments with new forms of art and critical practice, it's clear that these are the kinds of questions Ernst Logar has been asking himself, too. And if we pay close enough attention, we might find that he is also giving us some of the answers we so desperately need.

1 *The Treasure of the Sierra Madre*, directed by John Huston (1948); *Giant*, directed by George Stevens (1956); *There Will Be Blood*, directed by Paul Thomas Anderson (2007).

2 Oliver Millman, "Surge of new US-led oil and gas activity threatens to wreck Paris climate goals," *The Guardian*, March 28, 2024, https://www.theguardian.com/environment/2024/mar/28/oil-and-gas-fossil-fuels-report. In its recent annual reports. the International Energy Agency has indicated that oil demand will finally peak by the end of this decade. Even a decline in use from a peak would mean an enormous amount of oil would still be in use globally. See Alex Lawson,"Peak in Global Oil Demand 'In Sight Before the End of Decade,'" *The Guardian*, June 14, 2023, https://www.theguardian.com/business/2023/jun/14/peak-in-global-oil-demand-in-sight-before-end-of-decade.

3 The genre of environmental exposé, which draws attention to modernity's blinders, is large and growing. For a few recent examples, see Oliver Franklin-Wallis, *Wasteland: The Secret World of Waste and the Urgent Search for a Cleaner World* (New York: Hachette, 2023); Siddharth Kara, *Cobalt Red: How the Blood of the Congo Powers Our Lives* (New York: St. Martin's Press, 2023); and Henry Sanderson, *Volt Rush: The Winners and Losers in the Race to Go Green* (London: Oneworld, 2022).

4 My account of Manley Naitland's project as well as the Soviet's PNE program is drawn from William Marsden's *Stupid to the Last Drop* (Toronto: Vintage Canada, 2008), 1–34.

5 John Robert McNeill, *Something New Under the Sun: An Environmental History of the Twentieth-Century World* (New York: W. W. Norton & Co., 2000).

6 For some examples, see Alyssa Battistoni, "Bringing in the Work of Nature: From Natural Capital to Hybrid Labor," *Political Theory* 45, no. 1 (2017); Amanda Boetzkes and Andrew Pendakis, "Visions of Eternity: Plastic and the Ontology of Oil," *e-flux* 47 (2013); Warren Cariou, "Aboriginal," in *Fueling Culture: 101 Words for Energy and Environment*, ed. Imre Szeman, Jennifer Wenzel, and Patricia Yaeger (New York: Fordham University Press, 2017), 17–20; Stephanie LeMenager, *Living Oil: Petroleum Culture in the American Century* (Oxford: Oxford University Press, 2014); Andreas Malm, *Fossil Capital: The Rise of Steam Power and the Roots of Global Warming* (London and New York: Verso, 2016); and Leon Sealey-Huggins, "'The climate crisis is a racist crisis': structural racism, inequality and climate change," in *The Fire Now: Anti-Racist Scholarship in Times of Explicit Racial Violence*, ed. Remi Joseph-Salisbury et al. (New York: Zed Books, 2018). There are hundreds of books and articles in the field of energy humanities I could have listed which undertake the work of linking fossil fuels, culture, society, politics, and philosophy.

7 Elizabeth Shove, "Time to Rethink Energy Research," in *Nature Energy* 6 (2021), 118–120.

—02

—02

A Collective Imaginative Journey to Rethink Oil

Interdisciplinary Collaboration Between the University of Applied Arts Vienna and the University of Leoben

Alejandra Rodríguez-Remedi

experiments
interdisciplinarity
crude oil
laboratory
viscometer
arts-based research methods
systems thinking
thought collectives
reflection

Reflection—Experimentation—Reflection
"Arts-based learning engagements are more ideally suited for habit-forming exercises, rituals of perception, acts of reflection, personal expression, and social agency which, if they are to be sensibly evaluated for their effectiveness, must be assessed over the long run to document how the life practices, thinking habits, and communities of the learner have been transformed."[2]

Creative group discussions and reflection were placed at the heart of *Reflecting Oil's* five-year collaborative research processes. They were facilitated from the very outset, in late 2019, to encourage exchange between artistic and scientific approaches to crude oil, setting the ground for the planning and execution of a series of

oil experiments.

These interdisciplinary reflections, which brought oil's cultural meaning and significance to the forefront, helped to create the conditions for a fruitful dynamic of encounters, dialogue, and mutual learning, broadening the research team's understanding of art and science and also developing its members' consciousness about themselves as a "science-art" thinking collective.
An emotive dimension running through the reflection processes opened up for the

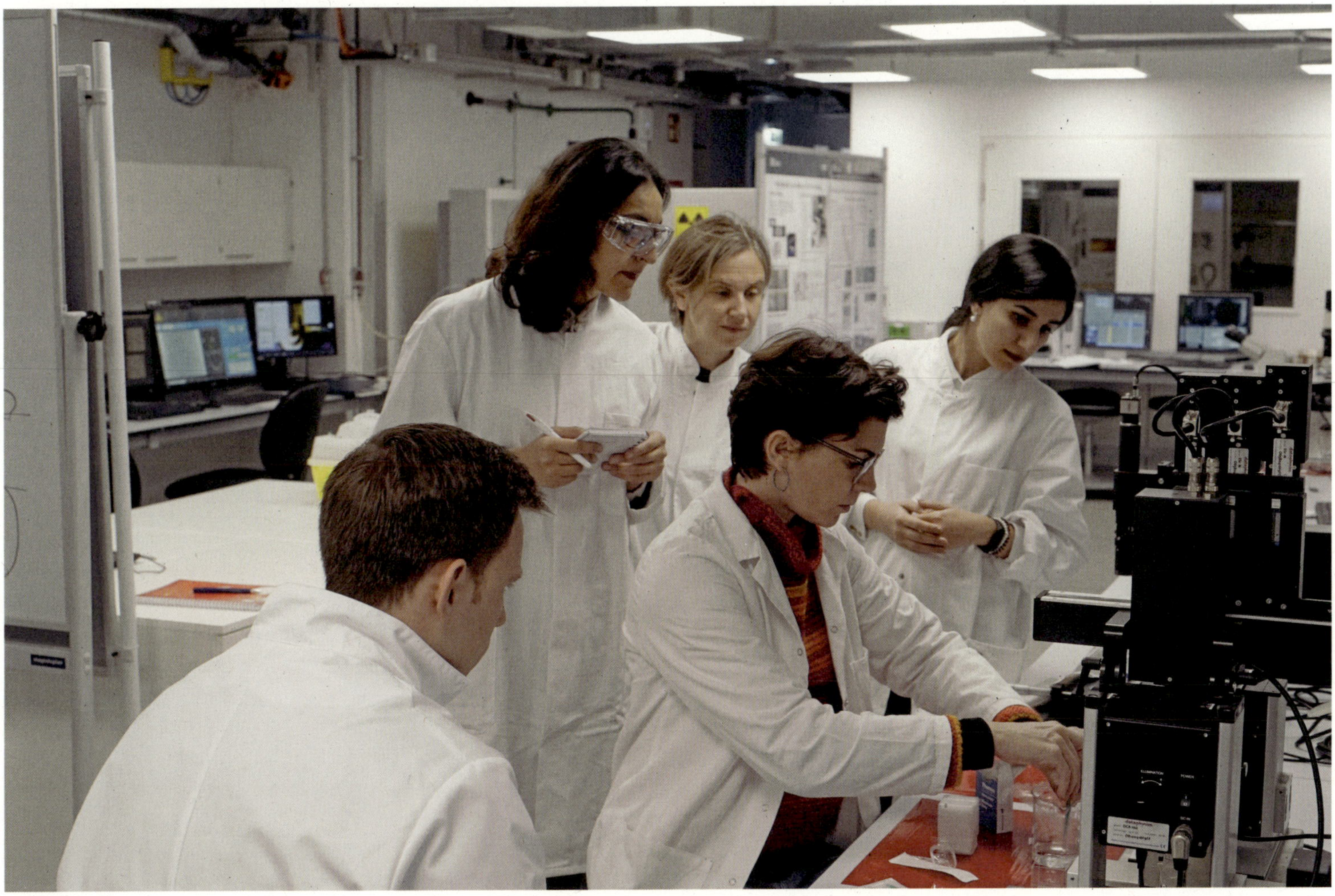

Crude oil experiments, Department Petroleum Engineering (DPE) laboratory, University of Leoben, 2019

team an opportunity to explore their feelings linked with the substance, thereby addressing issues of perception and behavior, an experience that became particularly meaningful for the team's petroleum engineering experts who were unaccustomed to acknowledging and making explicit the effect of emotions upon scientific thinking. The reflections often tapped into the ambiguous and contradictory qualities of oil (associated with both progress and environmental degradation), which encouraged team members to talk about what they described as their mixed feelings towards the substance, attesting to its complexity and reinforcing the relevance of the project's multi-perspective approach.

It is pertinent to point out that the Leoben experts had never engaged in an art-and-science research collaboration before and that, though some of the other team members had prior experience of collaborating with scientists, they too had never participated in an art-and-science collaboration on the scale of *Reflecting Oil*. The preliminary reflections unveiled the shared view that technology alone cannot make our oil-addicted societies transition to renewable energies and that creativity should play a more prominent role not only in raising wider awareness about our dependency on fossil fuels but also in (re)imagining transition. However, initial conversations also evidenced differences in expectations among team members, which did impact communication at times, prompting Ernst Logar as the Principal Investigator to facilitate further spaces for open dialogue so as to unveil barriers. A process of self-evaluation in the shape of in-depth interviews, which took place in early 2021, a year after the project had begun, became key to identifying issues perceived as either conducive or detrimental to a fruitful collaboration, like for example the unforeseen work conditions imposed by the COVID-19 pandemic (which made it exceptionally difficult for team members to interact in person) as well as the value systems and power relations at play within the two Austrian collaborating academic institutions housing the team. Neither the Principal Investigator nor the head of the University of Leoben's Department Petroleum Engineering (renamed Department Geoenergy in 2024 to reflect its research concentration on decarbonization and sustainability) leading the project's scientific contribution, Professor Holger Ott, shied away from speaking openly about their original expectations, which were based on their respective assumptions about what constitutes research and artistic practice and therefore *how* the project was going to be carried out. The Leoben experts had assumed that their quantitative research approach (characterized by a goal-driven linearity and strict timeframes) was somehow going to be the motor of the collaborative project. Though the Leoben experts described scientific processes as creative in their own right, they were quick to add that their approach was in fact dictated by the very technical and scientific nature of the urgent challenges posed by their ongoing research which focuses on securing sustainable energy supply and finding energy alternatives in an effort to mitigate climate change.

Seeking to encourage understanding about the diverse research stances held by team members at this early stage, the Principal Investigator facilitated a series of online sessions during which he introduced the team to his body of artistic work on oil, which he had initiated in the Scottish city of Aberdeen in 2008, and invited Professor Ott to present some key scientific parameters used in reservoir engineering and give an overview of the research on energy storage, simulation technologies, and enhanced oil recovery (EOR) techniques being conducted in his department. These sessions provided invaluable insights into artistic and scientific forms of inquiry. Logar used this instance to further contextualize *Reflecting Oil's* rationale holistically and also give a flavor of the *creative outputs* and the less tangible *outcomes* the project was striving for (like those involving perception shifts), while Professor Ott introduced basic subsurface processes involved in oil production and technical challenges, encouraging a more informed reflection about sustainability and environmental impact. Uncertainty about what specifically the final results to emanate from this explorative arts-based project were going to consist of created concern, an unknown that the team felt more comfortable working with as the project progressed and collaborators got to know one another.

Differences in expectations within the team unveiled a clash of the perspectives held by the Leoben experts and Vienna experts respectively, recalling what physicist Fritjof Capra and chemist Pier Luigi Luisi refer to in their book *The Systems View of Life: A Unifying Vision*[3] as "analytical thinking" and "systems thinking." They write: "Systems thinking is 'contextual,' which is the opposite of analytical thinking. Analysis means taking something apart in order to understand it; systems thinking means putting it into the context of a larger whole."[4] While systems thinking emphasizes "relationships, qualities, and processes,"[5] Capra and Luisi are quick to call for a "complementary interplay between the two perspectives,"[6] rather than one cancelling the other out. This complementarity of perspectives suggested here to propel a shift in ways of thinking about oil was precisely what the *Reflecting Oil* project strove for, demanding the development of a more inclusive decision-making process which eventually not only brought the team closer together but also contributed to a sense of cohesion and authorship. Interestingly, Capra and Luisi also write about the "changes of values"[7] attached to "changes of thinking,"[8] aligning thinking that privileges analysis and linearity with values such as competition and domination, and thinking that privileges synthesis and nonlinearity with the values of cooperation and partnership, calling again for a "dynamic balance"[9] between these tendencies. The research team's encounter with different forms of thinking thus went hand in hand with the encounter with the disparate methodologies associated with them, prompting discussions about diverse ways of knowing and doing, and particularly about the creative force at the center of arts-based research methods and about scientists' averseness to dealing with "subjective phenomena,"[10] which Capra and Luisi connect to "our Cartesian heritage."[11] *The Systems View of Life* was in fact useful as a key theoretical referent to facilitate the team's engagement with the holistic approach underpinning the project throughout, and thereby encourage the development of a shared understanding.

Once the team members had learned more about their counterparts' ways of thinking and working, a dynamic of mutual trust began to be established, and subjectivity (associated with artistic methodologies) and objectivity (associated with exact sciences) turned from a contested research territory into a broader field of possibilities which the group felt more at ease exploring together. Basic mathematical equations embedded in the language of petroleum engineering, for example, acquired new meanings not only for the Leoben experts, who were encouraged to contextualize them culturally and think about them as a potential source of imaginative thought, but also for the other team members who took part in these creative speculations. This playful exchange stimulated greater consciousness about limitations imposed by language, particularly scientific language, in a way that resonates with the physicists David Bohm and F. David Peat's claim, in their book *Science, Order, and Creativity*,[12] that most of the processes of language "take place largely unconsciously and unobserved and reflect the overall infrastructure of ideas embraced subliminally by the scientific community."[13] The ideas emanating from the exchange between diverse perspectives, "unimpeded by rigid attachments to particular points of view"[14] so as to be truly creative, according to Bohm and Peat, became the primary source for the experimental part of the project.

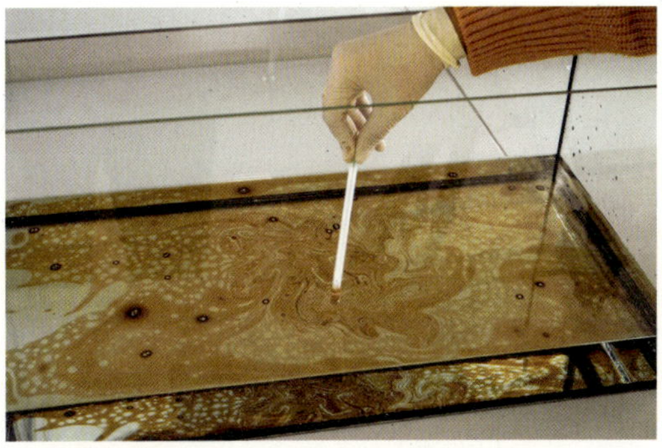

Emulsion formation experiment, DPE laboratory, 2021

Experimentation—Artistic Approximations to Oil

"We need to understand our societies as oil societies and our modernity as a *petro*-modernity to better grasp who and what we are."[15] "Scientific experience in particular derives from special conditions established by the history of ideas and by society."[16]

Throughout the project, a series of oil experiments was planned and executed in the laboratories of the University of Applied Arts Vienna and the University of Leoben's Department Petroleum Engineering, led by the Principal Investigator in collaboration with the research team, with the support of external guests on various occasions. These experiments sought to "rethink" crude oil using arts-based methodologies, focusing on the exploration of those sensory properties that are not usually researched—either for health reasons (in the case of smell, for example) or because they are difficult to quantify, measure, and describe objectively (in the case of color, for example).

The Leoben experts made a vital contribution during this experimental phase of the project with their research expertise and their acute sense of curiosity and ingenuity, offering meaningful advice about the feasibility of the proposed experiments. Here, once again, language and communication became a critical issue as the Leoben experts (often under time pressure) found themselves attempting to explain abstract concepts and sophisticated procedures (that could not be improvised) to the rest of the team. The imaging techniques used at Leoben to make visible the pore structure of rock samples retrieved from the subsurface, for example, captivated the Vienna experts from the start not only for their aesthetic qualities but also because they gave a more tangible idea of the way reservoir engineers look at oil (and its movement inside the rock) and a sense of the methods they use to measure the flow of fluids within the porous space of the reservoir, which are at the heart of their quantitative research approach. An introduction to petrophysics, which allowed the Vienna experts to familiarize themselves with fundamental petrophysical properties like porosity and permeability commonly analyzed to determine the interconnection of pores in the subsurface, proved essential to charging what initially looked like merely enigmatic visualizations with fresh scientific and artistic meanings. Patience and a predisposition to listen actively contributed to the team's trust-building process, which eventually paid off, as team members frequently praised the opportunity to engage in open dialogue and acknowledged the role that this openness played in forging mutual understanding.

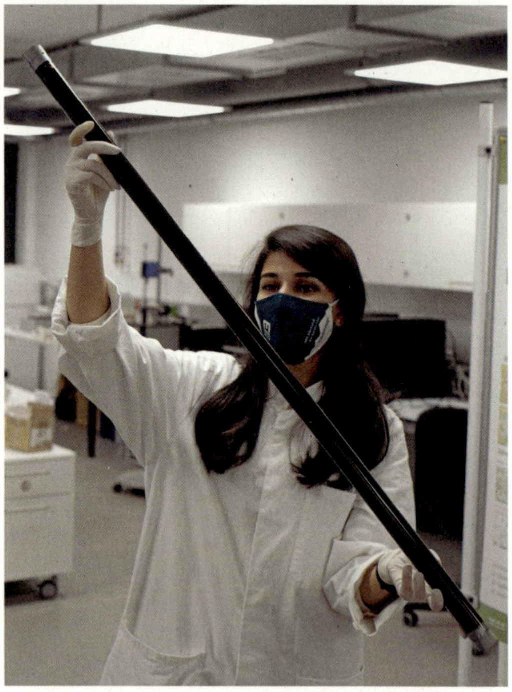

Viscosity experiment, DPE laboratory, 2020

Many of the experiments that were conducted privileged simple, hands-on procedures to facilitate direct manipulation of the substance and also the observation of unfolding processes that the Leoben experts do not normally get to see when they undertake highly mechanized procedures. However, some experiments that were conducted (like distillation to see the fractionating of oil's compounds, for example) were complex and did rely heavily on the scientific expertise of the Leoben specialists. Experiments such as this not only required a lot of preparation and waiting time but also highly specialized theoretical backgrounds to make profounder meaning of them, becoming particularly stimulating for the Leoben experts. A broad range of experiments was executed organically throughout the *Reflecting Oil* project, a sample of which can be found in the next section, responding to the explorative and intuitive impetus behind arts-based methods.

A sense of play was embraced during the experimental stage of the project, a case in point being the construction of a DIY viscometer, which offered a new perception of viscosity, a key property related to oil's resistance to flow. The viscometer consisted of an acrylic tube with a metallic ball inside, which was filled with oil and worked through choreographed body movements. The abstract property of viscosity was thus brought to life in unison with the team members' kinetic performance, giving participants not only the opportunity to *feel* the viscosity as the ball slid inside the stick but also to speculate about society's viscosity through questions like: is it because we live in a viscous society that we react very slowly to pressing global issues like the climate crisis?

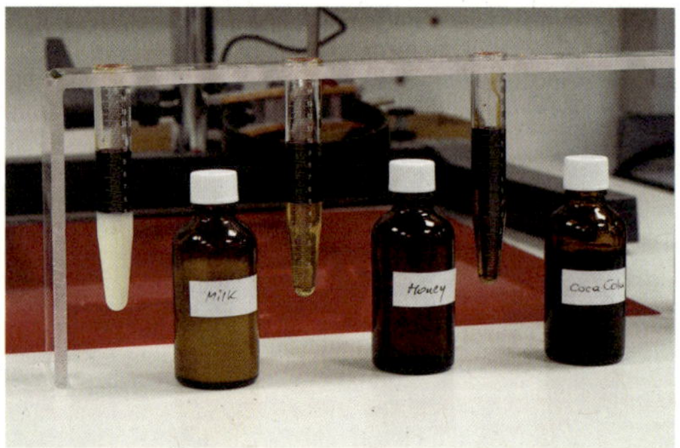

Emulsion experiment, DPE laboratory, 2020

Some of the experimental settings stipulated the execution of experiments in natural surroundings outside the laboratory's controlled environment, offering the team an opportunity to think about the formal space of the laboratory and its material culture differently and also to reflect about implicit epistemological implications behind given scientific parameters. Other experiments consisted of mixing crude oil with honey, milk, and Coca-Cola, which allowed the team not only to observe the oil's behavior under different emulsions, but also to reflect about the symbolic cultural meanings emanating from these mixtures, prompting multi-perspective discussions about "*petro*-modernity." Honey, for example, was associated with sustainable processes and the systems view of life while Coca-Cola was linked to the continuous flow of commodities feeding into our consumer societies, a movement fueled by oil and the ideology of unlimited growth. Experiments of this sort triggered the team's capacity to make imaginative connections and to extrapolate meanings, inspiring lively conversations about the ubiquity of oil, our modern consumer habits (that we find difficult to let go of), and their impact on the environment. Team members thus gained fresh awareness about the importance of narrative while attempting to describe contemporary societies' intricate interconnectivity with oil. This urge to narrate and even narrativize oil, propelled throughout the experimental phase of the project, turned the laboratory into an unprecedented site for the creative exchange of ideas and speculation.

The experiments were always followed by a time of reflection, both in writing and online group discussions, to give participants the opportunity to engage in the introspection necessary to integrate thoughts, make profounder sense of the experience, and also to raise new questions, which subsequently came to inform the project as a whole. The experiments entailed the production of artworks (creative artistic-scientific outputs in their finalized versions or preliminary sketches, led by the Principal Investigator, using various media like photography, video, and sculpture) that also fed into the research process. Artworks were conceived from the start as a means of encouraging a shift of perception about oil and also new imaginings of sustainable energy futures both within and outside academia. Some of the Leoben experts took direct part in the process of artistic creation, an experience they felt broadened their horizons, which will hopefully continue to bear fruit, now that what Bohm and Peat refer to as an "artistic attitude" that "is conducive to a sustained creative perception"[17] has been developed.

The alternative forms of perception and the associations resulting from the experiments set the grounds for the team's embrace of fresh thinking in a fashion that chimes with scientist and philosopher Ludwik Fleck's pioneering conceptualization of "thought collectives" and "thought styles" in his book *Genesis and Development of a Scientific Fact*[18] where he endeavors to apply the principles of sociology and culture to scientific knowledge production. Here Fleck argues that communities of researchers ("thought collectives") assimilate distinctive ways of doing research ("thought styles") that research communities perpetuate unconsciously, shaping the way they see and think about the world to the detriment of alternative forms of inquiry. Fleck claims that "even the simplest observation is conditioned by thought style and is thus tied to a community of thought"[19] but that thought styles can shift (and as a matter of fact have shifted throughout history) when members from different thought collectives cooperate and engage in an exchange of ideas and consequently embrace new thinking.

Fleck's theoretical framework illuminates the Vienna–Leoben cooperation (and its underlying epistemological implications), calling on us to defy those "habits of thought"[20] we latch onto when we stay within our comfort zones and instead engage in interdisciplinary and holistic thinking necessary to approach not only energy transitions but other interrelated pressing global challenges like biodiversity loss and world poverty. The collaboration empowered the entire research team in a way that superseded expectations, making an impact at an institutional level, now that the Universities of Leoben and Applied Arts Vienna have introduced curricular innovations that seek to initiate students into a holistic approach to oil transitionings grounded on an exchange between the arts and science to ignite novel post-oil imaginings.

By facilitating direct contact with oil's materiality, *Reflecting Oil's* series of experiments involved participants in a multisensorial experience of the substance and in new perceptions. The experiments carried out throughout the project with the support of experts from Vienna, Leoben, and beyond (attesting to the complementarity of perspectives that Capra and Luisi call for), can broadly be classified into two strands: those that were more explorative and artistic in nature (albeit having a scientific basis) and those that followed scientific principles and premises in the stricter sense. The six experiments discussed below, representing but a sample of the wide range undertaken, exemplify these two strands; while the *Petrolio* rock, loudspeaker, fingerprints, and color experiments fit more comfortably within the former strand, the smell and bacteria experiments (drawing on olfactory and bacteriology respectively) fit within the latter. Each experiment involved a creative approximation to oil, offering participants an opportunity to feel oil's sensory properties in a unique way, which in turn engaged them in reflection about their own entanglements with oil and those of society as a whole. To return to the James Haywood Rolling Jr. quotation that I began this chapter with, the effectiveness of "arts-based learning engagements" at the center of these experiments cannot be appropriately evaluated in the short run. However, seen from the long-term angle proposed in Imre Szeman's chapter in this book, the experimental dimension of *Reflecting Oil* illuminates "the collective experiments we need to undertake to move past the experiment of oil modernity.

1 Petrocultures Research Group, After Oil (Edmonton, Alberta: Petrocultures Research Group, 2016), 14–15, https://afteroil.ca/wp-content/uploads/2024/04/After-Oil.pdf

2 James Haywood Rolling, Jr., "A Paradigm Analysis of Arts-Based Research and Implications for Education," in *Studies in Art Education: A Journal of Issues and Research* 51, no.2 (Winter 2010), 111, https://www.jstor.org/stable/40650456

3 Fritjof Capra and Pier Luigi Luisi, *The Systems View of Life: A Unifying Vision* (Cambridge and New York: Cambridge University Press, 2014).

4 Capra and Luisi, *The Systems View of Life*, 66.

5 Capra and Luisi, 79.

6 Capra and Luisi, 83.

7 Capra and Luisi, 13.

8 Capra and Luisi, 13.

9 Capra and Luisi, 13.

10 Capra and Luisi, 262.

11 Capra and Luisi, 262.

12 David Bohm and F. David Peat. *Science, Order, and Creativity* (1987; reis., London and New York: Routledge, 2011)

13 Bohm and Peat, *Science, Order, and Creativity*, 67.

14 Bohm and Peat, 78.

15 Petrocultures Research Group, 69.

16 Ludwik Fleck, *Genesis and Development of a Scientific Fact* (1935; reis., Chicago and London: University of Chicago Press, 1979, translated by Fred Bradley and Thaddeus J. Trenn), 48.

17 Bohm and Peat, 263.

18 Ludwik Fleck, *Genesis*, 1935.

19 Fleck, 98.

20 Fleck, 104.

—02/01–04

Crude Oil Experiment Series

Alejandra Rodríguez-Remedi

Petrolio Rock Experiment
computed tomography
Petrolio
enigmatic stone
geology
artistic rock
metaphor

Loudspeaker Experiment
crude oil
sound
motion
Petrolio

Fingerprints Experiment
crude oil
tactility
fingerprint
identity

Color Experiment
crude oil
color
camouflage

—02/01 *Petrolio Rock* Experiment

The *Petrolio Rock* experiment, which entailed the creation of a manmade rock inspired by the book *Petrolio*, was one of a series of experiments with crude oil conducted at Leoben in 2022, employing various technologies used in the oil and gas industry. Dr Arianna Mondin, a guest participant for this series, contributed from an architect's perspective, most particularly through her expertise on how oil relates to space and shapes our everyday lives. At the outset, Mondin gave insights into *Petrolio*, the unfinished literary opus (posthumously published in 1992) by Italian writer and filmmaker Pier Paolo Pasolini (1922–75), which comprises a seemingly disparate collection of notes connected through a complex structure defined by the movement of oil.

Mondin introduced the following passage from *Petrolio*, which recounts the story of an enigmatic stone found in the desert that remained a mystery after scientists were unable to distinguish what was toxic and what was precious in it. Here Mondin found a metaphor for approaching oil in all its complexity and ambivalence:

"The geologists loaded that precious find into their Land Rover as well as they could and carried it to the civilized world to analyze it. But they do not succeed, and today that stone remains a pure enigma. The infinite variety of its soft colors corresponds to an infinite variety of materials, but none of them have really been identified, because each material presents contradictory characteristics, both in relation to itself and in relation to the other minerals with which it is amalgamated or compounded."[1]

This passage, which eventually informed every stage of the experiment, became the starting point for the construction of the manmade rock endowed with ambiguous qualities and properties, inviting participants to question positivistic assumptions about science. Logar built this randomly shaped *Petrolio*-inspired rock using

CT scanning of the *Petrolio Rock*
Department Petroleum Engineering
(DPE) laboratory
University of Leoben, 2021

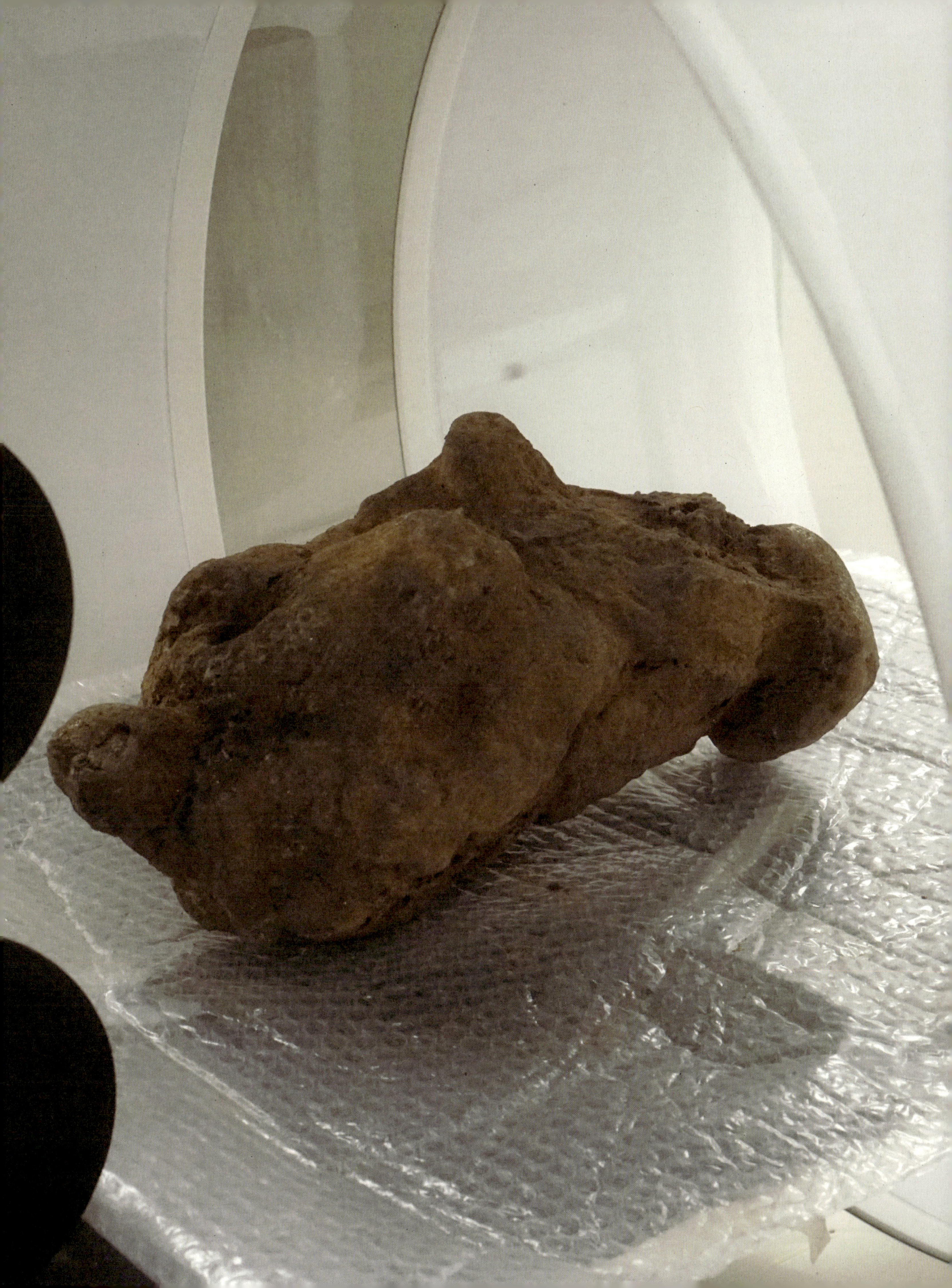

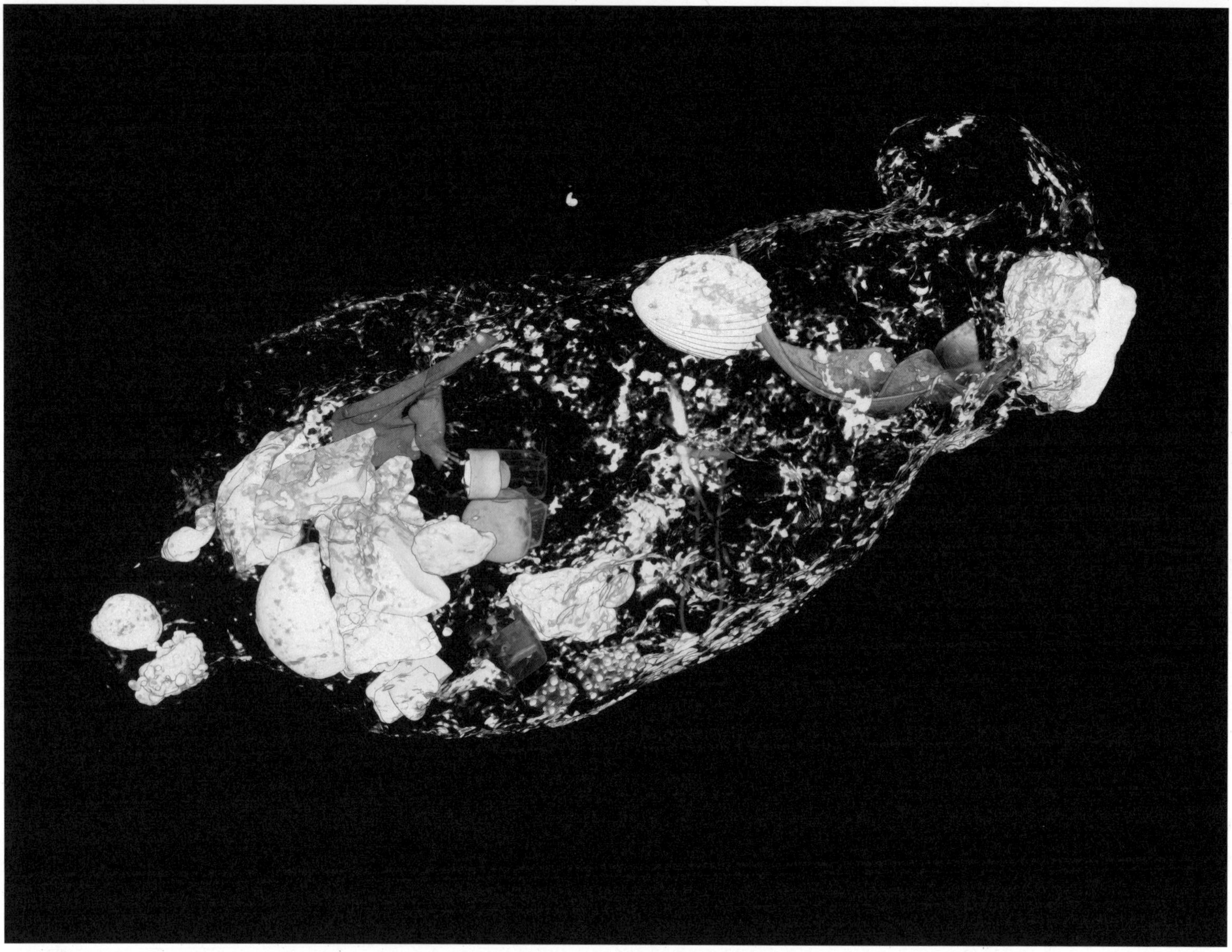

The image is a volumetric CT reconstruction of the *Petrolio Rock*, showing a heterogeneous composition.
Various embedded materials with different densities are distinctly visible, appearing as high-contrast inclusions within the foam matrix.

polyester foam, sand, and various hidden objects, like fossils and bits of plastic, which were especially selected to invoke geological and petrocultural meanings. At a later stage, a Computed Tomography (CT) scan visualized these hidden objects by detecting their different densities, without damaging the rock. The Leoben experts, upon examining the series of 3D images of the artificial rock, were quick to identify an anomaly: this manmade rock lacked the pore space and connectivity of the pores of a real rock. This abnormality ignited a creative discussion about how to bestow this artistic rock with network properties, that is, an interconnected pore structure to allow fluids to flow in it. This discussion eventually illuminated the idea of looking at networks (and their properties) from different perspectives to encourage the connection of oil with the social and the cultural, for example, becoming another potential metaphor to approach our entanglements with oil.

The oddness of Logar's rock was also recognized at a haptic level. Though it resembles a rock on the outside, it does not feel like one to the touch, as it is both warm and light. The experiment inspired participants to reflect on "scientific looking" (and its inevitable subjective angle). Despite the technological mediation, which supposedly safeguards objectivity, it is the scientists themselves who set up technological instruments (in this case a CT scan) to show them what to see.

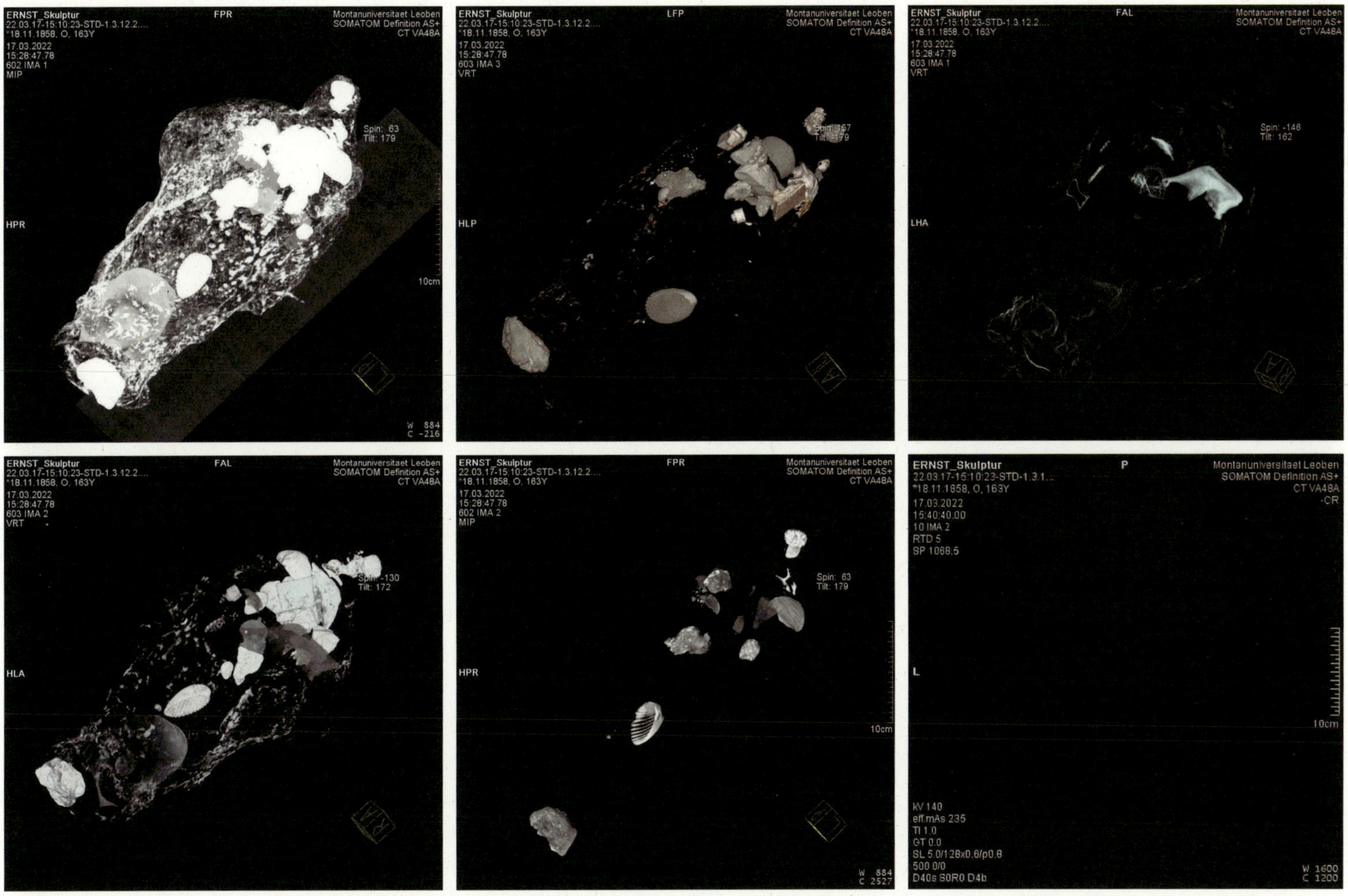

The CT image series shows specialized post-processing filters and reconstruction techniques to enhance contrast and distinguish materials by their attenuation properties. X-ray attenuation depends on electron density and atomic composition, measured in Hounsfield Units (HU). Higher atomic number elements (e.g., metals) show greater attenuation, while lower-density materials (e.g., organic matter, soft tissues) attenuate less.

The cultural dimension behind the act of seeing the precious properties and qualities of things, in this case a rock, was also acknowledged and discussed creatively.

Pasolini expands on the above-mentioned passage, informing us that ongoing research, which is still trying to understand the mysterious stone, only gives “partiality of results,” in a way that resonates with the partial, almost fragmentary quality of the image series produced by the CT scanner itself. The *Petrolio Rock* experiment, originally conceived to explore the metaphor emanating from Mondin’s close reading of *Petrolio*, generated unexpected conditions to defamiliarize the material culture associated with the lab, triggering a critical conversation about oil’s elusiveness and the unique contribution that artistic methods can make to approach its complexity.

1 Pier Paolo Pasolini, *Petrolio* (New York: Pantheon Books, 1997). / Pier Paolo Pasolini, Petrolio (Turin: Einaudi, 1992), 115.

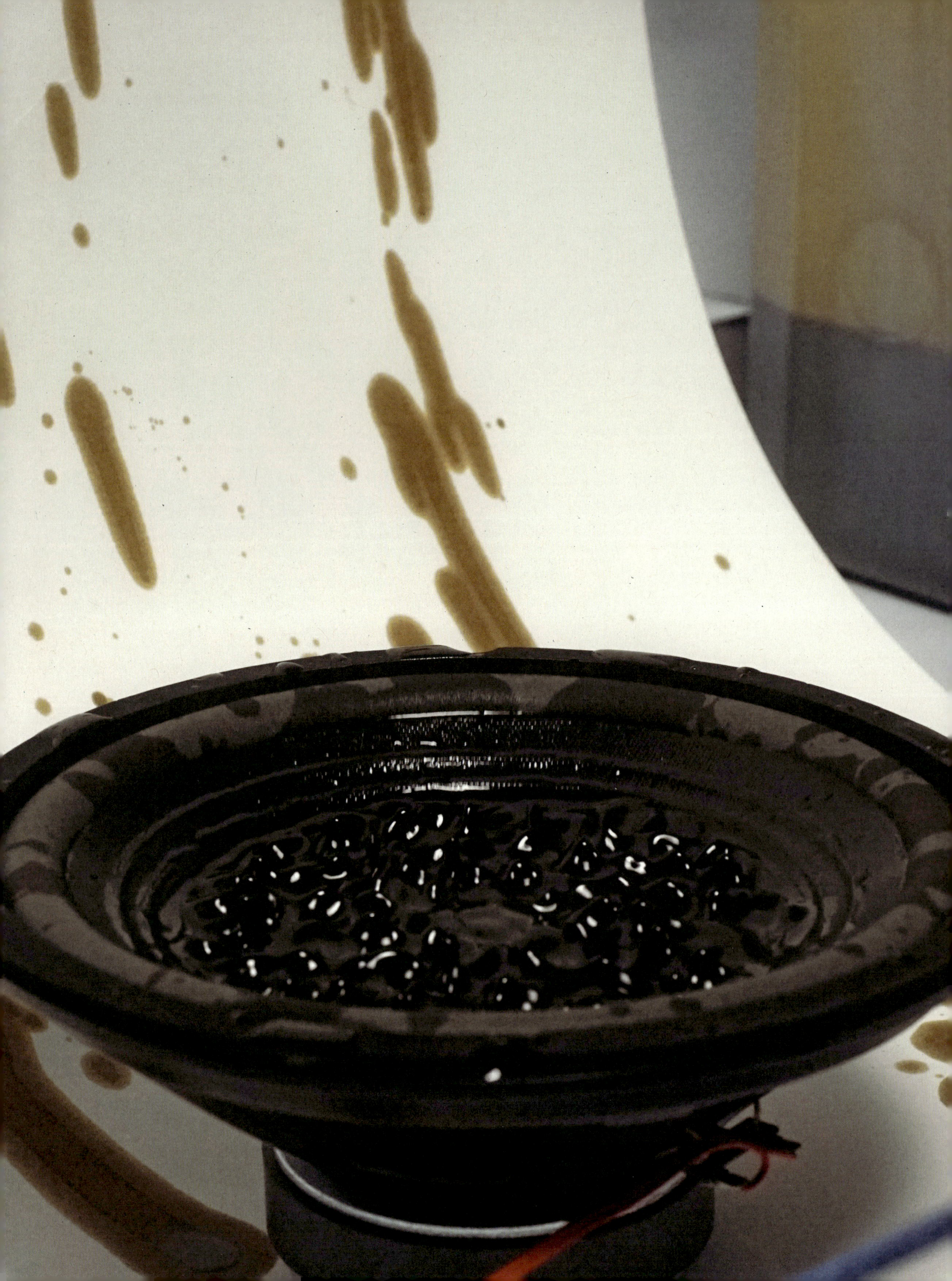

—02/02 Loudspeaker Experiment

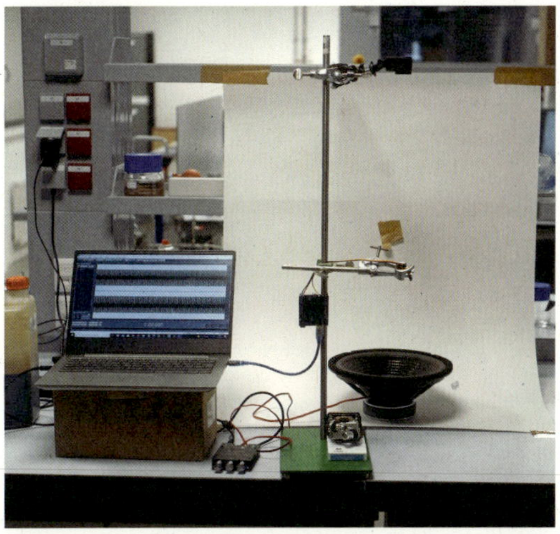

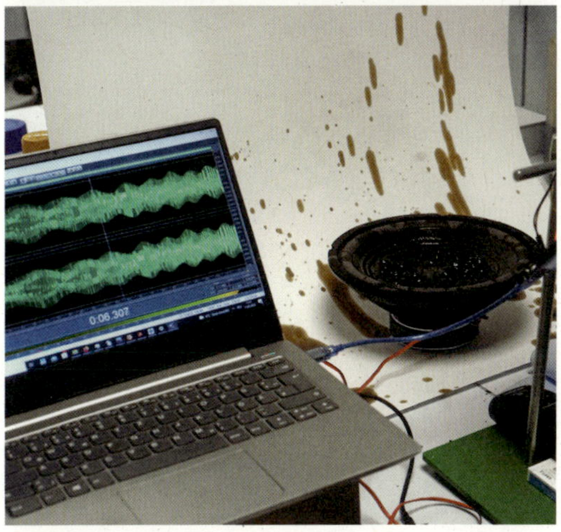

Loudspeaker experiment, experimental setting
Subwoofer, amplifier, laptop, laser diode, paper, crude oil

The loudspeaker experiment was another of the series carried out in 2022 that Mondin was invited to take part in. This experiment sought to explore oil surfaces in motion, a concept that Logar had looked at previously when researching the North Sea oil and gas industry, especially through his *Reflecting Oil* (2008), an installation consisting of a mirror made of moving oil. In that art piece, a pump made the oil move, whereas here sound was used to create motion. Geologists commonly use sound as a subsurface parameter and, like light, it is often deployed as an explorative tool. Geologists collect subsurface sounds and analyze them with software to help them visualize the porous medium quantitatively.

Once again, Mondin contributed to setting up the experiment with her expertise on *Petrolio*, a novel that Pasolini had conceived from the outset as being in transformation, a magmatic form of reality in constant movement. The magmatic concept and sense of motion that Pasolini strove to evoke through his writing provided the germinal idea for this experiment that offered a creative interpretation and materialization of Pasolini's approach to oil.

The experiment involved the use of a sound generator, an amplifier, a laser beam, and a loudspeaker filled with crude oil. After trying a range of high and low frequencies, the team decided that the lower frequencies came closest to creating an effect that fitted Pasolini's vision: 10 hertz and below (frequencies inaudible to the human ear) triggered vibrations that not only made the oil move, and emit sound as it moved, but generated regular patterns that made the oil look as if it were boiling. Mondin equated this regular pattern formation with what Pasolini referred to as a "swarm" movement that made the substance look alive; or, in Mondin's own words, made it appear as if it were "beating like a heart and moving like monsters of the deep."

A red laser was directed towards the surface of the oil and a laser beam was emitted and projected onto a makeshift paper wall, following the movement of the oil to create an enhanced visual effect. The oil spurted as it moved in various directions, hitting the paper in a way that recalled Jackson Pollock's action painting. Participants reflected about the striking effect caused by this visualization of oil's animation through sound in terms of an enigmatic manifestation, which felt as if oil, a non-living substance resulting from ancient life, had been awakened by a primordial ritualistic beat. For some, it seemed as though the oil were speaking, an illusion triggered by the fact that the oil was moving inside the diaphragm of a loudspeaker. Speculative questions arose: if crude oil had a voice, what sort of voice would this be? What would a language of oil entail? Would there be a plurality of languages depending on the place of origin or other unique properties of the oil in question?

Participants were thus encouraged to make gender, class, and race-related issues explicit.

The loudspeaker experiment set the grounds for the exploration of scientific sonic parameters in an imaginative way. Like the *Petrolio Rock* experiment, this experiment prompted ideas for further multisensorial experiments and an open conversation about artistic methodologies' capacity to convey embodied experiences and thus ignite fresh perceptions.

Loudspeaker experiment
DPE laboratory, 2021

—02/03 Fingerprints Experiment

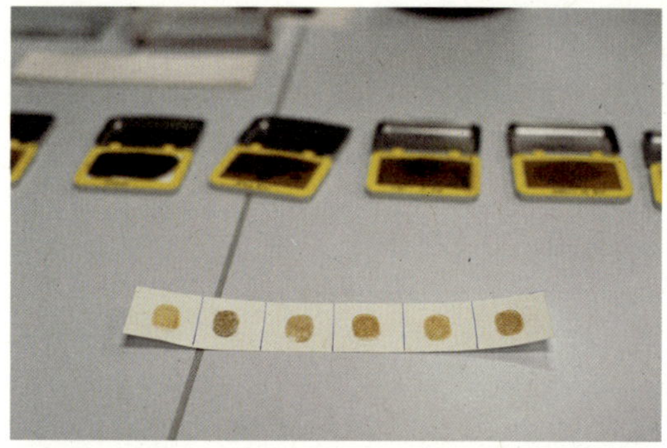

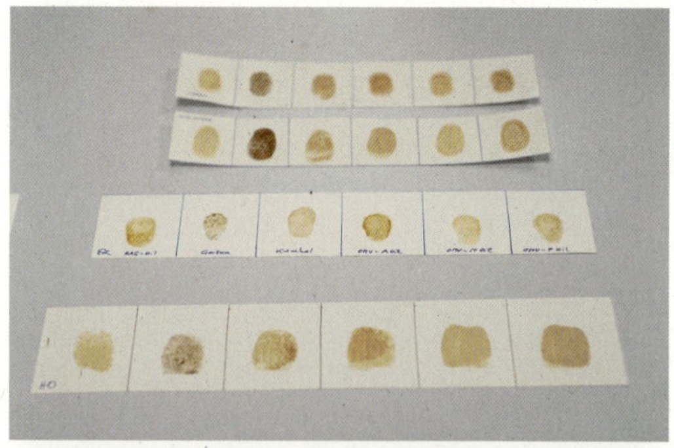

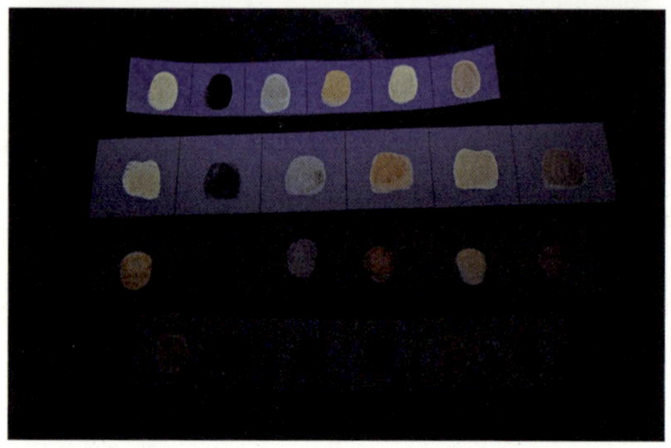

Top: Six different crude oils in stamp pads
Center: Crude oil fingerprints on watercolor paper
Bottom: Crude oil fingerprints under UV light

The fingerprints experiment, one of a series conducted in 2023, engaged the *Reflecting Oil* research team in a haptic perception of crude oil and in novel visualizations of the substance. As a guest participant, I sought to propel the group discussion from a visual culture standpoint by focusing on what the tactility and visuality at the heart of oleaginous identity could potentially unveil about our petrocultural condition.

The starting point of the experiment derived from Logar's extensive hands-on research on oil as well as from his wish to offer others a similarly transformative encounter with the substance. As he has noted, "My experience with the substance is changing my thinking about it." Discussions with geologists also informed the experiment, in particular a conversation that followed a presentation delivered to the *Reflecting Oil* research team by Leoben geologist Prof. David Misch in 2021 about the basics of the petroleum system. Misch had spoken about how crude oils from different regions possess unique fingerprints that can actually be identified through biomarkers—hydrocarbon molecules that geologists use to determine the relative age and environment in which an oil is formed.

All those taking part in the experiment were given cotton paper strips divided into six cells. Meanwhile, six different crude oil samples—RAG (Austria), Geisum (Egypt), Kumkol (Kazakhstan), OMV-A (Austria), OMV-M (Austria), and OMV-P (Austria)—were poured onto six stamp pads. Participants then took turns to cover their thumbs with one of the crude oil samples before stamping their thumbprint onto a cell on the cotton paper strips. Participants repeated this for all six samples, making sure to wipe their hands clean between stamps. Before cleaning the oil off, however, they took time to *feel* the oil between their thumb and index finger and verbalized how it felt. Because all the oils had a distinctive smell and color, comments on the oils' tactile properties inevitably extended to their olfactory and visual qualities. The thumbprints on the paper strips were examined under UV light (often used by geologists to identify traces of hydrocarbons in rocks by making oil's fluorescence visible), revealing the participants' fingerprints to striking visual effect. The UV light enabled the group to see nuanced differences in color between oil samples.

Human fingerprints and oil fingerprints were amalgamated into one.

The participants were thus invited to make symbolic connections, such as between the heterogeneous identities of oil and the plurality of humankind itself. The experiment opened the floor to reflection about our identities as human beings (bestowed with unique fingerprints that are symbolically smeared by the oil-infused commodities that make up petroculture) and our ethical accountability for the carbon footprint responsible for climate change that each of us leaves upon the environment. Participants discovered in fingerprints, a concept that the Leoben experts had solely looked at as a scientific approach in petroleum exploration and refinement, a powerful metaphor to reflect creatively about our embeddedness in petroculture. The haptic experience and novel visualizations of oil facilitated by the fingerprints experiment gave participants an enhanced awareness of themselves as petro-subjects, a key step in the conception and development of a sustainable subject.

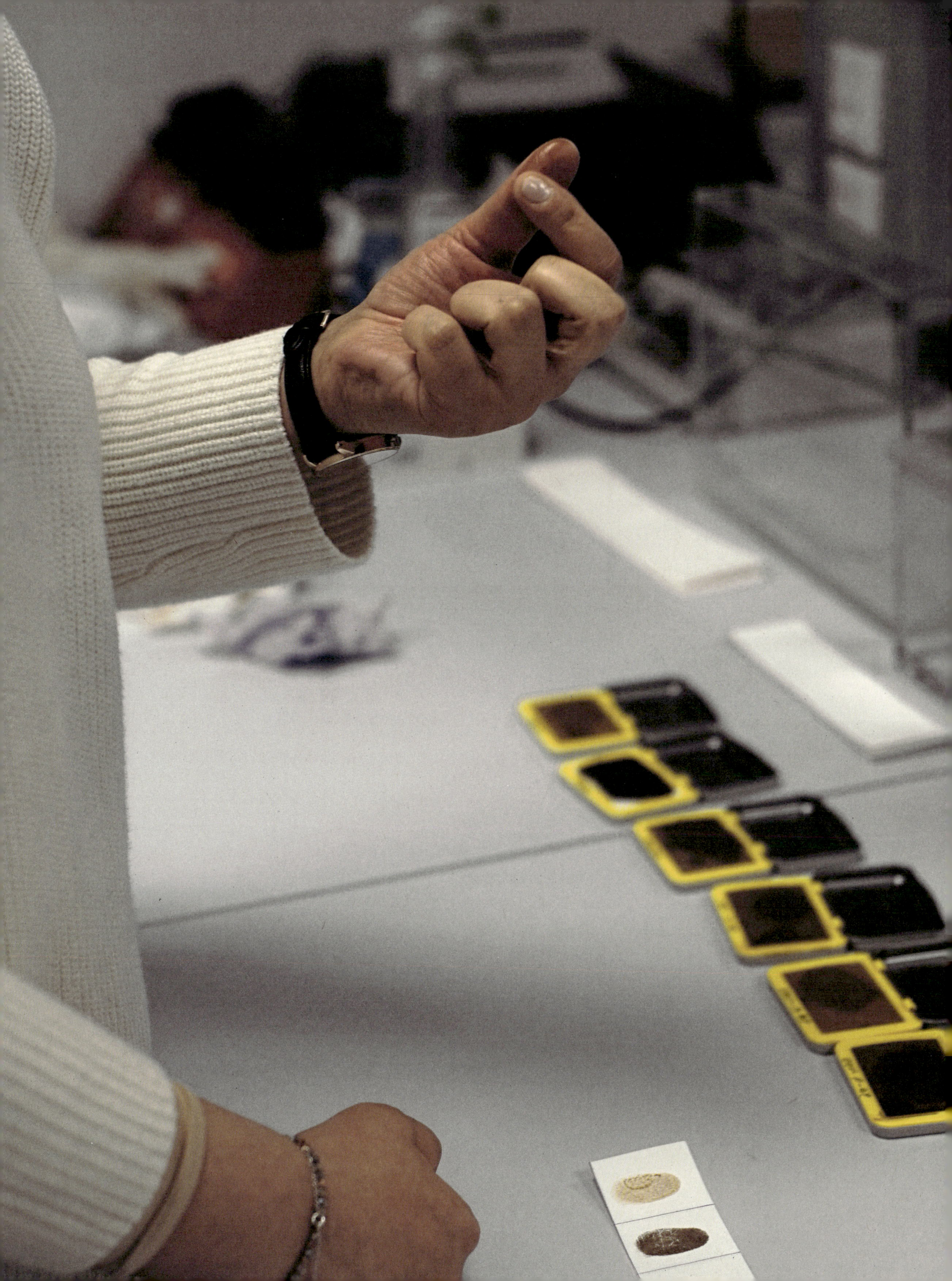

—02/04 Color Experiment

From the outset, and from an artistic perspective, Logar envisaged great potential for creative experiments on crude oil's visual appearance and aesthetics, particularly its color. Soon after the project began, when he and the Leoben experts were planning for possible experiments that would not only open room for the imaginative exploration of the physical properties of crude oil but also guarantee maximal hands-on manipulation of the substance, it became evident that the property of color did not customarily receive the same level of attention as did crude oil's other physical properties like its viscosity.

Although the Leoben experts spoke about the ASTM Color Scale[1] used to determine the color of petroleum products, both to measure quality and to indicate the degree of refinement, they acknowledged that there was no color system in place distinguishing crude oils' different black and brown tones.

It was not until the *Reflecting Oil* project was approaching its conclusion, when Logar had gained enough appreciation of the distinct visual properties of crude oils, that he was able to design an exploratory color experiment. Its execution involved 20 different samples of crude oil which were first displayed in separate glass plates and then photographed. The eventual application of additive synthesis with red, green, and blue (RGB) primaries to the resulting image allowed Logar to estimate the color of the different oil samples.

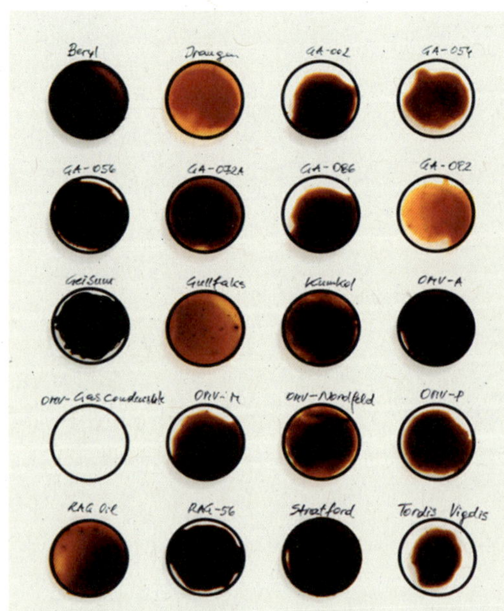

Crude oil color experiment
20 different oil samples

This joyfully not-so-accurate experiment makes an important contribution to the visualization of lighter and darker crude oils (an approximation of black and brown tones), constituting a meaningful effort to address oil's ambiguity. It is relevant here to mention *Six oils* (2024), an art piece where Logar alludes to the very color palette produced in the crude oil color experiment to evoke a camouflage effect that conceals instead of making visible, reminding us of the pervasive power relations and geopolitics underpinning oil's invisibility and elusiveness.

The crude oil color experiment provides a basis for what could potentially comprise a comprehensive crude oil color system able both to advance verbal descriptors of the color of crude oils and group the oils by their main compounds. By broadening the research to the physical property of color through the inclusion of cultural and artistic parameters, a nuanced understanding of the materiality of the substance could potentially be achieved alongside the promotion of inventive representations of oil capable of propelling new post-oil imaginings.

1 ASTM D1500-12(2017)
Standard Test Method for ASTM Color of Petroleum Products (ASTM Color Scale)
https://www.astm.org/d1500-12r17.html

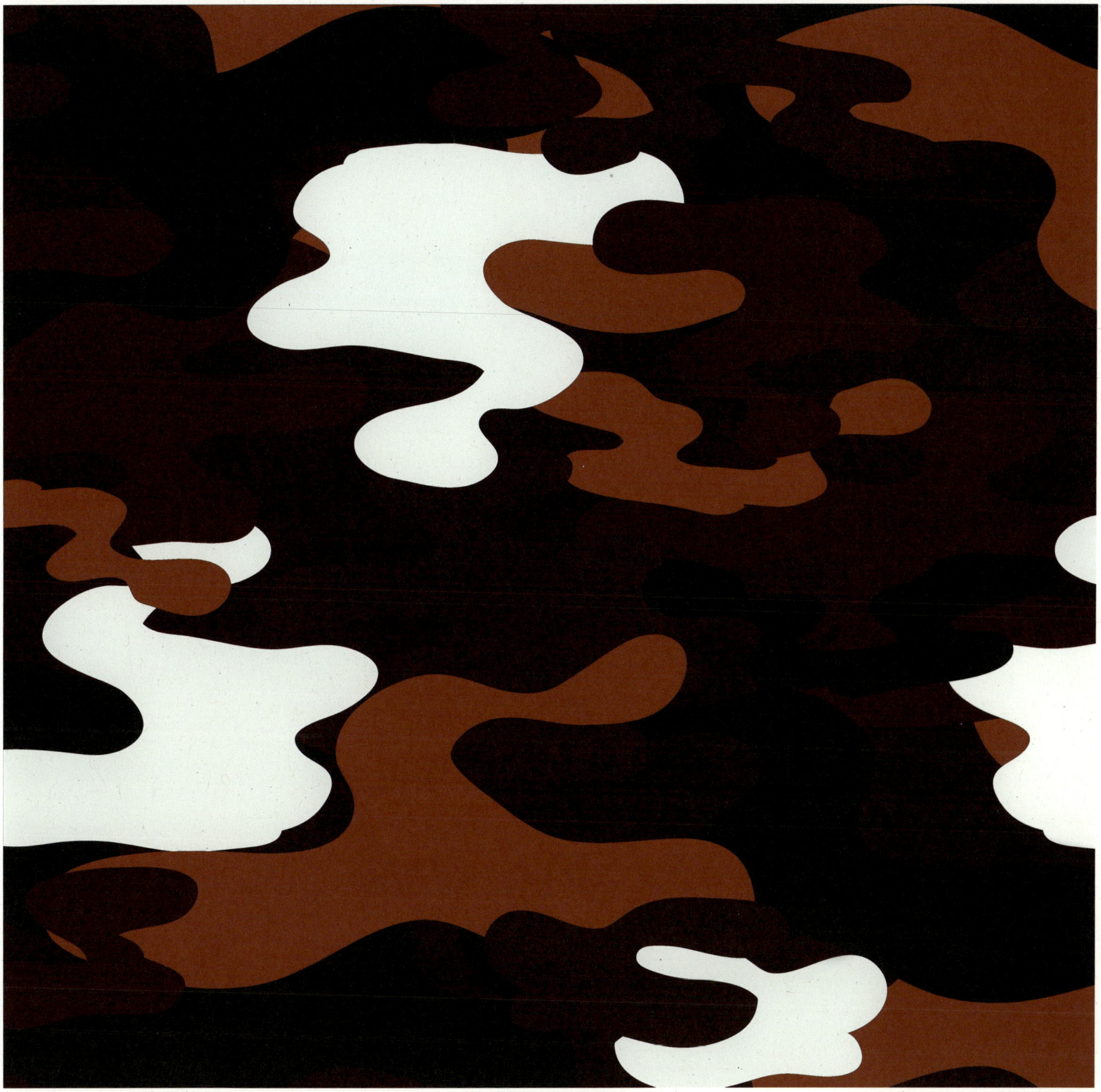

Ernst Logar, *Six oils—Beryl oil, Draugen oil, GA-086 oil, OMV-Gas condensate, RAG oil, Tordis Vigdis oil*, 2024, Inkjet print

—02/05

How Does It Smell?

An Experimental Approach to the Odor of Crude Oil

Iris Stappen, Johannes Novak

experiment
smell
crude oil
fragrance wheel
odor analysis
gas-chromatography
spectrometry
toxicity
olfactory crude oil wheel

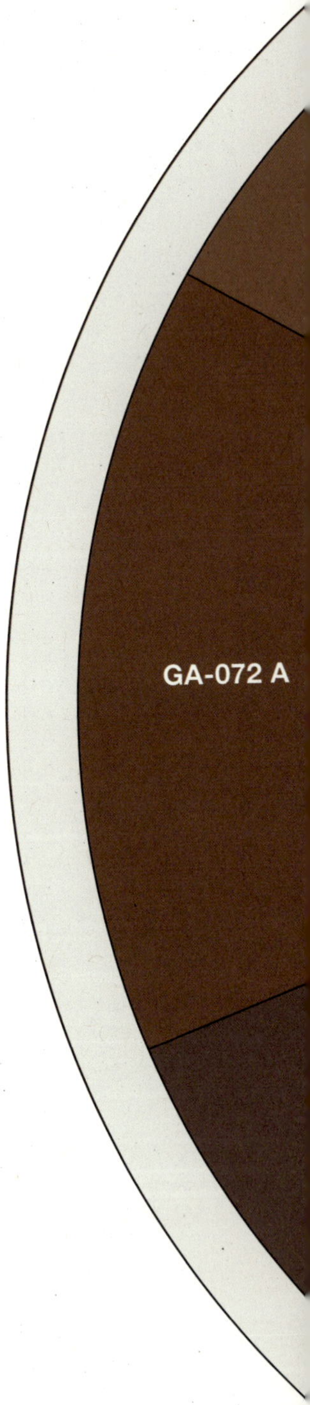

For a very long time, the human sense of smell was neglected by scientists. Humans were believed to be "microsmatics" with an indiscriminate olfactory ability. However, starting from the 1980s, researchers became increasingly interested in the nose and the underlying mechanisms of olfaction. This peaked in 2004, when Linda Buck, a US-American neurophysiologist, and Richard Axel, a US-American physician, were awarded the Nobel Prize in Physiology or Medicine for their investigations on the olfactory receptor gene family.[1] Meanwhile, scientific research has confirmed that the human sense of smell is better than its reputation and, further, that odors have a noticeable psychological impact, a finding that has been discussed in various journals and books.[2]

In 1997, the German psychologist and perfumer J. Stephan Jellinek published his model of the psychodynamic mechanisms of odors, pointing out the powerful, individual psychological effect of fragrances on humans. These reactions are mainly due to a person's attraction to certain smells (be they pleasant or unpleasant—the "mechanism of hedonic valence") as well as past emotional experiences of a particular scent (the "semantic mechanism").[3] Furthermore, a high overlap and strong connection between the olfactory and emotional regions of the brain were discovered, confirming and explaining this psychological impact. This makes smells important in the treatment of minor psychological disorders, such as anxiety, depression, and insomnia.[4]

In recent years, olfaction and/or odors have been the subject of various art projects, including the piece *Fear of Smell / Smell of Fear_12_24* performed by Norwegian artist and olfaction researcher Sissel Tolaas in St. Pölten, Lower Austria.[5] This investigation aims to characterize the scent of crude oil within an art context. To this end, two approaches were performed: first, to smell the target oil sample and describe its odor, and second, to fragment the mixture of volatiles into their individual components and characterize the sample by the sum of odors released by its main compounds.

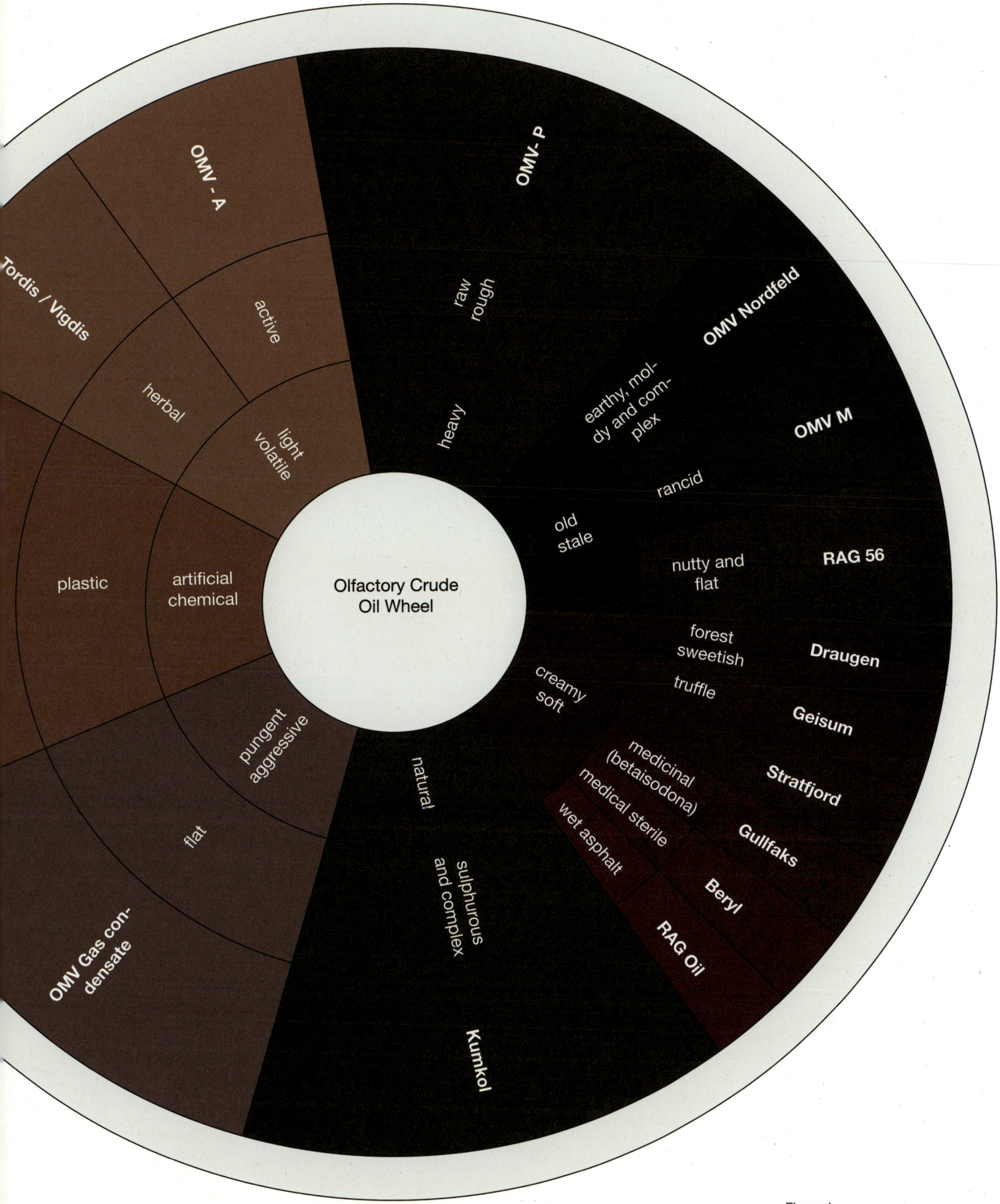

Figure 1
Crude Oil Olfactory Wheel with descriptors for the odors of oil fractions

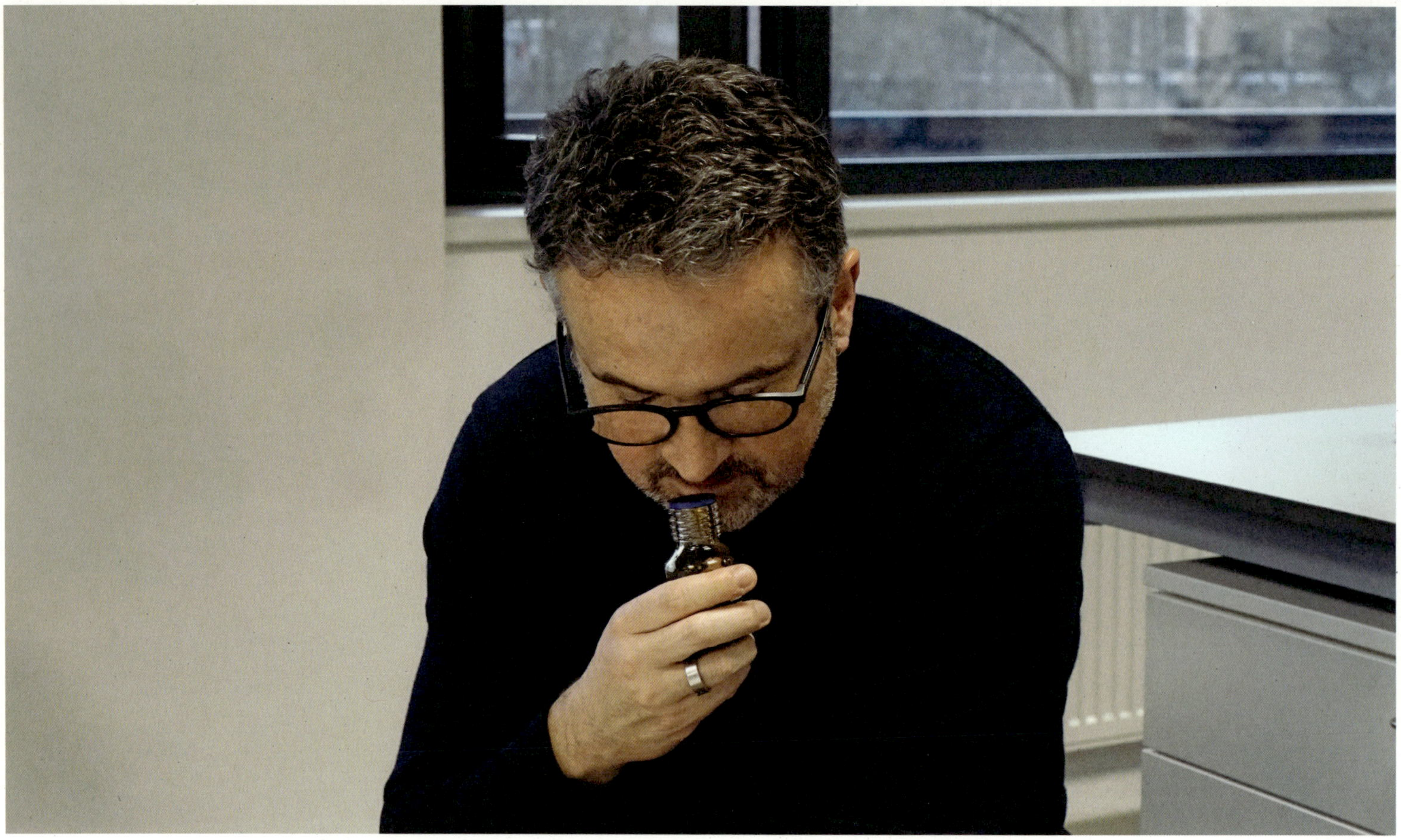

Crude oil smell experiment, Department Petroleum Engineering (DPE) laboratory, University of Leoben, 2024

Odor Description

Crude oil is a complex mixture of hundreds of organic compounds. Some of these substances are volatile and therefore emit an odor. This odor depends on the oil's composition, which varies widely depending on the region it was extracted from.

As a starting point, we asked colleagues and friends to describe the smell of crude oil. First, most of them experienced it as unpleasant. Second, they started comparing the smell to something they know, for example, "it smells like petrol/a petrol station" or "it resembles the odor of the [heating] oil tank in our basement." People do not have the words to describe the smell of crude oil because this important raw material has never been looked at from an olfactory point of view. This had to be changed.

In 1984, feeling the need to help retailers suggest perfumes to their customers, fragrance expert Michael Edwards published the largest independent guide for fragrance classification: *The Fragrance Manual*. In 2000, it was renamed *Fragrances of the World* and since then it has been reprinted annually. Edwards noticed that the smell of perfumes do not necessarily fall into the four main, previously defined olfactory groups (woody, floral, oriental, and fresh) but could be more precisely characterized by additional subgroups that are linked to each other (e.g., soft oriental, oriental, woody oriental etc.). He created the Fragrance Wheel (also called Aroma Wheel or Fragrance Circle), a circular diagram that shows the relationships between the four olfactory groups, based on the differences and similarities between smells, and defines 14 different fragrance families. The relationships between these odors and aromas derive from similarities in their chemical compositions.[6] The wheel was adapted to include food and beverages, leading to even more descriptors for (food) aromas.[7]

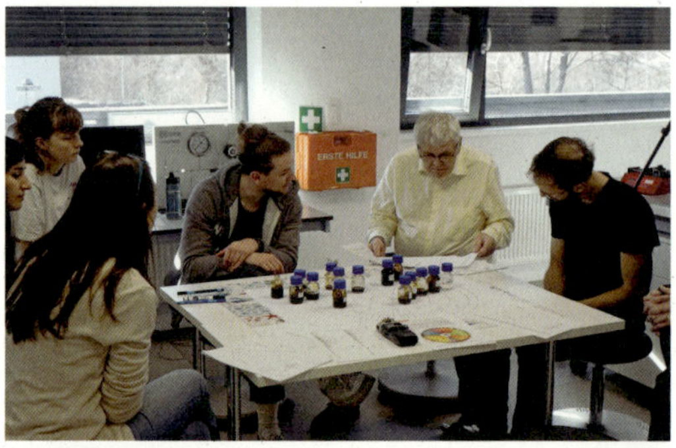

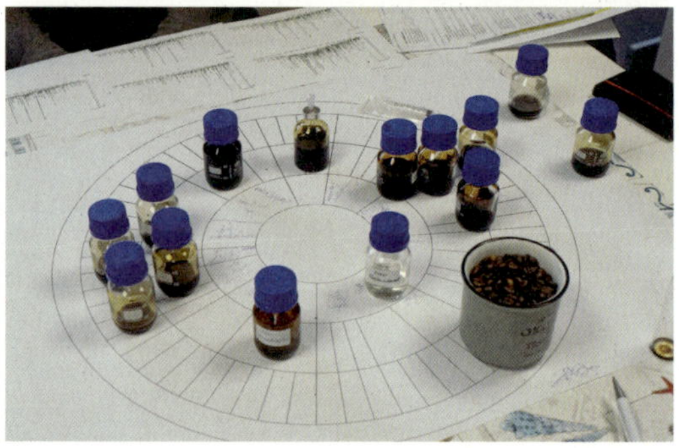

Crude oil smell experiment DPE laboratory, 2024

Although a lot of fragrance or flavor descriptors exist already, we had to face the fact that—not surprisingly—the smell of none of the crude oil samples we were examining fitted any of the existing perfume or food odor descriptions. Therefore, a panel of eight men and women, professionals working in either crude oil or odors, got together at the University of Leoben, in Austria, to think of words that might best describe the smell of these oil samples, but also to try to put them in relation to each other according to the fragrance and aroma wheels. The resulting Crude Oil Olfactory Wheel can be seen in Figure 1.

Odor Analyses

Additionally, the volatiles of the oil samples underwent gas-chromatography/mass-spectrometry (GC/MS) analysis, using the headspace (HS) technique, to provide clues for possible odor-leading structures within the mixture. The aim was to underlay different smells of diverse originsof oil with chemical data. GC is an analytical technique mainly used on liquids and gases in order to separate and detect the chemical components of a sample mixture through a column in time. That way, the presence, absence, and quantity (in relation to each other) of the individual substances can be evaluated. The MS further measures the mass-to-mass ratio (m/z) of each single substance detected by GC. By comparing the MS spectra of these substances with the spectra of defined compounds from databases, these unknown chemicals could, in best cases, be identified.

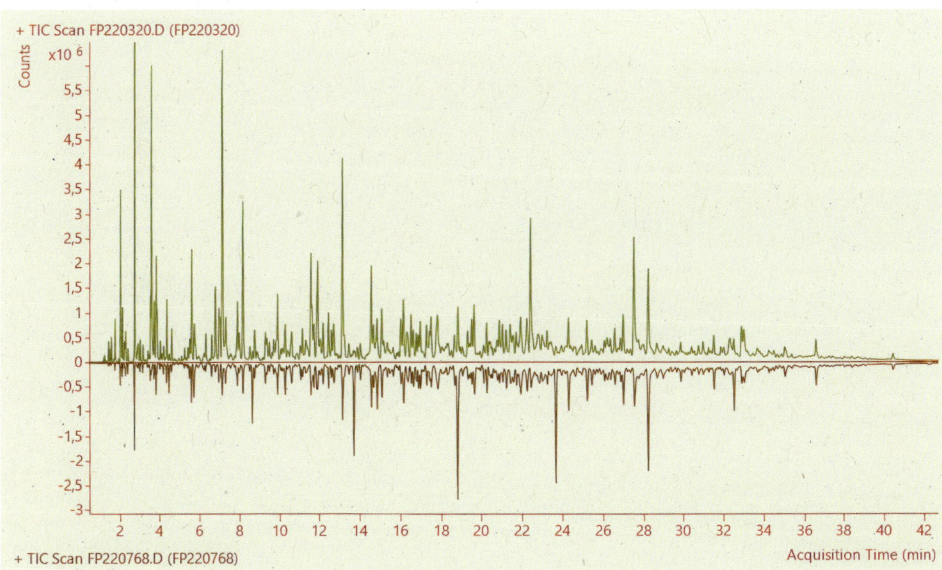

Figure 2a
Difference plot of the volatiles of two crude oils (above 'GA-072a', below 'Statfjord')

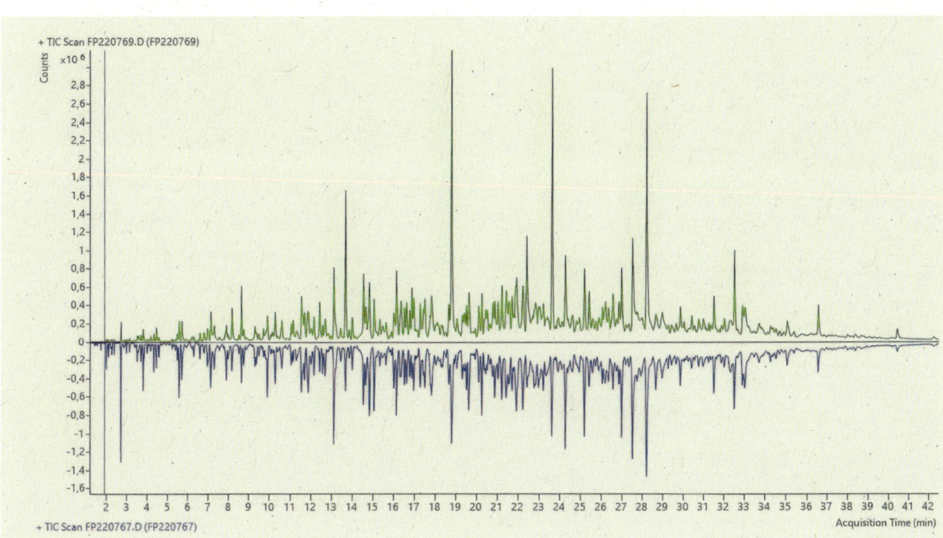

Figure 2b
Difference plot of the volatiles of two crude oils (above 'Beryl', below 'Gulfaks').

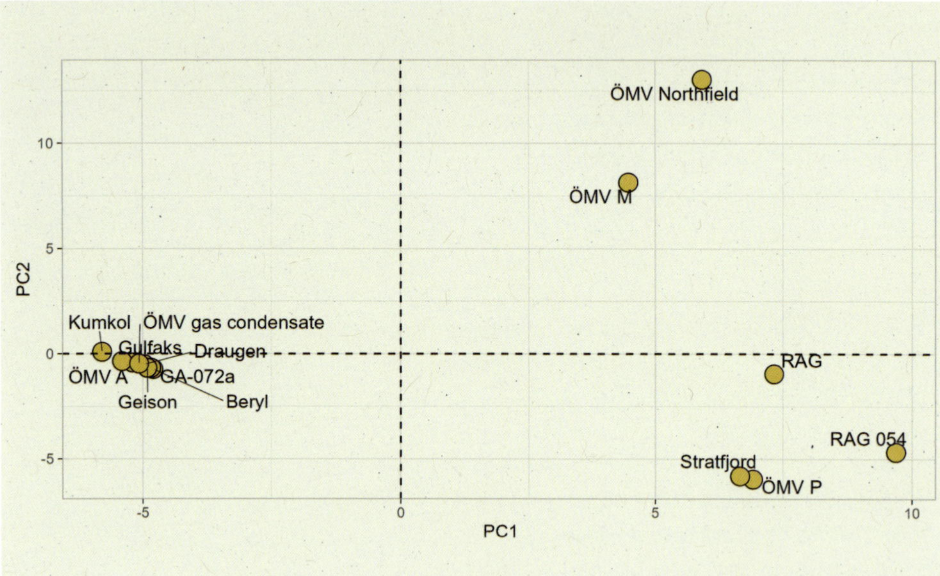

Figure 3
PCA crude oils: first two dimensions of principal component analysis of the volatiles of 14 crude oils.

Since the focus of the investigation was on the odorous (i.e., volatile) compounds in crude oil, the HS technique was used. Therefore, the oil samples were heated to either 30°C or 50°C in a closed vial for 30 minutes. The vapor was then collected by means of a special HS device. This was then injected into the GC for the volatiles to be separated and identified as described above.

Crude oil mainly comprises more than 500 hydrocarbons (aliphatic, aromatic, cyclic) in combination with sulfur, oxygen, and nitrogen, all showing similar molecular weights and fractions, so it was impossible to reliably identify most of the components. However, looking at the GC chromatograms (visual representations of the intensity of the individual compounds [y-axis] separated in time [x-axis]), it was noted that the samples' compositions varied more or less widely depending on the origin of the oils. Nonetheless, comparing the pattern of peaks separated by GC, one could see that some of these chromatograms resembled each other in retention time and relative quantity of single compounds. This means that the composition of the vapors escaping from these oils was similar. Figure 2a and Figure 2b show, exemplarily, two pairs of chromatograms demonstrating this similarity and disparity, respectively.

Although an identification of odor character compounds could not be achieved by GC/MS, similarities and dissimilarities in the vapor composition of oil samples were identified.

By comparing the composition of the different oils statistically, similarities and dissimilarities become obvious, as visualized in Figure 3. According to their components, as identified by GC, the Austrian and Norwegian samples were clearly separated whereas the RAG 054 and GA-072a samples were two outgroups with completely different aroma profiles.

Results and Discussion

First of all, it must be mentioned that crude oil contains many chemicals that are considered toxic. This toxicity concerns dermal and inhalation exposures. Animal cancer models subjected to long exposure durations and high concentrations showed signs of tissue hyperplasia. Mainly, it is the water-soluble fraction, with its polar chemicals, that seems to be responsible for the oil's toxicity, a toxicity which was intensified by sunlight: the hydrocarbons oxidized leading to more dangerous substances.[8] As such, the intense sniffing of crude oil and its products, such as diesel fuels and gasoline, is to be avoided! It was only performed for this investigation to characterize a raw product, one that is well known to almost everyone who comes from an industrialized country but that has never been looked at in the context of olfaction/art.

We noticed that it was difficult to describe an odor without previously defined verbal descriptors. Although the odor of crude oil is familiar to people, they lack the words to describe a smell they have never experienced from an olfactory point of view. Further, the volunteers involved in this project were not trained in olfaction. People who work with taste and smell (perfumers and "nosers") are taught to be able to detect and identify up to 3000 odor chemicals.[9] However, once we focused on the smell, verbal descriptors were found (Figure 1). Additionally, splitting the volatile fraction by GC helped us to find the similarities or dissimilarities between crude oils derived from different regions. This way, the oils could be grouped (Figures 2a, 2b) and the outcome confirmed the olfactory evaluation.

Conclusion

In contrast to vision ("reflecting oil"), olfaction ("sensing oil") is a chemical sense where molecules interact with receptors in the nose. It is also directly connected to the emotional center of the brain, which evokes an immediate response (without reflecting) after smelling odors. As we noted in this experiment, this response was mainly negative—the odor of crude oil was rated as unpleasant, with people avoiding the odor source rather than approaching it. On the "second sniff," several pleasant odor descriptors were found. The oil was looked at from another perspective and grew a body rather than being viewed as just a raw material. Therefore, the experiment of exploring crude oil from completely different perspectives, such as art or olfaction, improved the character of this product.

Furthermore, our instrumental approach provided us with data from a measuring instrument (gas chromatography) that made us more aware of the significant differences between the oils than smelling alone. The results of the data have sharpened, or rather, refined our sensitivity to the diversity of scents.

1 David Julius and Lawrence C. Katz, "A Nobel for smell," in *Cell* 119, no. 6, 747–752.

2 Matthias Laska M. (2011), "The Human Sense of Smell—Our Noses are Much Better than We Think!" in *Senses and the city: An interdisciplinary approach to urban sensescapes*, ed., M. Diaconu et al., (Vienna: Lit Verlag, 2011), 145–153; Johannes Frasnelli, *Wir riechen besser als wir denken* (Graz: Molden Verlag in Verlagsgruppe Styria GmbH&Co.KG, 2021).

3 J.S. Jellinek, "Psychodynamic odor effects and their mechanisms: Failure to identify the mechanism can lead to faulty conclusions in odor studies," in *Cosmetics and Toiletries* 112 (1997), 61–71.

4 E. Heuberger, I. Stappen, and R. Rudolf von Rohr, *Riechen und Fühlen. Wie Geruchssinn, Ängste und Depressionen zusammenspielen* (Munderfing: Verlag Fischer & Gann, 2017).

5 Sissel Tolaas, *Fear of Smell / Smell of Fear_12_24*, 2024, July 14, 2024, Tangente St. Pölten, Austria, https://www.tangente-st-poelten.at/de/kunstparcours/Sissel-Tolaas.

6 Michael Edwards, *Fragrances of the World: The Reference Book 2020 & 2021*, https://www.fragrancesoftheworld.com/TheReferenceBook.

7 Prof. Dr. Thomas Simat et al., "Geruchs- und Aromaschulung in der Sensorik," DLG.org, January 2017, https://www.dlg.org/de/lebensmittel/themen/publikationen/expertenwissen-sensorik/geruchs-und-aromaschulung.

8 Ionan Marigómez (2014), „Oil, Crude," in *Encyclopedia of Toxicology* (Third Edition), P. Weixler (Publ.), Academic Press/Elsevier Inc.

9 Perfumer/in – Hintergrund: mit dem richtigen Riecher zum Erfolg – abi.de https://abi.de/studium/berufspraxis/naturwissenschaften/parfuemeur-in-hintergrund#:~:text=Eine%20staatlich%20geregelte%20Ausbildung%20zum,%2C%20Chemie%2C%20Lebensmitteltechnologie%20oder%20Pharmazie (July 14, 2024)

—02/06

How Toxic Is It to Bacteria?

The Interaction of the Components of Crude Oil with *Escherichia Coli* Bacteria

Michael Duchêne

experiment
bacteria
crude oil
thin layer chromatography
toxicity

Bacteria are the most ancient form of life on Earth, for which fossil records (called stromatoliths) of more than three billion years old exist. Due to their small size, they were discovered only around 350 years ago, and Antoni van Leeuwenhoek is credited for this scientific breakthrough. In 1882, Robert Koch discovered the mycobacteria as a cause of tuberculosis. In recent years, it has become clear that the human body is an open ecosystem containing many different bacteria in almost all tissues, with the largest numbers found in the colon (large intestine).[1] Taken together, the number of bacteria is comparable to the total number of cells in the human body.[2] The bacteria do not only help to digest the food we eat, but they also provide nutrients and vitamins to the cells in our large intestine. *Escherichia coli* bacteria (Figure 1) are found in the human intestine, so if they are found in water samples, this is a sign of fecal contamination. On the other hand, *E. coli* is the old workhorse for biochemistry and genetics. Here we describe the interaction of living *E. coli* bacteria with crude oil samples, a non-living material derived from ancient life.

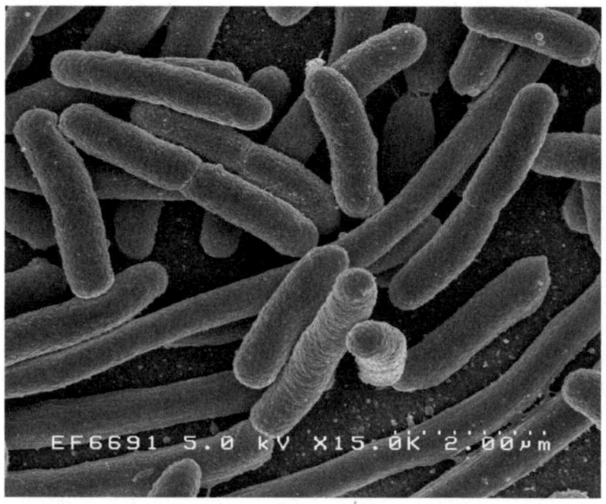

Figure 1
Electron microscopic image of *E. coli* bacteria (© National Institute of Allergy and Infectious Diseases NIAID).

Interaction of Bacteria with a Crude Oil Sample
Crude oil is a mixture of hundreds of components in widely different concentrations.[3]

How can we find out if some components are toxic to normal bacteria like *E. coli*?

In an altogether different field, extracts from *Stemona collinsae*, an Asian plant, were investigated for their toxic activity against the common fungus *Cladosporium herbarum*.[4] Plant extracts were separated by thin layer chromatography (TLC) and the fungal spores were directly sprayed onto the TLC plate. Areas of reduced fungal growth were tested for toxic components of the plant extract.

Figure 2
LB agar plate with *E. coli* bacterial colonies expressing the green fluorescent protein.

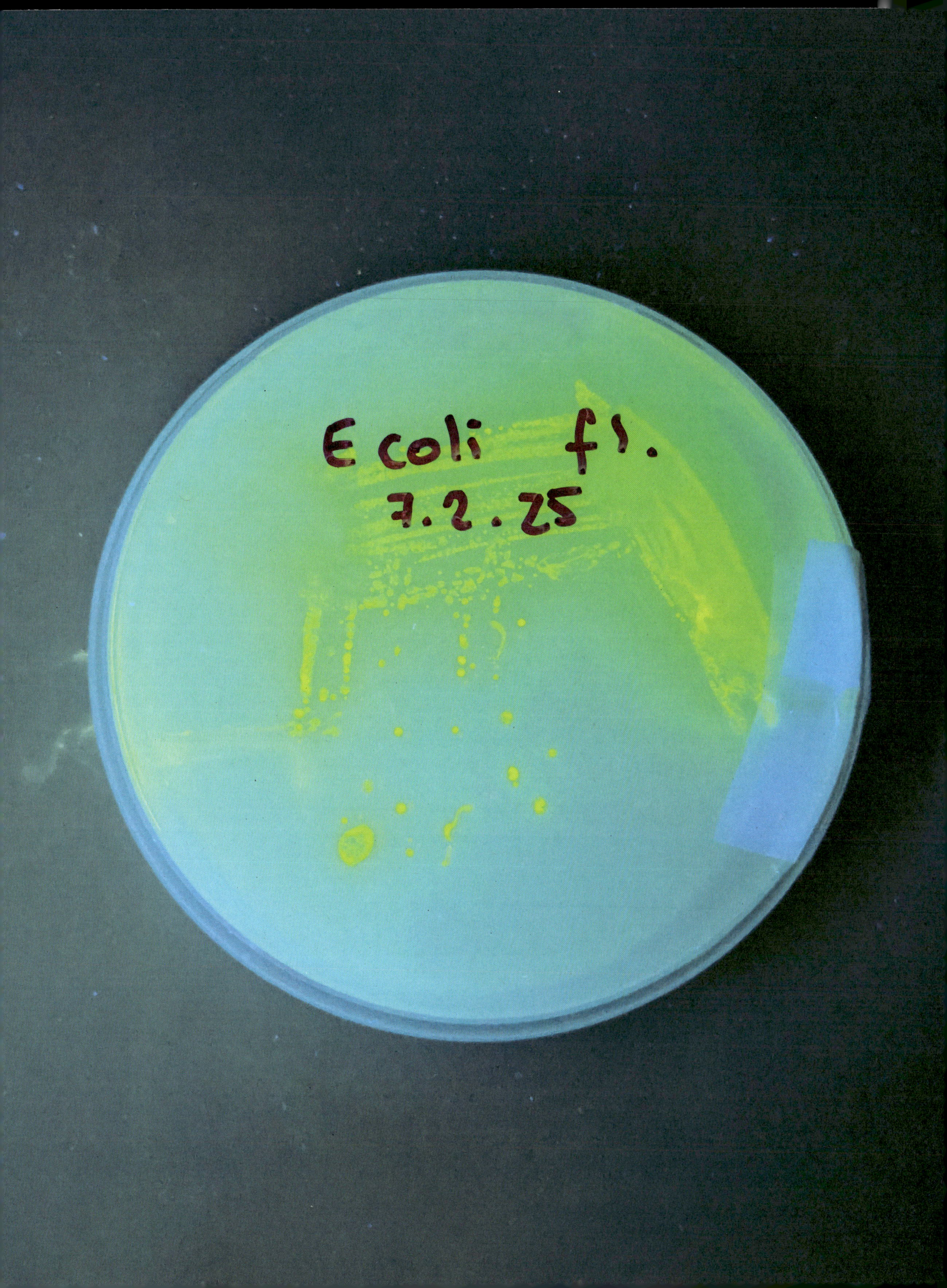
E coli f1.
7.2.25

In a similar manner, we planned to test the interaction of *E. coli* bacteria with crude oil components. In order to generate clearly visible fluorescent bacteria, *E. coli* bacteria were transformed with a plasmid directing the synthesis of green fluorescent protein, according to the protocol from the supplier (Edvotek, Washington DC, USA). The fluorescent bacteria were streaked onto a suitable LB plate and photographed under UV light (Figure 2).

For the main experiment, we applied a sample of crude oil from the Beryl oil field, a major oil field in the UK sector of the North Sea, to a 10 x 15 cm TLC plate, separated the components with decane as a mobile phase and dried the plate. The bacteria were added to warm classical LB (lysogeny broth) medium containing 0.7% agar, then the mixture was poured onto the TLC plates and incubated at 37°C for 48 hours. The bacteria were then visualized with a UV lamp. Although the experiment was rather crude, the bacterial growth was seen all over the plate, no areas were detected without bacterial growth (Figure 3).

Figure 3
Bacterial growth on a TLC plate with a separated crude oil sample from the Beryl oil field. The large black spot in the top middle of the plate shows where the sample was loaded. The separated components are below the black spot.

The greenish-blue fluorescence of the bacteria (modified by the agar) is seen on the whole area and is not strongly inhibited by the crude oil components.

Conclusion

So, roughly, the components of crude oil were not highly toxic for *E. coli* bacteria. In a way, this was not altogether surprising as crude oil is transformed living matter, often originating from other bacteria.[5] On the other hand, human exposure to crude oil in oil drilling regions is known to cause cancer, liver damage, immunodeficiency, and neurological symptoms.[6] So, although this strange material is transformed living matter and drives our economy, it can also harm us directly and its combustion contributes to the drastic climate change that is currently being observed.

1 Ed Yong, *I Contain Multitudes: The Microbes Within Us and a Grander View of Life* (New York City: Ecco, 2016).

2 Ron Sender, Shai Fuchs, and Ron Milo, "Revised Estimates for the Number of Human and Bacteria Cells in the Body," in *PLoS Biol*, (August 19, 2016), https://doi.org/10.1371/journal.pbio.1002533.

3 Nagham Mahmood Aljamali and Nuha Salman Salih, "Review on Chemical Separation of Crude Oil and Analysis of Its Components," in *Journal of Petroleum Engineering and Technology* 11, no. 2 (2021), 35–49.

4 T. Pacher, C. Seger, D. Engelmeier, S. Vajrodaya, O. Hofer, H. Greger, "Antifungal Stilbenoids from *Stemona collinsae*," in *Journal of Natural Products* 65, no. 6 (May 11, 2002), 820–827.

5 Vasily Simanzhenkov and Raphael Idem, *Crude Oil Chemistry* (Boca Raton: CRC Press, 2003).

6 Jill E. Johnston, Esther Lim, and Hannah Roh, "Impact of upstream oil extraction and environmental public health: A review of the evidence," in *Science of The Total Environment* 657 (March 20, 2019), 187–199.

—03

—03

A Critical View from the Perspective of Art and Science

Interdisciplinary Workshops

Michaela Geboltsberger

Reflecting Oil Colloquium
interdisciplinarity
art
science
workshops
crude oil
collaboration
energy transition

It takes millions of years for crude oil to form, but its consumption—almost exclusively through combustion—occurs in the shortest of times. It is a process that unites prehistoric nature with state-of-the-art technologies. As the key resource of the twentieth and twenty-first centuries, oil has been at the heart of conflicts and a vital source of prosperity, too. A material full of contradictions that spans the entire globe and yet is barely visible.

The research project is centered around the substance crude oil. The team and invited guests investigated the role of this material on a geopolitical level, as a cause of environmental pollution and disasters, and as a socio-cultural asset between power and conflict. A constituent part of the project were 34 online workshops[1] organized between 2020 and 2023, which explored different approaches and models for a transition to sustainable energy and a future life without oil. In the framework of these digital meetings and interdisciplinary dialogues, scientists, artists, curators, and activists presented their work and reflections on the topic of crude oil. Scientific analyses, artistic forms of expression, and practical strategies were juxtaposed and combined to prospect creative horizons and find innovative solutions to the challenges associated with the substance.

The workshops were conceived to cover a broad spectrum of topics and perspectives. For example, **Holger Ott**, head of the Department Geoenergy (formerly Department Petroleum Engineering) at the University of Leoben, reported on the environmental aspects of oil production and the associated technical and scientific

Keynote speech by Cleo Reece
Reflecting Oil Colloquium, 2022
University of Applied Arts Vienna

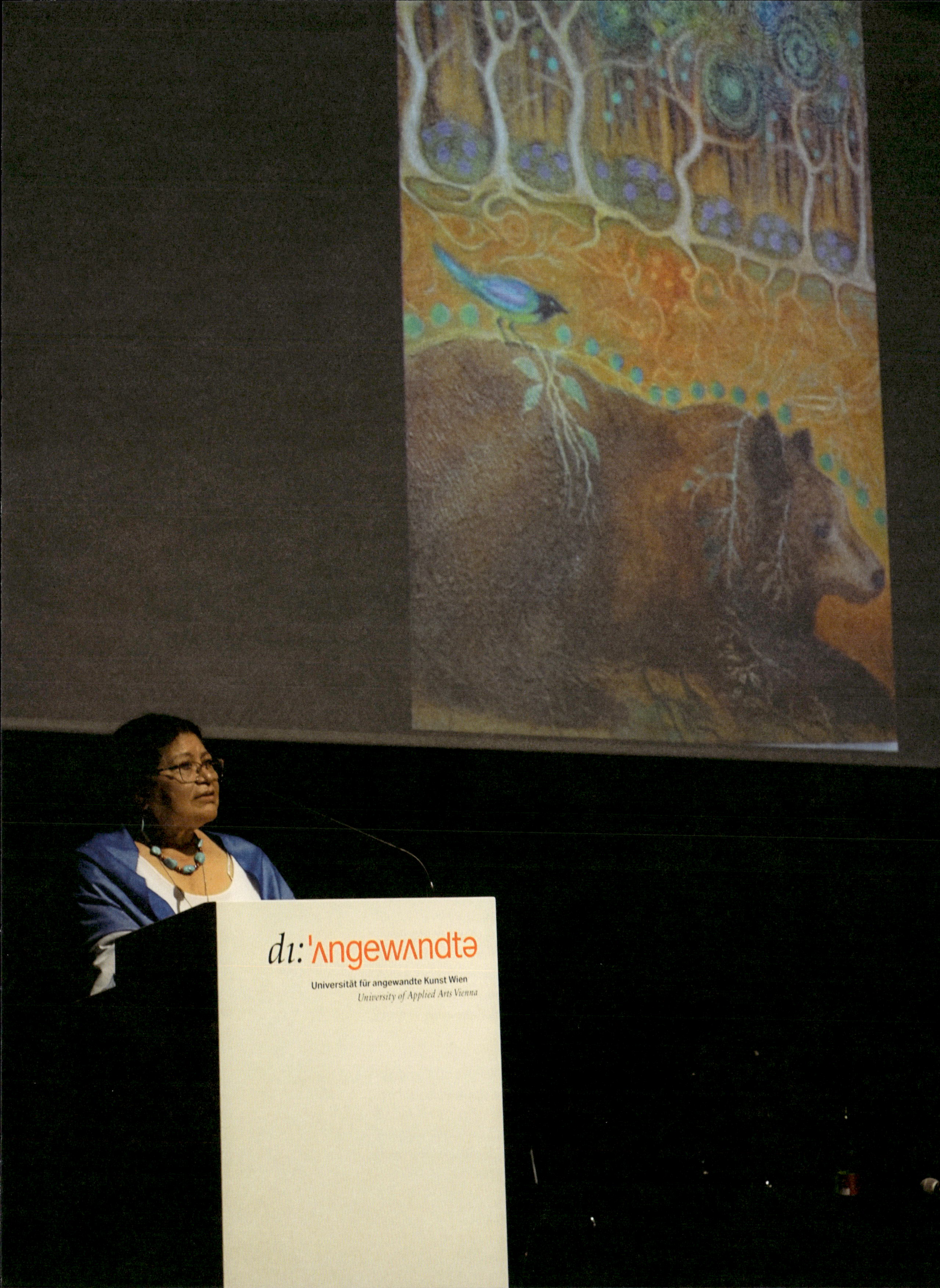
di:'ʌngewʌndtə
Universität für angewandte Kunst Wien
University of Applied Arts Vienna

challenges. Brazilian artist **Mari Fraga** presented her works, which deal with human interventions in nature, the dichotomy between the natural and the artificial, the Anthropocene, climate change, fossil fuels, mining, and industrial land use. In her workshop, she introduced her artistic approach to the world's key oil and gas production sites and the connection between oil and the advancement of Western civilization and culture. Inspired by ecofeminism and her Latin American perspective, she developed analogies between the human body and the Earth. Italian architectural researcher **Arianna Mondin** drew parallels between oil and architecture on the basis of the unfinished book *Petrolio* by Italian author and filmmaker Pier Paolo Pasolini. She researches the history of power and oil, taking the Italian energy company Eni as an example. An important contractor for the construction of highways, petrol stations, and large residential complexes for employees in the oil industry, the company continues to leave its mark on the Italian landscape to this day. The Austrian artist **Herwig Turk** discussed his interdisciplinary work about routines and gestures in the laboratory setting: Turk asked scientists to perform scientific procedures, but without the familiar instruments—their hand gestures are so precise that fellow scientists can easily read and interpret them. **Imre Szeman**, director of the Institute for Environment, Conservation and Sustainability and professor of Human Geography at the University of Toronto Scarborough, examines the history of energy transitioning. His workshop framed the COVID-19 pandemic as a window of opportunity for a shift to a green, solar-powered future. **Cleo Reece**, an environmental activist and filmmaker who actively campaigns for the rights of Indigenous peoples—in particular, the Fort McMurray 468 First Nation community in Canada—spoke about the "healing walks" organized by the local community to raise awareness about the effects of environmental pollution from the tar sands industry and its impacts on the population.

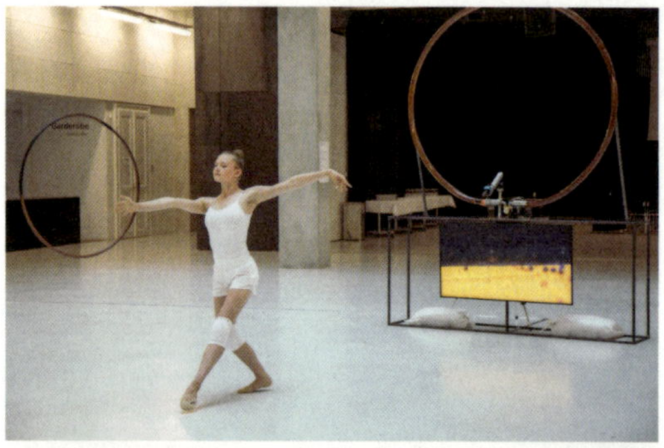

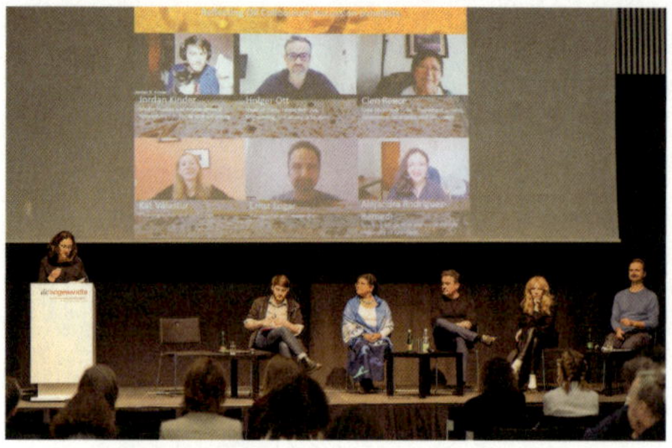

Top: *Spinning Melancholy*, performance by Mia Lietke, choreography by Kat Válastur
Bottom: Panel discussion, moderated by Alejandra Rodríguez-Remedi, *Reflecting Oil Colloquium*, 2022

> A central and recurring theme in the workshops was the question of the long-term effects of crude oil use, and if and how the substance can be more sustainable or even substituted altogether.

One workshop in this domain was hosted by **Peter Troxler**, an independent researcher at the interface between business administration, society, and technology, who presented the techniques he uses to encourage people to imagine a future without oil. His research focuses on the circular economy, the recycling of plastic waste, and how to close this loop of plastics and create clean materials from waste. In his contribution, **David Misch**, deputy scientific head of the Chair of Petroleum Geology at the University of Leoben, asked if fossil fuels can actually be replaced. He anticipates that global players in the energy sector will increasingly switch to renewable energies. However, the sustainability of these new energy sources is still largely unclear and a highly political issue.

How can artistic and scientific strategies address and reimagine the challenges of our petromodernity? Curator and art historian **Elena Sorokina** spoke about her exhibition *Petroliana* (2007), which explored the entanglements of politics and ideologies. She examined the relationship between humankind and the environment against the backdrop of modernist notions of the domination of nature. Her work, too, envisions an end of oil from an artistic and curatorial perspective.

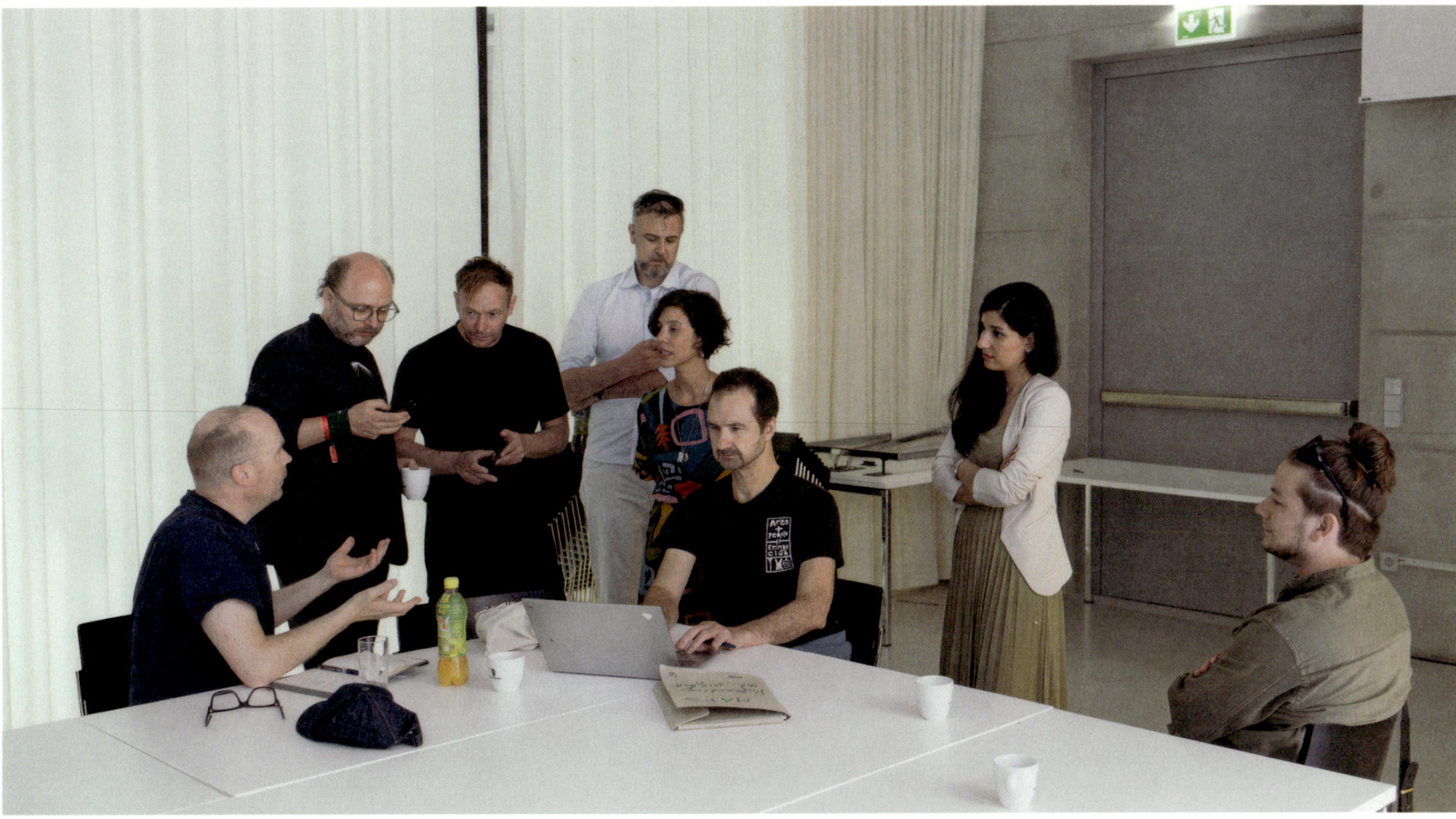

Working group 1, preparation of the final workshop presentation, *Reflecting Oil Colloquium*, 2022

In an atmosphere of open dialogue and collaboration, the participants shared ideas, formulated critical questions, and identified new perspectives and innovative ways of dealing with oil and its impacts on contemporary society and the environment. The workshops not only fostered a deeper understanding of crude oil as a substance: the interdisciplinary exchanges and collaborations exemplified how a synthesis of art and science can tackle complex problems and overcome conventional ways of thinking. The result is a host of findings, creative works, technological innovations, policy recommendations, and—most importantly—a strong network of stakeholders who are committed to working towards a sustainable future.

The content and reflections from the 34 online workshops paved the way for the *Reflecting Oil Colloquium*, which took place at the University of Applied Arts Vienna from June 9 to 12, 2022. Three working groups explored the substance of crude oil using different methods. On one hand, crude oil was examined through the lens of arts-based research methods in a working group led by **Ernst Logar**. Working on a more theoretical trajectory, another group dealt with the implications of the visibility and invisibility of crude oil and prepared texts about its cultural representation and social perception. This group was moderated by **Alejandra Rodríguez-Remedi**. A third, experimental working group supervised by **Ulrike Payerhofer**—with the support of artist **Olaf Osten**—developed narratives for a graphic novel about possible transitionings out of the oil age and imagined a future after oil.

1 Summaries of the workshops can be found on the website www.reflectingoil.info

—03/01

Crude Oil as a Substance for Artistic Experimentation

Ernst Logar

workshop
experiments
crude oil
art-based research methods
laboratory
interdisciplinarity

"forms of things were regarded as indicators marking the historical evolution of cultures, but substances were never in the focus of interest"[1]

Crude oil, the leading substance of our petromodernity, is primarily perceived and discussed as an abstract concept. Extracted from the geological depths of the Earth and often characterized as "buried sunshine," this resource has remained invisible throughout the course of its cultural transformation, while tangible opportunities to truly fathom it or its many liquid derivatives are rare. The complex chemical-physical properties of crude oil are one reason behind its obscurity—it is a substance that comes most clearly to light in the wake of an oil tanker disaster or the contamination of ecosystems such as the Niger Delta. To fully comprehend crude oil, sensory perception represents a useful technique and an important departure point for knowledge production in the transformation towards a post-fossil society.

In the framework of the *Reflecting Oil Colloquium*, the *Arts-Based Research Methods* working group adopted this approach in their examinations of crude oil in the chemistry laboratory of the Institute of Conservation and Restoration at the the University of Applied Arts Vienna. The chemistry lab was specifically adapted for this purpose with the necessary equipment and materials to provide the participants with hands-on starting points for creative work with crude oil as well as its diverse effects and meanings. The working group consisting of six participants from different disciplines came together in advance during the *Reflecting Oil* online workshops.

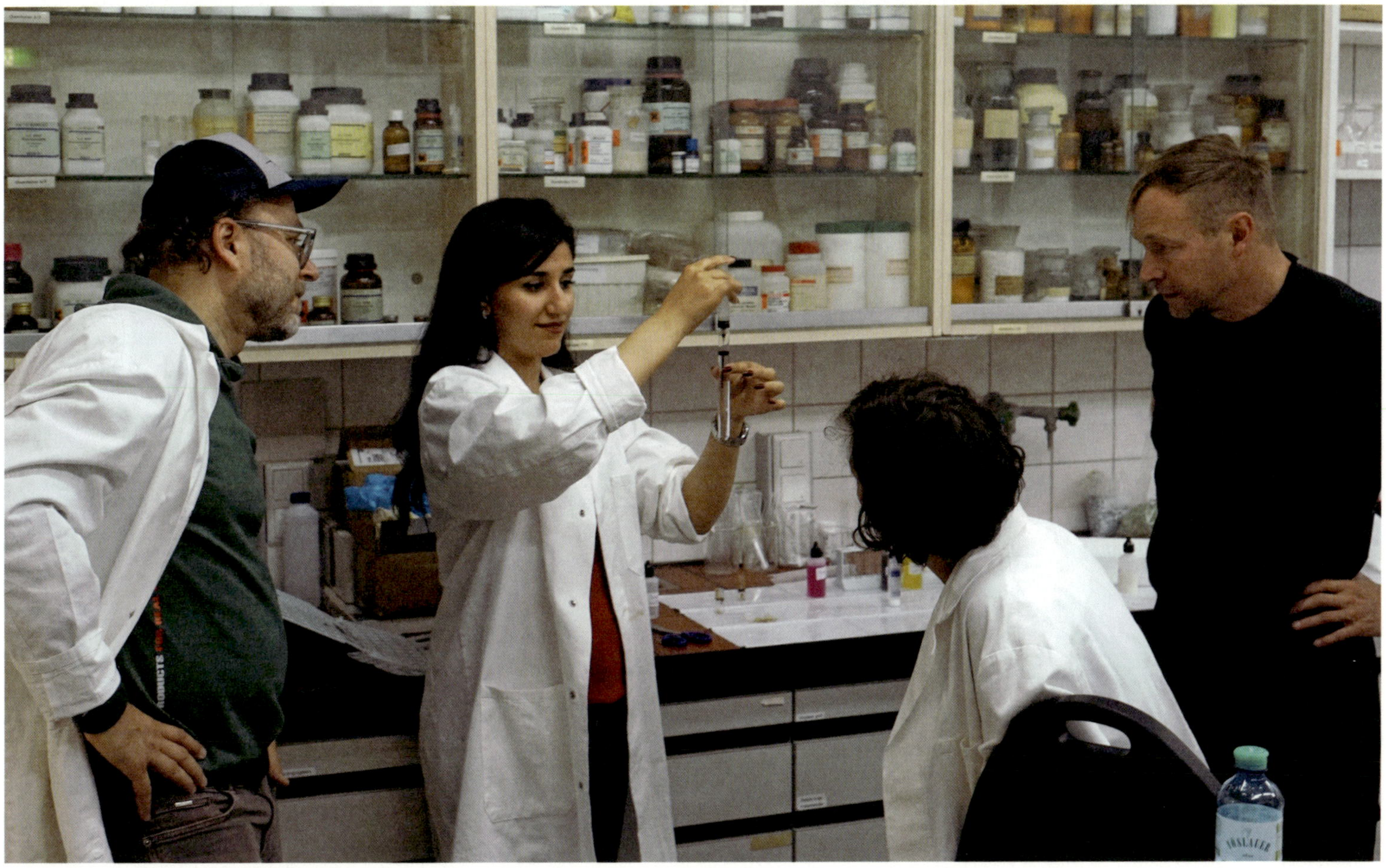

Working group 1, chemistry laboratory, Institute of Conservation and Restoration
University of Applied Arts Vienna, 2022

The Participants
Brazilian artist **Mari Fraga** explores analogies of the human body in relation to fossil fuels in her arts-based research project *Fossil Time: oil, art and the body in the cosmopolitics of the Anthropocene*. In her work *63 Perforations*, the outlines of a map of the world were transferred onto Fraga's body through several days of exposure to targeted sunlight. In a performative setting, the map was then perforated with 63 acupuncture needles marking key oil extraction sites around the globe.

Iraqi petroleum scientist and master's student **Karez Abdulhameed** is specializing in drilling technology at the University of Leoben. She is currently developing the research project *Hydrogen Transportation—Compressor Station Modelling and Market Cost Analysis* to evaluate and enhance the economic feasibility of hydrogen distribution networks in Europe.

Crude oil is a central component in the artistic practice of the Russian-born, France-based conceptual artist **Andrei Molodkin**. In his hollow Plexiglas sculptures shaped as letters, words, and symbols and flooded with oil, the artist tackles the political and economic implications of crude oil in a precise, critical, and often radical manner. Molodkin's current focus on the war in Ukraine and the role of autocratic ruler Vladimir Putin led to the work *Putin Filled with Ukrainian Blood*.

Austrian artist **Herwig Steiner** is active in the fields of film and music and currently works with the medium of sculpture in a site-specific context. Situated at the interfaces of diverse genres and disciplines, his experimental and playful multimedia projects investigate phenomena in which the virtual permeates the real world.

PhD student **Patrick Jasek** works at Department Petroleum Engineering at the University of Leoben with a focus on reservoir technology. In his research, Jasek investigates microfluid processes in geological formations in their relation to energy recovery and energy storage.

Austrian artist **Herwig Turk** explores the connections between art, technology, and science. In many of his works, Turk interweaves the material culture of the laboratory with his reflections on the concept of landscape. He currently investigates notions of landscape in the context of river basins.

The six workshop participants had two full days to experiment with crude oil and explore different dimensions of the substance through creative processes in interdisciplinary groups and joint collaborations.

The works created during the workshop address the topic of crude oil from different perspectives and with various media. The artistic approaches spanned from an investigation of the substance's origins as primordial elements in prehistoric landscapes or an aesthetic analysis of crude oil on a microscopic level from the perspective of the researchers' cultural background to tackling the political impacts of oil in the context of wars and struggles for resources or the ubiquity and (in)visibility of crude oil as the foundation of our everyday lives.

—03/01.01
Oil Dialogue
Karez Abdulhameed and Mari Fraga

In their joint experiment, Mari Fraga and Karez Abdulhameed examined crude oil in its interaction with salt and water. This symbolic set-up was inspired by Fraga's preoccupation with Brazilian oil extraction (artistic work *Fossil Pit*, 2016),[2] the political circumstances, and the geological formations on the coastline. Their work dealt with the interplay of substances on a microscopic scale. In a joint dialogue between the participants, the visual material was interpreted from the perspective of different disciplines and cultural contexts.

—03/01.02
Primordial Soup: Dance of Exchange Systems and Variables
Patrick Jasek and Herwig Turk

The departure point for the collaboration between Patrick Jasek and Herwig Turk was the primordial elements of prehistoric planet Earth. In the experiment, they attempted to physically and figuratively reproduce the ancient dynamics of primordial landscapes, which led to the formation of oil as they slowly sank below the Earth's surface. A video work documents these fluid dynamics as part of the experiment.

—03/01.03
Hello my name is Peter Lumo
Herwig Steiner

In *Hello my name is Peter Lumo*, Herwig Steiner worked on printing techniques with crude oil in combination with bitumen. He used the medium of screen printing to explore the technical potentials of this hard-to-handle substance. The artist approached the topic on a linguistic level, taking humorous angles to address the omnipresence and simultaneous invisibility of oil. By translating this concept to the format of a T-shirt printed with ink containing crude oil, Steiner transfers the work into the public sphere, where the ubiquitous substance becomes readily visible, albeit in an encrypted manner.

—03/01.04
PUTIN – TO THE NEW LIGHT – WAR
Andrei Molodkin

In the workshop, Andrei Molodkin continued his ongoing work about Vladimir Putin and the war in Ukraine, which has been raging on since February 24, 2022. In the work entitled *Putin Filled with Ukrainian Blood*, he literally floods a portrait of Putin with the blood of Ukrainians. It was on display as an installation and—given its iconographic aesthetics—altarpiece at once in a church in central London in May 2022. As Molodkin commented in an interview: "In every barrel of Russian oil, there is Ukrainian blood. Money for gas and oil is continuing this war."[3]

In Vienna, Molodkin worked with mixtures of (animal) blood and crude oil in his experiments with silkscreen printing. The artist also further developed his augmented reality work, a part of the *Putin Filled with Ukrainian Blood* project: he visited the Russian embassy in Vienna's third district, produced video footage of the embassy building, and drastically combined it with the blood-streaked image of Putin.

1 Hans Peter Hahn and Jens Soentgen, "Acknowledging Substances: Looking at the Hidden Side of the Material World," in *Philosophy and Technology* 24, no. 1 (2011), 19–33.

2 Mari Fraga, "Fossil Time: oil, art and the body in the cosmopolitics of the Anthropocene," *Revista Brasileira de Estudos da Presença / Brazilian Journal on Presence Studies* 8, no. 1 (Jan./Mar. 2018), 31–62.

3 James Cox, "Artist attempting to display portrait of Putin filled with Ukrainian blood in Moscow," *The Irish Times*, May 8, 2022, https://www.breakingnews.ie/ukraine/artist-attempting-to-display-portrait-of-putin-filled-with-ukrainian-blood-in-moscow-1300751.html.

—03/01.01

Oil Dialogue

Karez Abdulhameed, Mari Fraga

experiment
artist
oil engineer
crude oil
microscope
laboratory
dialogue

Mari Fraga: *We meet at the laboratory. I am from Brazil, you are from Iraq. I am an artist, you are an oil engineer. We are both women who come from countries with complex histories. In Brazil, centuries of colonialism, centuries of the capture and slavery of black people, centuries of Indigenous genocide and decades of violent dictatorship are historical wounds that are still open and bleeding. Our past is alive in the present. Our land is our body, and the body doesn't forget trauma—the pain always returns, re-incarnates; the plot constantly re-enacts itself, in spite of our individual or collective will. At the same time, resistance is also always alive, embodied in cultural manifestations that are full of music, color, dance, and joy.*

Karez Abdulhameed: The historical complexity of Iraq is rooted in its long, rich, and diverse history where successive empires, dynasties, and cultural influences marked its legacy of conflict and resilience. A sinuous history of prosperity and rapaciousness due to its resources and geographical location. Crude oil, as an ancient commodity, played a significant role in Iraq's modern history and shaped its economy, and its political and international interactions. Today, the world's thirst for more energy has grown to a scary level and has created confusion for how the world operates.

We experiment with oil, but I can't stop thinking about the layers of violence that are inseparable from the substance. For me, oil means energy and hopes of development, but also coups, corruption, cruel geopolitical power dynamics, and disappointment. The exploitation of natural resources is analogous to the exploitation of vulnerable bodies.

I've feared and detested this natural resource all my childhood and teenage years. I viewed crude oil as a curse rather than a grace. It brought dictatorship and isolated my country from the rest of the world for the longest time. We grew far from modern societies. I didn't choose to study petroleum, it chose me. Back then, I was fascinated by the science and technology of oil, by its vital side, and the fact of it driving our civilization forward. I want to share the importance of understanding the value of this commodity both as an ambitious engineer and as an optimistic individual. Engineering happens to be my destiny, as now I am able to change what I once viewed as a beast.

Inside the lab, we experiment with oil, water, and salt. One of the largest reserves of crude oil found in Brazil sits at the bottom of a deep underwater salt layer. The

Mari Fraga, *Oil Dialogue*, 2024
Microscopic photograph of crude oil, water, and salt

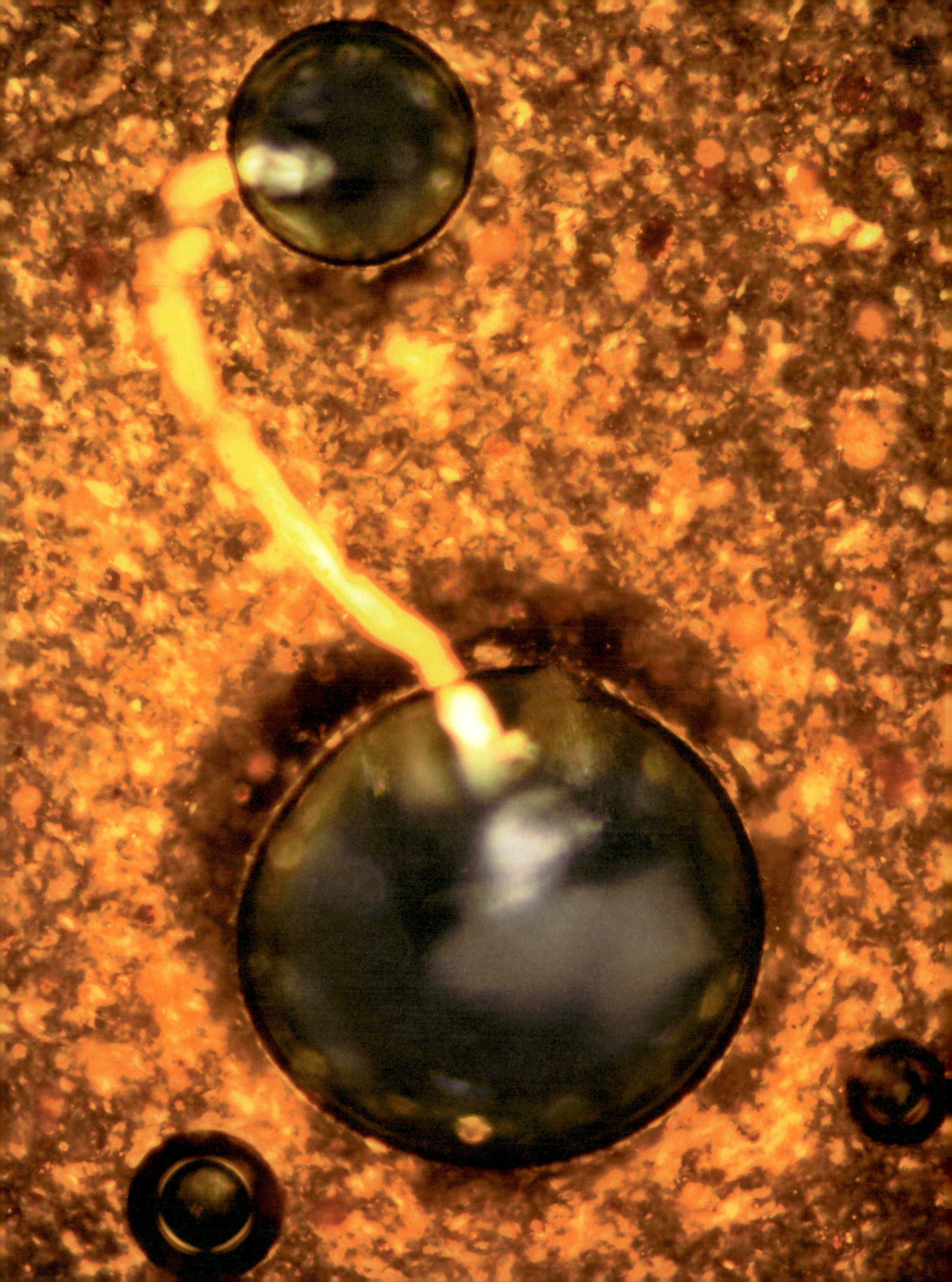

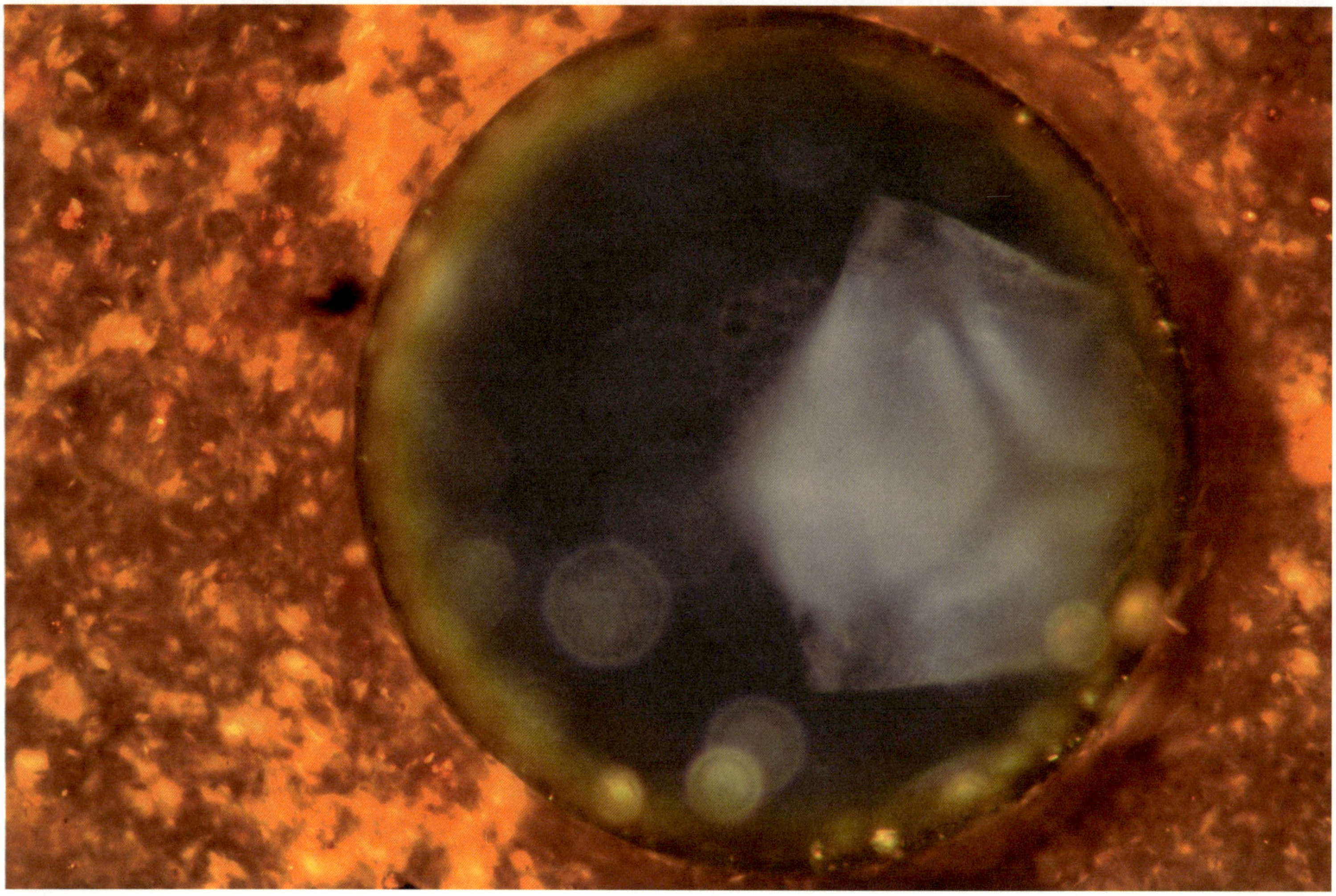

Mari Fraga, *Oil Dialogue*, 2024
Microscopic photograph of crude oil, water, and salt

political events that happened after this discovery also made me think of oil as a curse. In my culture, salt is a matter used for spiritual healing. I brought salt and oil together in past works hoping that some alchemic-poetic cure could be imagined—through substances, an encounter between the death drive and the healing drive can be dreamed of. Water is elementary for life. Crude oil is a substance that results from aquatic life that inhabited the Earth millions of years ago. But oil and water don't mix, and crude oil effects can be toxic for our living planet. Can we control a substance that transcends us in space and time?

The subsurface, where different substances flow, is packed with wonders. These include, to name but a few, the secret of living water, blasting lava, gas, and oil. Crude oil has contributed wonders to our world today. It has brought us energy in easier and cheaper forms. It has built our lifestyle and allows us to tour the globe and the universe. An ancient substance that now has the time to shine brighter during both day and night. It builds societies and grows the economy, but it can burn and kill when handled with greed. It took millions of years for nature to make it. We need to be more cautious with how we treat it. The sea doesn't mix with oil because life cannot be mixed with what's now a potential death sentence.

We look inside the microscope and see a water bubble surrounded by crude oil. Another image shows two bubbles connected by a mysterious string-like thread.

The first thing that comes to my mind is the connection between a mother and her baby growing in her belly. A connection that remains even after birth. A connection that nourishes and grows an important being. The immiscibility of crude oil and water, yet the salt seems to bring them slightly together.

The way you look to these images makes me think how love can be present even in the most contrasting and ambiguous contexts. Maybe you and I are like these tiny globules, weaving an oil dialogue. In the other image, we see a cubic salt crystal inside the water bubble.

The salt crystal is embraced by a water droplet thanks to the molecular attraction between these two substances. The oil layer showcases the immiscibility of these disparate substances as in a war of polarity where the salt crystal is shielded by the water bubble. This microscopic image magnifies the beauty of these molecular forces that interplay with each other and reflects meanings of microcosmic tensions.

Even when immersed in a toxic environment, we can create the poetic space and time for beauty and imagination to be born.

—03/01.02

Primordial Soup: A Dance of Exchange Systems and Variables

Patrick Jasek, Herwig Turk

experiment
artist
oil engineer
primordial landscape
Hele-Shaw cell
geology

This art-enhanced scientific laboratory experience aimed to observe the interaction between Earth-abundant elements and the uniqueness of phenomenological, reconstructed archaic dynamics.

The project, titled *Primordial Soup: A Dance of Exchange Systems and Variables*, focuses on bringing back the primordial landscapes of the world that are now buried in the subsurface, with the ultimate goal of exploring crude oil dynamics and its early-stage movement in the presence of artificially recreated landscapes.

For the recreation of the primordial landscape, various elements were selected. The presented results deliver unique insights into the intricate interplay of archaic systems and provide a new perspective on the origins of buried hydrocarbons.

Materials and Methods

Substance	Elements	Properties and abundance
Water	Hydrogen	Most abundant element in the universe
Water, Air	Oxygen	49.2% of the Earth's mass
Air	Nitrogen	78% of the atmosphere
Sodium chloride	Sodium	2.8% of the Earth's crust
Silicon oxide	Silicon	10% of the Earth's crust
Lugol's Iodine	Iodine	Heaviest of the halogens
Iron (III)- oxide	Iron	Most abundant by mass
Activated coal powder	Carbon	Fourth most abundant element in the universe

Table 1
List of elements and substances representing primordial constituents of prehistoric Earth.

Principle

The setup is inspired by the Hele-Shaw experiment, a flow visualization technique traditionally used in engineering and scientific research to examine flow and displacement characteristics in porous environments, e.g., rocks. It involves observing different flow configurations between two glass plates equipped with a mechanically controlled syringe injection system. However, we adopt an art-based approach that bridges the realms of art and engineering. By combining these disciplines, we aim to create an immersive experience that stimulates both intellectual and aesthetic engagement, providing a unique perspective on the interaction between matter and forces.

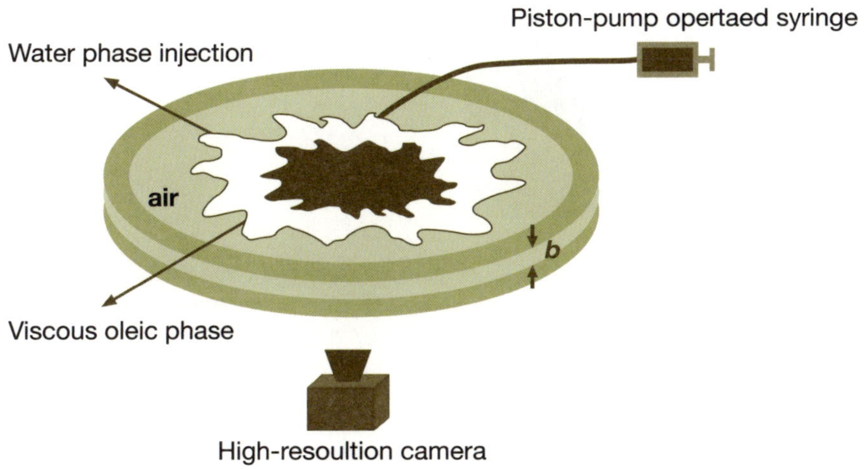

Figure 1
Schematic Hele-Shaw cell configuration.

Methodology

The Hele-Shaw cell (L: 42.4 x W: 32.3 x H: 0.5 cm), with an integrated high-resolution imaging setup with an underlying LED board, allowed for the visualization of primordial landscape dynamics and to capture crude oil's mobility. The interaction of various elements, under standard conditions, show advective and diffusive flow characteristics resembling natural processes. To realize the artistic vision we selected elements that address their abundance and high stability within the lithosphere.

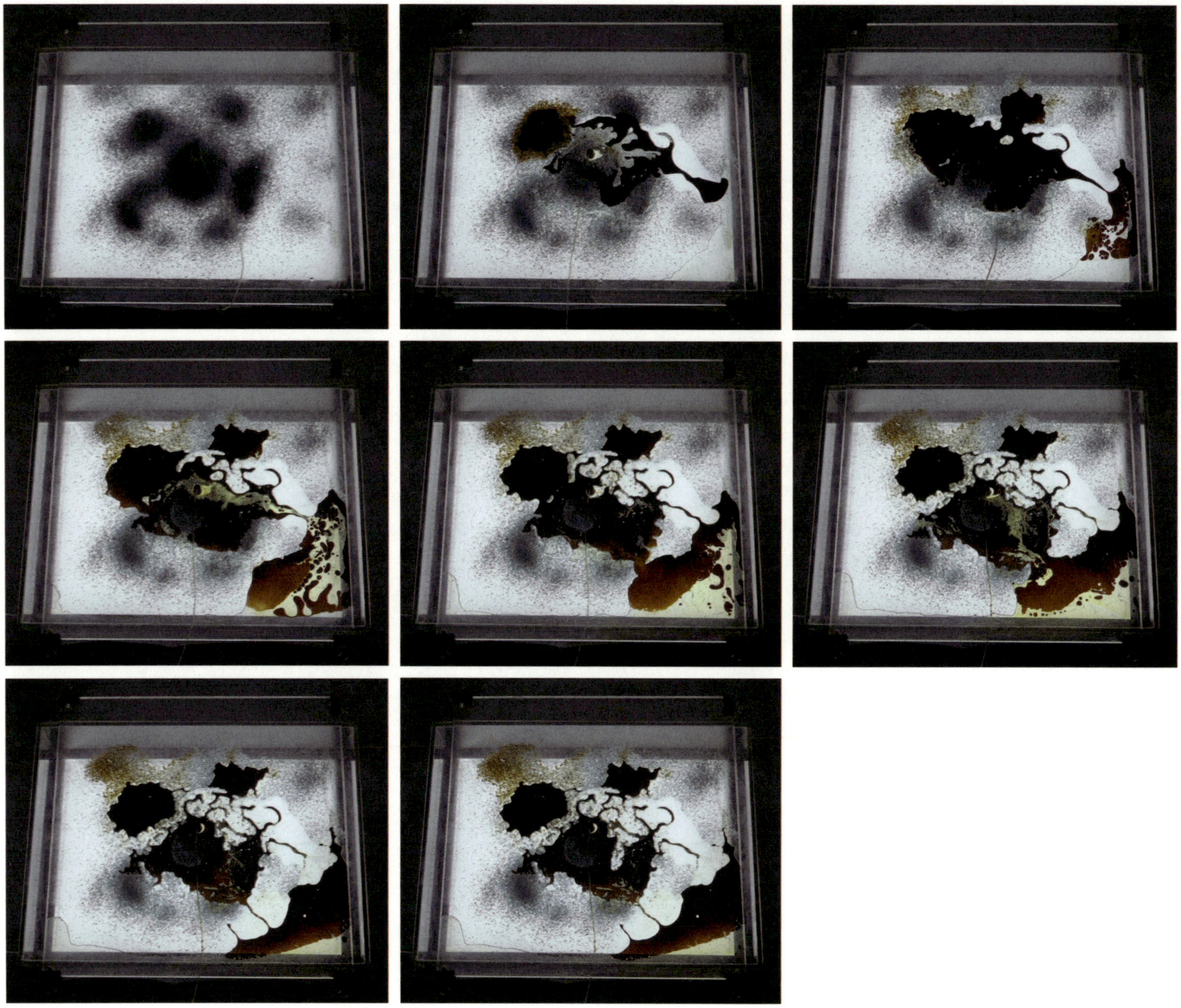

Figure 2
Time-lapse sequence of fluid displacement dynamics within a Hele-Shaw cell, capturing interactions of crude oil with selected lithospheric elements. The high-resolution imaging setup with LED backlighting reveals anisotropic flow patterns driven by advective and diffusive processes at different time-scales. It illustrates the evolution of landscape-like structures under controlled experimental conditions (4K video).

Procedure

1. Coating elements selection and application.
2. Injection fluid selection and rates.
3. Setup: Hele-Shaw cell with two glass plates.
4. Initialization: creating flow configurations to simulate the dynamics of archaic systems.
5. Data collection: observation and recording of flow patterns and matter interaction.
6. Analysis and interpretation of image data to describe system variables.

Remarks and Observations

To avoid the uncontrolled displacement of the glass plates caused by high pressure, the plates were fixed with clamps. A thin layer of grease was applied to the interior edges of the glass plates to avoid spill events. Experiments were not carried out under air-tight conditions.

During the investigation several fluid sequences where tested. The observed displacement and fluid propagation patterns resulted in unique schemes of an anisotropic nature (Figure 2). Localized homogeneities were the subject of detailed ROI (Region of Interest) analysis. Further, time resolved observation revealed significant changes in configuration at no-flow conditions (stopped injection). The rearrangement of the formed landscapes was triggered by the imbalance of system forces. Natural driving forces of capillarity and concentration, and gradient-driven diffusivity, dominated the system. Significant differences, controlling the sensitivity of variations with time, were subject of further analysis and were predominantly a function of drag forces and selected fluid viscosity.

Results and Discussion

The experiment explores the implications of the dynamics and their connection to the early stages of hydrocarbon formation below the surface. It examines the interplay between solid, liquid, and gaseous substances resulting from forced imbalance and the equilibration-driven process post injection. Finally, the rearrangement of solids during fluid injection unravels mechanisms relevant to river systems, meanders, sliding slopes, and other depositional environments. The aesthetically appealing forms are created by the substances, their interactions, and exchange systems. The aesthetic configurations that are formed are elemental and structurally connected to images of geodynamics. What is lost in the individual images is the speed of propagation, and thus resistance, of fluids to flow. The movement is not continuous but repeatedly delayed, jammed, and recurrently sudden. This missing time variable can be compared with the lack of human perception of the change in landscapes which happens constantly at geological time scales. Through this physically well-described technique, we explored the temporal aspects of beginnings in a science and art-fused manner of "tempus initiis," or time of beginnings. The recreation and examination of subsurface mass movement at observable time scales under controlled laboratory conditions enabled us to unravel the intricate processes that shaped archaic landscapes and shed light on their uniqueness.

These experiments provide an illustrative view of the complex and fascinating processes within the Primordial Soup, shedding light on the underlying physical concepts. By using crude oil as a substance, the experiments offer a new perspective on the relevance of hydrocarbons and their impact on Earth's history.

—03/01.03

WHO IS PETER LUMO?

Herwig Steiner

identity
crude oil
petroleum
Peter Lumo
screen print

The search for Peter Lumo's identity begins with a discussion about the relationship between humans and petroleum. Where do we come from, what are we made of? Who are we, and where do we want to go? These questions were the starting point in the search for Peter Lumo in the framework of the *Reflecting Oil Colloquium*. Given our origin, identity, and biosphere, we are inextricably linked to nature and all its traits for all eternity of human time. Even if we try, as Icarus did, to physically transcend the world and its nature and our earthly existence with all available means, we too will hit the glass ceiling of our era with its axioms and set limits to fossil fuels. Looking backwards, taking off with crude oil is like falling and constantly sinking deeper into quicksand the more we move. The higher we soar, the faster we move, the farther we will fall once again. Peter Lumo should not let us forget this.

"Everyone is an artist"—Beuys's quote sparked the conceptual journey to Peter Lumo.

Every individual is also a Peter Lumo. So Peter Lumo makes up our own identity. Peter Lumo is each and every one of us. A fictional character in conflict with himself.

That's why each of us can playfully crack the alphabetical code behind Peter Lumo. Except for one person, himself…

If you forget to read the words as they obviously appear to you, Peter Lumo will emerge on the screen of your visual cortex as if by magic, at the very moment you are no longer thinking about it --> Just like Scrabble.

Herwig Steiner
Peter Lumo, 2024
Crude oil print on cotton T-shirt. Edition: 50

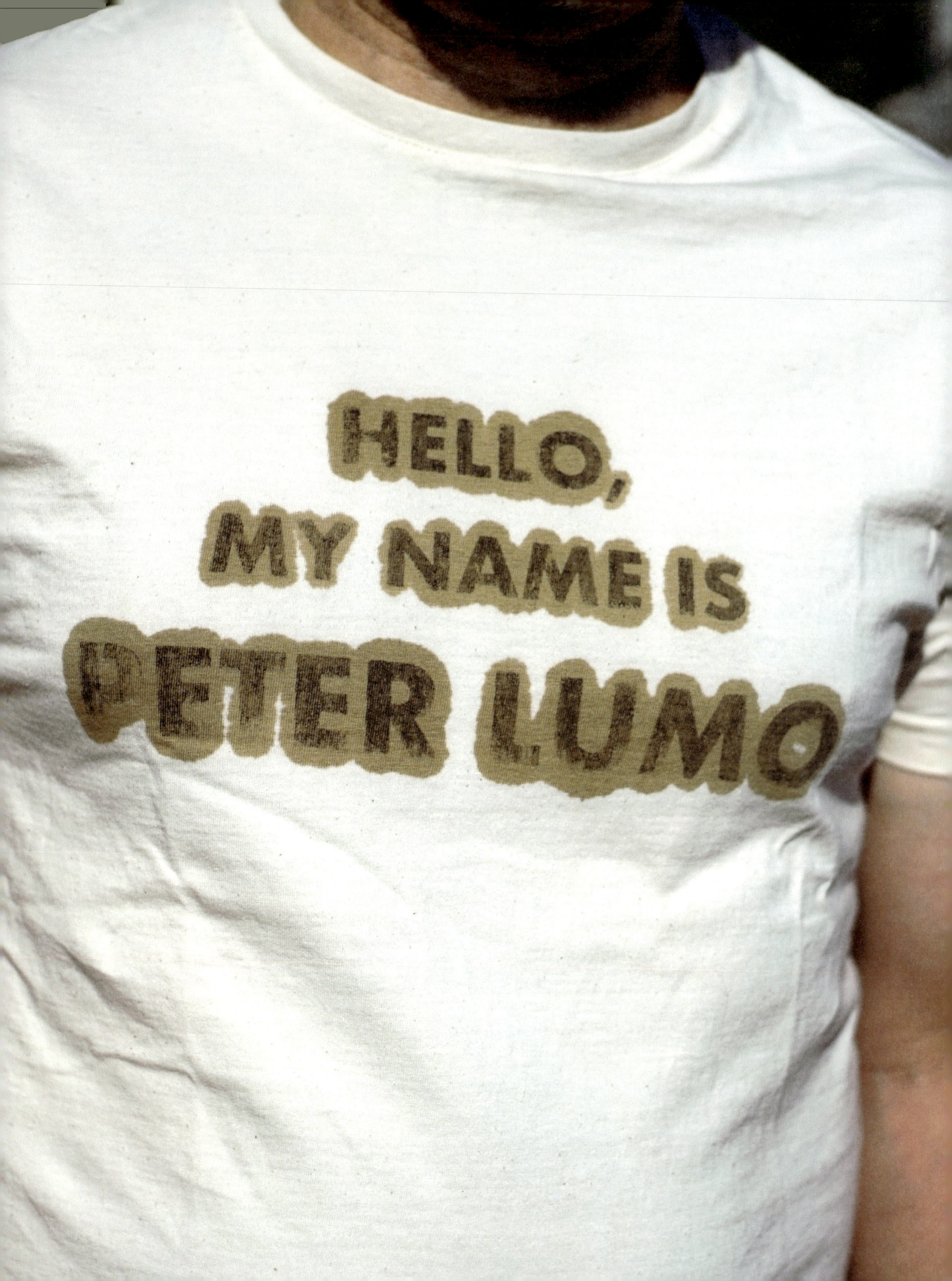
HELLO,
MY NAME IS
PETER LUMO

—03/01.04

Putin WAR

Andrei Molodkin

war
crude oil
blood
Ukraine
Augmented Reality
Putin

Andrei Molodkin produced the portrait of Vladimir Putin filled with Ukrainian blood as a direct response to the invasion of Ukraine.

Ukrainian friends and co-workers living with Molodkin at The Foundry, in the southwest of France, symbolically donated their blood before returning to their home country to fight.

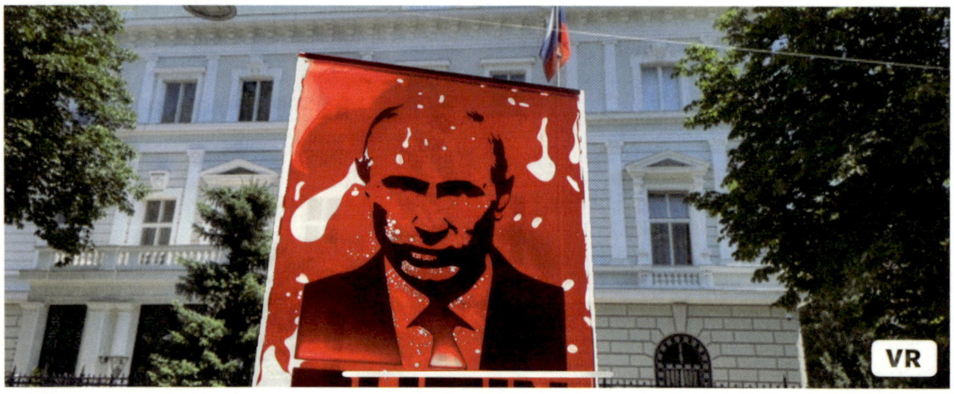

Andrei Molodkin
Portrait of Vladimir Putin filled with Ukrainian blood, 2022
Augmented Reality in front of the Russian embassy in Vienna
June 11, 2022

Andrei Molodkin
War, 2022
Oil, blood, Perspex box

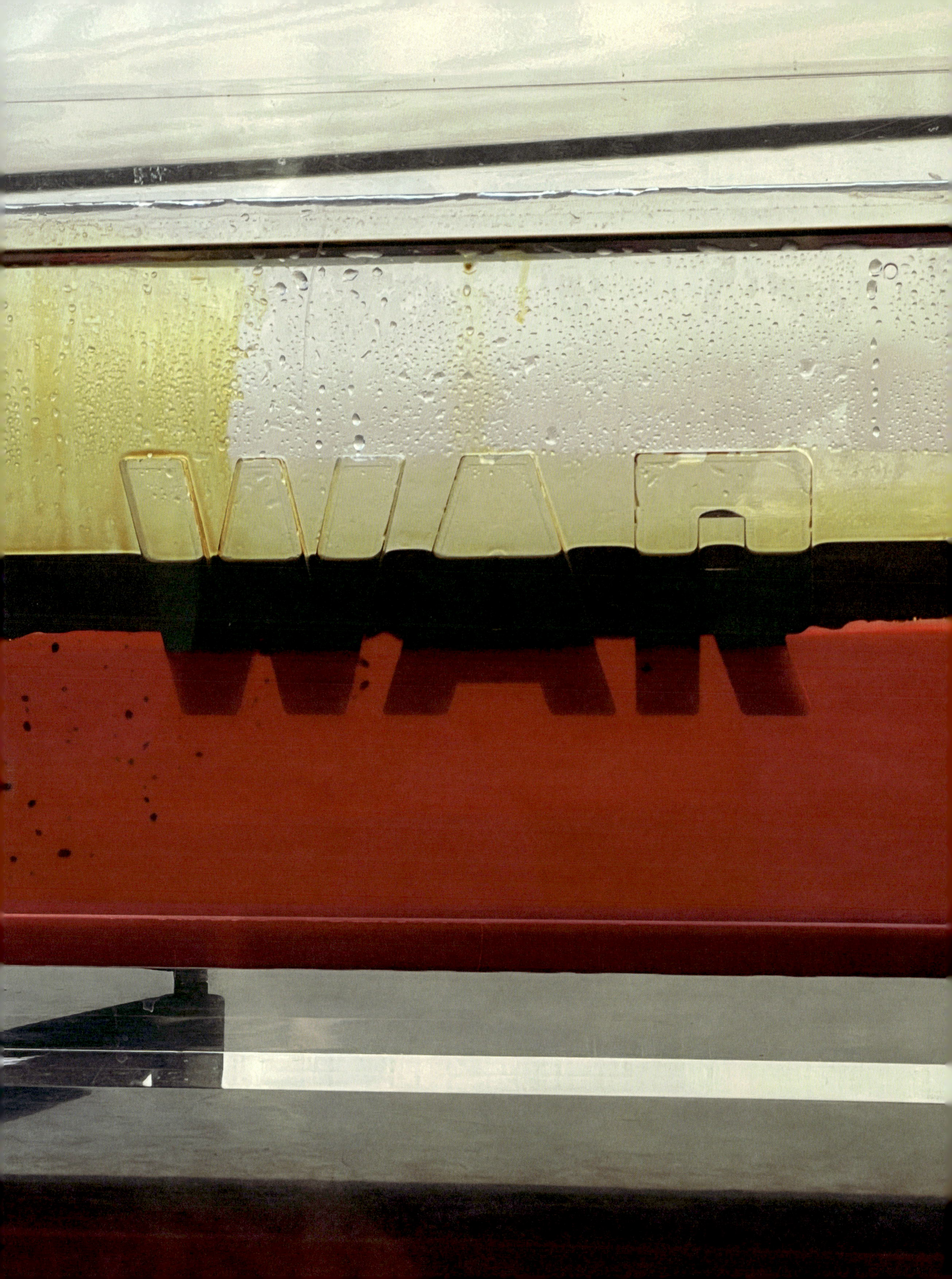
WAR

—03/02

The Visibility/Invisibility of Oil

Alejandra Rodríguez-Remedi

workshop
visibility
invisibility
crude oil
Niger Delta
interdisciplinarity
holistic understanding
knowledge exchange

Within the context of the *Reflecting Oil Colloquium*, working group 2 set out to make an interdisciplinary contribution to the understanding of the (in)visibility of crude oil and its industrial infrastructure. The seven participants engaged in discussions about how oil is represented culturally and perceived socially, producing the texts below. These texts retrace the (in)visibility dynamic which characterizes crude's journey through the production chain: from its extraction to the flow of commodities into our consumer societies. Though these texts were written individually to reflect each author's unique perspective, they all connect to the project of the sole artist in the group, Nigerian photographer **George Osodi**, whose work documents oil's impact on the environment and peoples of the Niger Delta, Africa's most important oil-producing region. The region has gained visibility in part thanks to Osodi's provocative work, inviting those in the Global North to question the provenance of the oil we consume to fuel our lifestyles. The idea of individual texts gravitating around his photographic project emerged organically at the colloquium when he presented his work to the group.

Osodi's evocative images became a catalyst for participants to relate to oil's (in)visibility intellectually and emotionally.

Osodi has said that his highly aesthetic, beautifully framed photos seek to arrest people's attention, to connect them deeply with those underlying narratives of the region he grew up in. The photos brought an unforeseen creative dimension, recalling US sociologist Patricia Leavy's claim that the arts "can connect on an

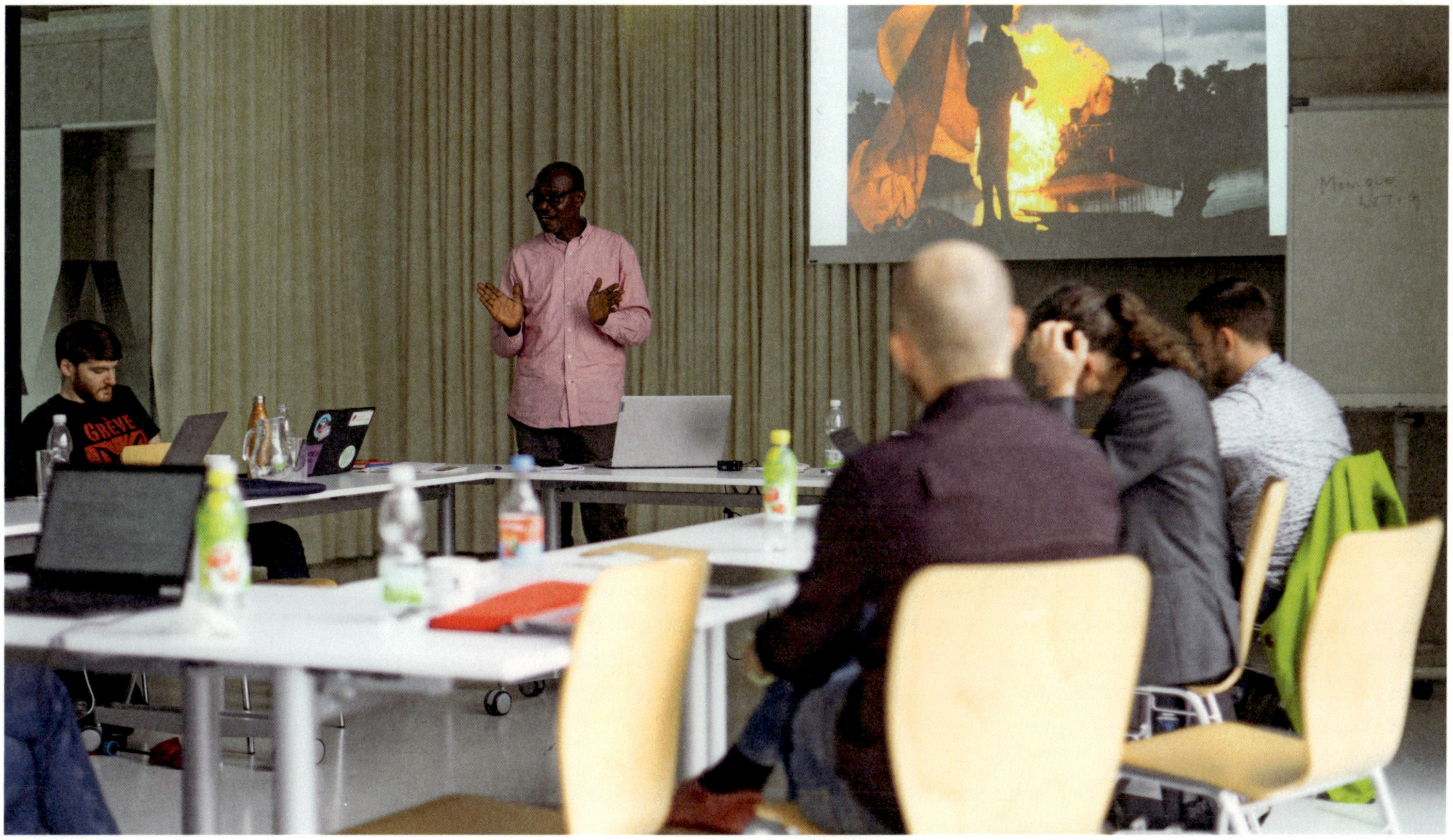

Working group 2, George Osodi's presentation on the Niger Delta, *Reflecting Oil Colloquium*, University of Applied Arts Vienna, 2022

emotional level, can create micro/macro links so that we can look at one person's individual story and connect it to something much larger in our culture."[1]

Conversations at the heart of the group's creation of "micro" and "macro links," as Leavy puts it, encouraged participants to share and learn from each other's perspectives. **Pit Arnold**, a reservoir engineer at the University of Leoben, shared his research on the topology of the pore spaces of rocks carrying oil, and his latest findings using 3D to visualize networks of paths and patterns as oil flows in a porous medium. Canadian environmental humanities scholar **Jordan B. Kinder** contributed his experience of the materiality of Athabasca's bituminous sands and his research on petrocultural imaginaries. **Simone Gingrich**, an Austrian social ecologist specializing in sustainability, contributed her expertise on social changes caused by industrialization, especially in terms of fossil energy and land use. Leoben petroleum geologist **David Misch** shared his knowledge of Austrian hydrocarbon provinces, his experience working with the oil and gas industry, his applied research on shale gas and oil, and his interest in technological solutions to alternative energies. Cultural theorist and science/technology historian **Benjamin Steininger** shared his knowledge of Austrian oil and gas as well as his theories about the place of oil as a hypermodern fossil substance in petromodernity. Italian architect **Arianna Mondin** contributed her expertise on how oil relates to space, shaping cities and our everyday lives, through a reading of Pasolini's *Petrolio*.[2]

In preparatory online meetings, that I led, the group's members got to know one another and learned about each other's perspectives. During these sessions, participants had spoken of the complex ambiguity of oil, connecting it to economic and political power. Societies, they argued, have not benefited equally from the economic growth resulting from fossil fuel use. Less developed parts of the world are experiencing a slower transition away from oil and gas. At the outset, participants questioned what some perceived as an aestheticization of oil, a highly toxic substance, sounding a note of caution about the implications of a research project driven by artistic practice which indulges in subjectivity. However, the group identified in the project's multi-perspectival approach a meaningful effort to foster holistic understanding of the omnipresent yet elusive nature of oil, which they agreed is needed to tackle the challenges of just, sustainable transitions. Though participants spoke different "research languages" and held different understandings of research, they all, explicitly or implicitly, alluded to the value system underlying their own work, acknowledging its ethical dimensions and expressing appreciation for the chance to engage in interdisciplinary talks.

At this initial stage, the group proposed producing individual texts as an alternative to the original output format suggested by the project team (a single collaborative text, a format not everyone felt comfortable with). Conversations began about how these texts could be articulated to reflect interconnectivity *formally*, so that the pieces became an integrated whole. Mondin suggested the holistic structure of *Petrolio*, a novel composed of seemingly disparate notes, as a model to connect the group's individual contributions. Her suggestion evolved into a plan to write a *Petrolio*-inspired metatext, a task she herself undertook: an individual output where she deconstructs and reconstructs those "oil-spaces" visualized across texts.

From these discussions, a plan for the group's two days of collaboration at the colloquium was designed. It included activities to encourage exploratory and more focused conversations. A reader, collated by the project team in collaboration with participants, was a shared referent circulated to the group before the colloquium. It included Hans Peter Hahn and Jens Soentgen's 2010 article "Acknowledging Substances: Looking at the Hidden Side of the Material World"[3] which fed into the group's reflection about oil's (in)visibility. Artworks by Logar and others were also included in the reader to draw participants' attention to creative methods of inquiry and thus set the grounds for informed discussion about "artistic ways of knowing"[4] which emanate from the arts-based methodologies underlying the project. A key question propelling the group's discussions was: how can we approach oil's (in)visibility from our respective disciplines? Put another way: what do our respective disciplines offer to the understanding of oil's (in)visibility?

During the colloquium, the participants exchanged views about science and technology, the oil industry's infrastructure, consumer societies, political will, education, and more. Conversations took on what Mondin called a "mobile dynamic": feeling ideas (and participants) move as they adopted different perspectives. The last half-day of the colloquium, devoted to a plenary when all three participating groups gathered to offer insights into their work, gave this group an opportunity to present its reflections. This moment of introspection allowed participants to retrace their steps to make profounder meaning of the territory they had explored collectively over two days. It was clear that Osodi's photos, which offer at least two readings (an immediate one conveying the materiality and impact of the substance, and a symbolic one inviting multiple layers of meaning), had facilitated an attempt to build a narrative of oil's (in)visibility. The collective reading of the photos revealed narratives of colonial influence, power relations, social inequality, and corruption. That it was Osodi himself who led the narrativization of the selected photos, presented as an embodied experience of oil, made this participatory exercise yet more compelling. Wanting to give their outputs significance and coherence, the group envisioned Osodi's project as a thread tying their contributions together. There was also a recognition of the key role Osodi's artistic methodology played in facilitating knowledge exchange during the group's discussions—this proved particularly rewarding for the scientists in the group with little experience of working with artists.

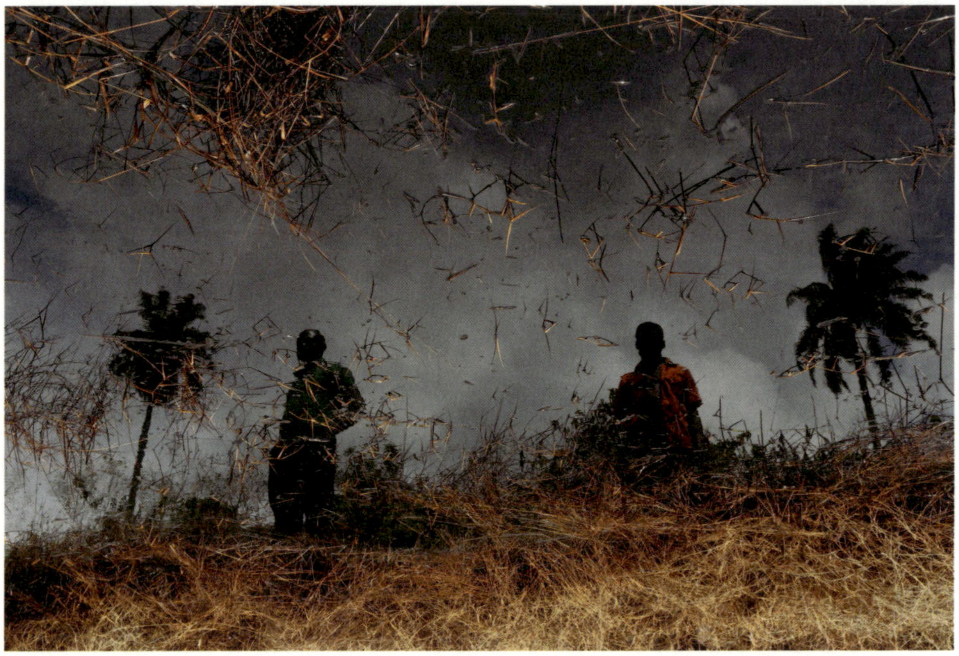

George Osodi
Black Gold, 2015

While reflecting on how to summarize their work to date, the group thought it relevant to give insight into the scope of their discussions and work dynamic. It was agreed that the most effective way to communicate this to the plenary would be to select two images which visualized the art/science territory the group had explored and conveyed the role that images had played in igniting thinking. The group selected *Black Gold*, an Osodi photo from 2015, which he described as a holistic picture of the Niger Delta evoking the periods before and after oil, giving visibility to the substance and its impact on people and the land. The second visual was a 3D simulation of oil movement in the pores of a rock which Arnold had introduced in a presentation about his research. The group found this scientific visualization of the flow of oil to be especially enigmatic. *Black Gold* and the 3D simulation are thought-provoking germinal images which facilitated creative knowledge exchange. Participants wrote preliminary outlines of their individual contributions which were subsequently shared with the group to convey an idea of how they intended to navigate the common ground they had delineated at the colloquium.

After the colloquium, the participants finalized their texts, which became the primary source for Mondin's metatext. Written from an oil-as-space perspective, the metatext offers a horizontal and vertical reading of the group's individual contributions, unveiling a complex structure reminiscent of what she has theorized as the "architecture of oil." Mondin's nonlinear approach illuminates not only points of encounter between texts but also expressive points of diversion and paradox. Her metatext is a creative exercise in interconnectivity which encourages explorative engagement with the texts until a common site, "the rooms of a building" (in her words), is revealed where new understandings of oil's (in)visibility can be unveiled.

1 SUNY New Paltz, "Arts-Based Research Keynote Speaker: Dr Patricia Leavy," March 13, 2018, YouTube video, 26:43–26:55, https://youtu.be/CJu4At61n2E?t.

2 Pier Paolo Pasolini, *Petrolio* (Turin: Einaudi, 1992).

3 Hans Peter Hahn and Jens Soentgen, "Acknowledging Substances: Looking at the Hidden Side of the Material World," in *Philosophy and Technology* 24, no. 1 (2011), 19–33.

4 Patricia Leavy, ed., *Handbook of Arts-Based Research* (New York: Guilford Press, 2017), 13.

—03/02.01

We Need a Delta!

Pit Arnold

Niger Delta
crude oil
greek letter delta
pore-scale physics
oil pollution
renewable energy

The growth and development of our modern society are strongly connected to the discovery and mass production of crude oil. Each variant of crude oil has a unique composition and physical characteristics, making it an enthralling and multifaceted substance. This intricate nature seems to have percolated into our contemporary relationship with oil. It paradoxically straddles between being an indispensable cornerstone of our daily existence and an emblematic harbinger of environmental degradation.

In contrast, the narrative of the Niger Delta, as portrayed by George Osodi, paints a divergent portrait of the relationship with crude oil. Despite the abundance of reserves in Nigeria, the riches have trickled down to only a tiny sliver of the population. In the early chapters of oil production, the locals were swathed in promises of affluence, which largely proved to be ephemeral. As the hands of time moved, skepticism and aversion, especially among the elders, began to surge against oil production. Fast forward to the present, and a burgeoning number of youths perceive it as a gateway to entrepreneurship. They engage in illegal siphoning of oil from pipelines and carry out makeshift refining operations deep within the forest. While this practice turns a blind eye to the ecological calamities it spawns, it ironically bestows the once-promised prosperity upon those who dabble in the clandestine production and sale of gasoline, with some even forsaking conventional employment.

In scientific parlance, the Greek letter delta symbolizes change and, in this narrative, it poignantly illustrates the stark divergence in the associations and transformations wrought by oil between the Western world and the residents of the Niger Delta.

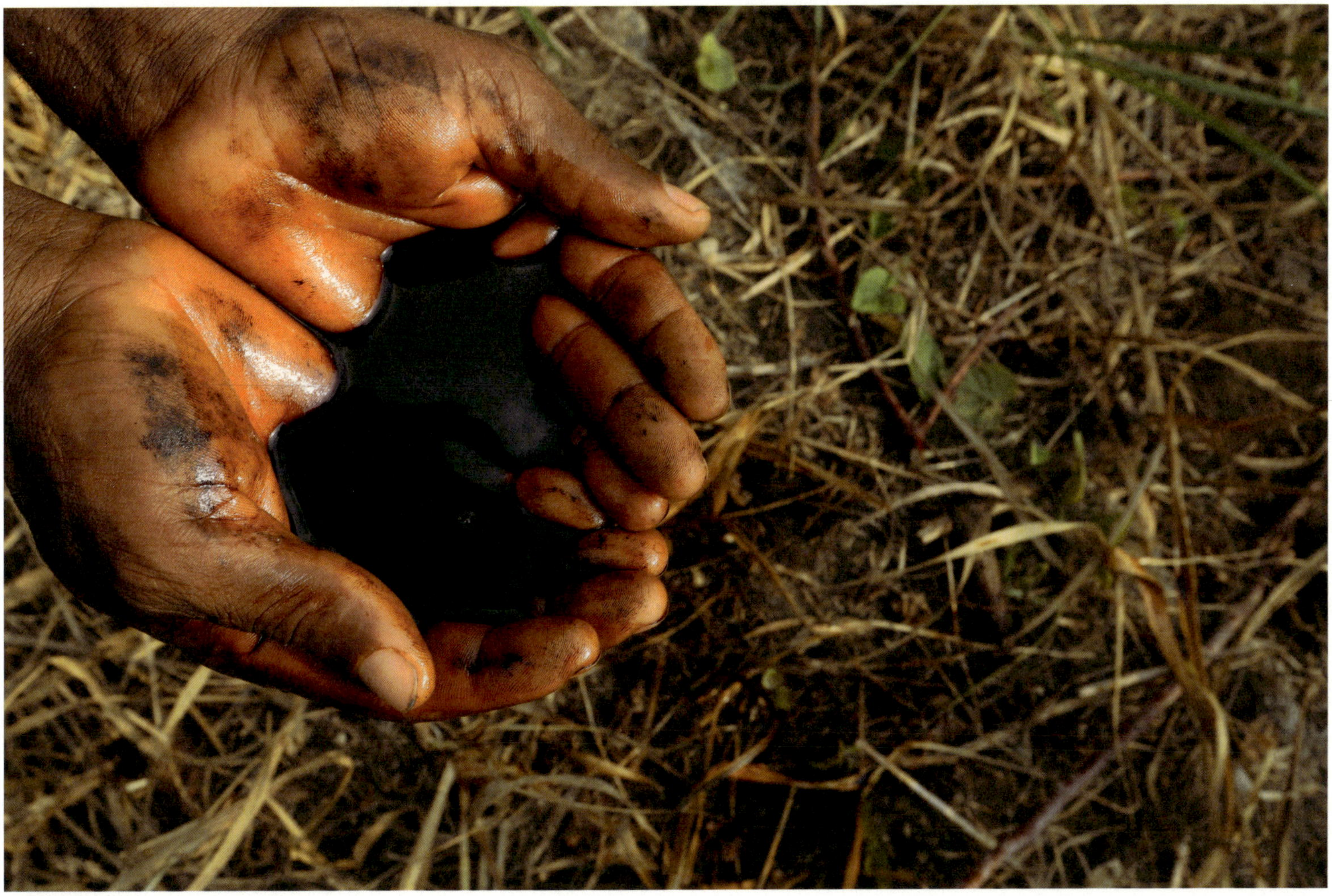

George Osodi
We Crude, 2016

Change has also unfurled its wings among the delta's inhabitants, where oil is now perceived as a conduit to financial ascendancy. Meanwhile, the global narrative is shifting, with a growing yearning to break the shackles of oil dependence. Austria serves as a role model in the realm of renewable energy production, with approximately 80 percent[1] of its electricity being harnessed from renewables such as wind, solar, biomass, and hydro energy.

However, a deeper inspection of the nation's overall energy consumption, inclusive of electricity, reveals that fossil fuels—oil, gas, and coal—still hold dominion over two-thirds of the energy portfolio.

This exemplifies a conundrum: a mere pivot towards renewables is insufficient in the face of colossal energy demands. It is an incontrovertible truth that the specter of energy consumption is an exigent issue that demands immediate attention and cannot be casually dismissed. Additionally, it is imperative to recognize that numerous regions across the globe are still in the crucible of development, ardently pursuing economic growth. In 2020, Scott W. Tinker, director of the Bureau of Economic Geology at the University of Texas at Austin, made a poignant remark: "I work in the oil and gas industry and I lift the world from poverty. What do you do?" While audacious, this statement bears an important truth: access to energy is a catalyst for affluence and, historically, fossil fuels have offered the most economical avenue for energy production. The question that looms large is: what is the true cost of this "inexpensive energy"? The repercussions are manifest in the toll taken on the

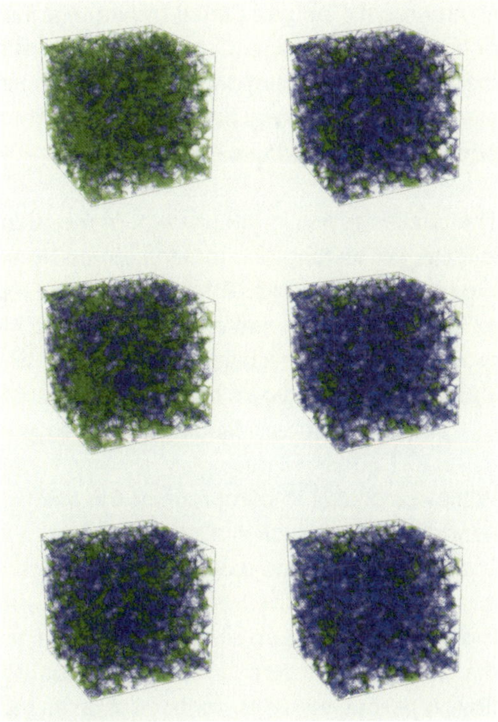

Displacement of oil (green) by water (blue) over time in a porous medium.

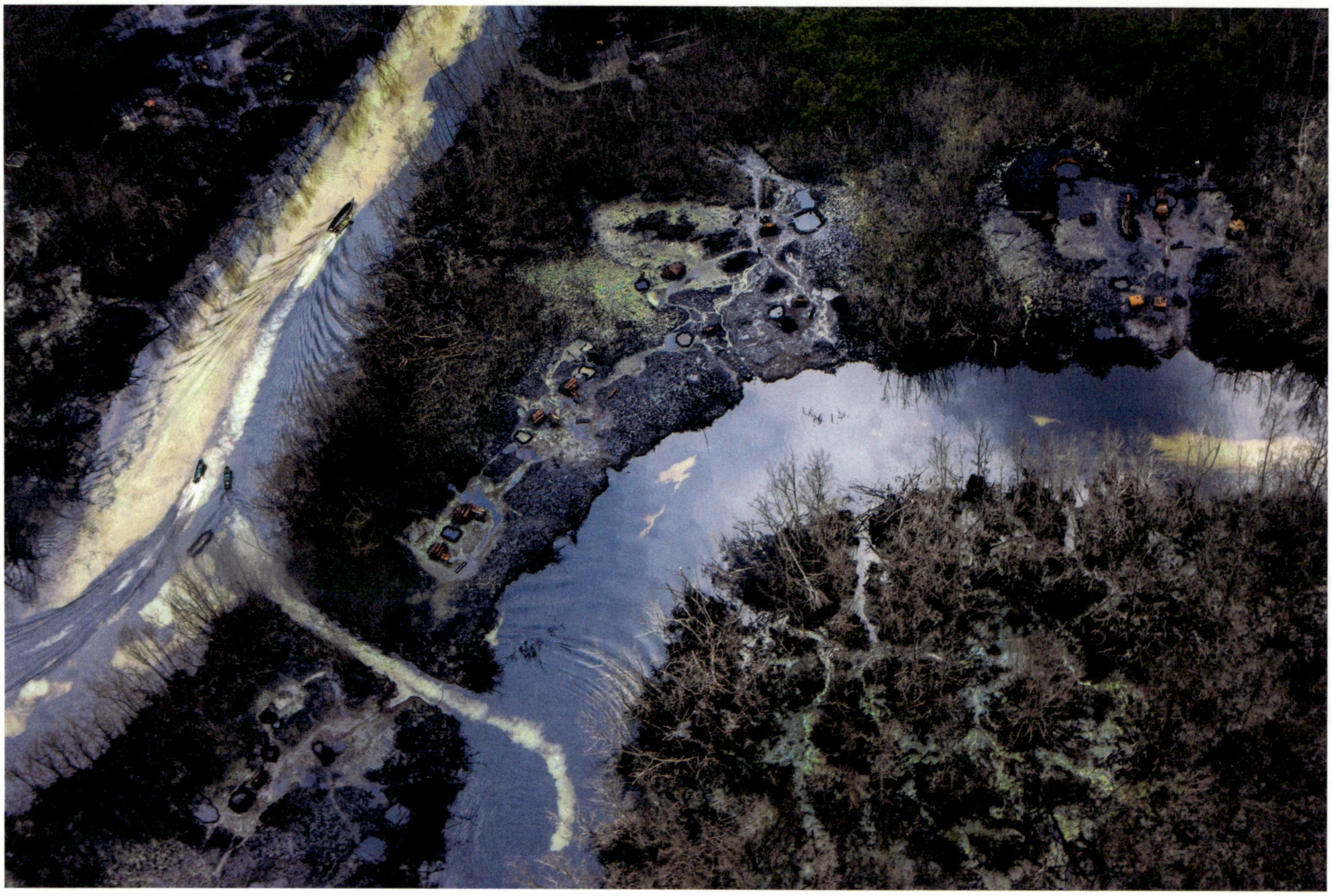

George Osodi
Oil Theft, 2013

environment. The plundering of nature is incalculable, with every passing day compounding the damage. Osodi's portrayal of the Niger Delta is but a microcosm of the pervasive destruction. Additionally, the insidious effects of daily CO2 emissions, stemming from energy consumption, might not be as immediately discernible, but pose a more formidable menace.

The challenge lies in the unseen. In the realm of pore-scale physics, our resolution is finite, yet wetting phenomena, crucial to understanding porous media flow, span a broad range of scales. The environmental repercussions of illegal refining processes extend far beyond what a single overhead image reveals. The oil seeps into porous ground, resulting in a lasting formation of oil-filled soils. Even after surface films are washed away and years of rainfall, remnants of oil persist on mineral surfaces within the ground, potentially leading to a change in the wetting state of the soil.

While our goal is to comprehend the mechanisms driving displacement—such as water replacing oil in a porous medium, leading to optimized production—this is a predicament one would prefer to sidestep in the Niger Delta. However, since it is already there, the transport of oil by water depends on the flow velocity of the river, which in turn relies on the river's flow path. This might seem obvious on the surface, but it also hinges on the composition of the riverbed. Similarly, the flow in porous media is contingent on its topology and can only be accurately modeled with three-dimensional information. As in a river, there are faster and slower flow paths, introducing intricacies to the transport dynamics.

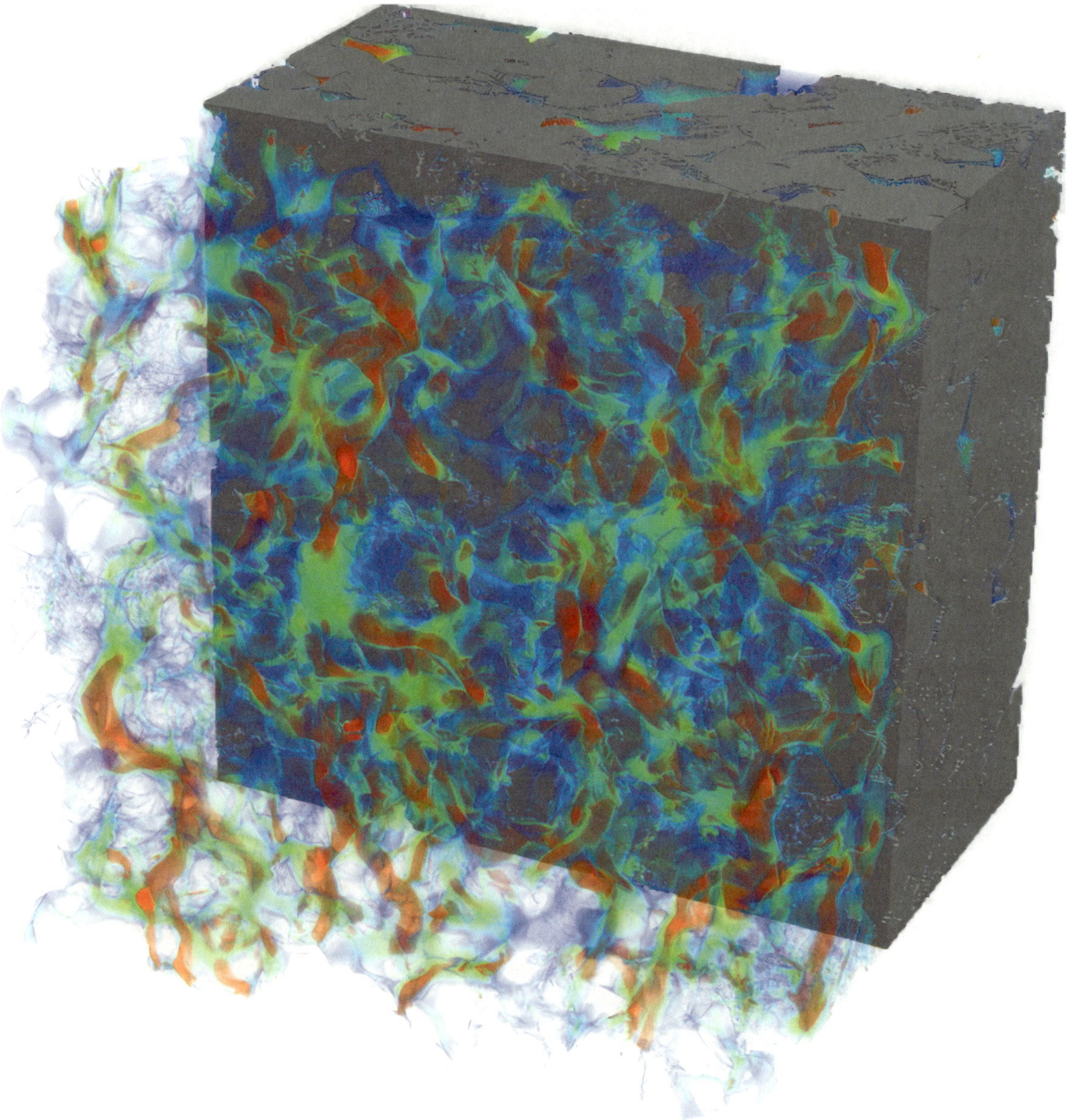

Illustration of flow velocities within a porous medium.
Red: high speed
Green/Yellow: medium speed
Blue: very low or near-zero speed

Hopefully, in the near future, the insights derived from porous media flow research will be applied to soil remediation, offering a means to mitigate the effects caused by oil pollution.

While curtailed consumption and a shift towards renewable energy are laudable long-term goals, they do not diminish the gravity of the current quandaries that demand resolution. These challenges will remain our constant companions in the decades to come, as the global appetite for energy and growth intensifies. For the immediate future, large-scale solutions such as carbon capture and storage, ironically gleaned from expertise in oil and gas extraction, offer a modicum of respite in the transition to a more sustainable future. However, such technical interventions are mired in bureaucratic red tape and remain prohibited in numerous jurisdictions.

What is requisite is a multifaceted approach encompassing sacrifice, the honing of extant technologies, and innovations, all the while not turning a blind eye to the present crises that plague us. The road ahead demands a collective will for transformation, judicious policymaking, and an unwavering commitment to sustainable progress.

We need a change Δ!

1 Federal Ministry for Climate Action, Environment, Energy, Mobility, Innovation and Technology (Republic of Austria), "Energie in Österreich" [Energy in Austria] (2022), https://www.bmk.gv.at/dam/jcr:3820f7e7-4abb-4324-b8e0-aa090325eb4a/Energie_in_OE2022_UA.pdf.

—03/02.02

From Oil Encounters to Oil Reflections

Jordan B. Kinder

Niger Delta
Arcitc
oil encounters
crude oil
fossil econmomy
Alberta tar sands
oil spill

To *encounter* oil is to *experience* oil in one or more of its formats—as a crude raw material, as an abstracted commodity circulating on the world market, as a refined substance beyond the crude such as petroleum. Well-travelled as an animating concept in the study of petrocultures and its umbrella field of the energy humanities, the "oil encounter" was first articulated by Amitav Ghosh in a review of Jordanian oil economist and writer Abdelrahman Munif's series of novels on the petroleum industry's formation in the Gulf Emirates, including *Cities of Salt*.[1] Here, the oil encounter presents oil to readers of *Cities of Salt* as a particular and peculiar historical and political economic force, a force mediated by the encounter between an emergent American petroleum industry and an existing Arab community whose ways of life would be forever altered. In his review, Ghosh meditates on how such an oil encounter has largely been absent in literary production, the result of a kind of intentional obscuration by the agents and architects of the fossil economy, which relegated oil as a substance of such political-economic significance to the domain of the invisible, inflected as it has been with "muteness."[2] In 1992 when Ghosh named the oil encounter, from the vantage point of these architects and agents, the less we collectively knew about oil as a fuel for global capital, the better. This remains true today.

Yet, the alarm has been sounded. Twisting the dial from mute to ten, IPCC reports, news headlines, and journal articles continue to repeat the present and future impacts of climate change propelled by the burning of fossil fuels. Perhaps, then, it is more appropriate to speak of *oil encounters* today than an oil encounter. George Osodi's documentary photography offers some such encounters in the Niger Delta where sweet crude sits so close to the surface that it bubbles up in a kind of perpetual spill. These spills are the dregs left by the handful of multinational oil companies

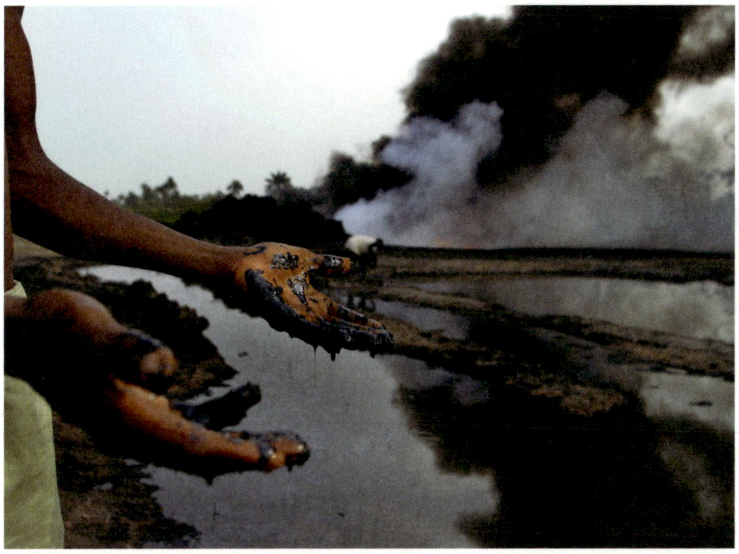

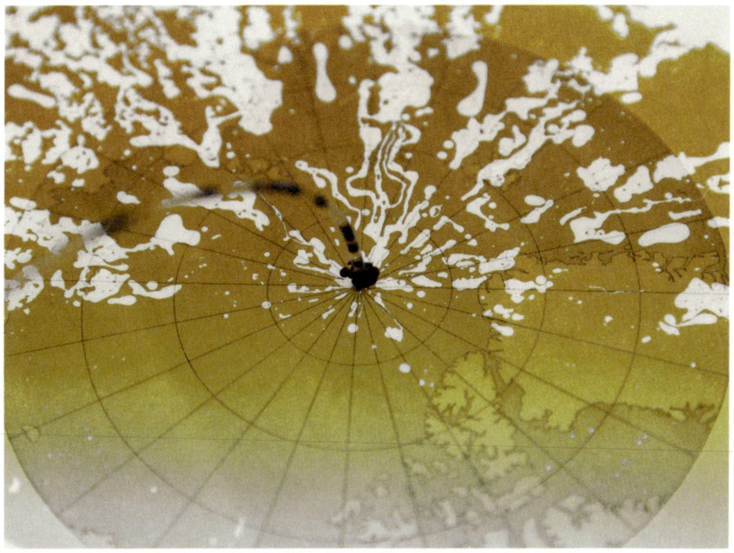

Left: George Osodi
Oil Stains, 2004

Right: Ernst Logar
Artic Circle, 2021
Crude Oil Experiments
lecture performance
Kunstraum Lakeside, 2021

operating in the region such as Shell, whose hands remain stained in blood through, for instance, their role in the execution of the Ogoni Nine. The oil-soaked hands in Osodi's photo are an embodied reminder that, while production may be moving offshore, the costs of extraction persist. Ernst Logar's *Arctic Circle* creates and documents another kind of oil encounter. Produced in a laboratory setting following safety protocols as part of an arts-based research practice, *Arctic Circle* was made using the Hele-Shaw flows. Logar's work speaks both to the planetary character of oil's ubiquity, as well as the emergent oil frontier in the Arctic made all the more viable due to melting icecaps. Set and setting prove paramount as, together, Osodi's and Logar's works register the tensions between scale and proximity that form oil's totality—the immediate, embodied experience of oil's materiality on the one hand and an abstracted one that figures oil as a planetary substance on the other. Some are in conditions to control their relation to and contact with oil; others are compelled into these relations by forces beyond their control. The boundary between these experiences is more porous than may first appear.

Our collective material and aesthetic encounters with oil are defined by uneven pluralities.

Material encounters with oil, bound as they are to these aesthetic ones and the imaginaries they inform, are often shaped by proximity to the raw material itself and the sites of production, like refining and transportation, or they occur solely at sites of consumption. For some, oil encounters begin and end at the gas pump. In the setting of Northern Alberta, Canada, which is home to the tar sands, Métis anthropologist Zoe Todd pivots from an oil spill that happened on her home territory to figure the agents and architects of the fossil economy as participating in a weaponization of oil, asking "how we may de-weaponize the oil and gas that corporate and political bodies have allowed to violate waters, lands and atmospheres across the prairies."[3] Todd's provocative line of questioning highlights the powerful role of energy imaginaries in shaping our past, present, and future relations to oil. Todd's answer is to approach oil as kin in a move that adds another dimension to existing oil epistemologies, or "how to know about oil."[4] But are we limited to only knowing about oil in these terms? Or can artistic interventions like those of Osodi and Logar help us to better know oil directly, an experience sitting somewhere between encounter and reflection that demarcates horizons of de-weaponization?

1 Abdelrahman Munif, *Cities of Salt*, trans. Peter Theroux (New York: Random House, 1987).

2 Amitav Ghosh, "Petrofiction: The Oil Encounter and the Novel," in *The New Republic* 206, no. 9 (March 2, 1992), 29–34.

3 Zoe Todd, "Fish, Kin and Hope: Tending to Water Violations in amiskwaciwâskahikan and Treaty Six Territory," in *Afterall: A Journal of Art, Context and Enquiry* 43 (2017), 102–7.

4 Imre Szeman, "How to Know about Oil: Energy Epistemologies and Political Futures," in *Journal of Canadian Studies/Revue d'études Canadiennes* 47, no. 3 (2013), 145–68.

—03/02.03

What a Difference a Substance Makes

Reflections on the Delta Oil

Simone Gingrich

Niger Delta
crude oil
climate crisis
ecosystem
christmas tree
energy transition

Oil makes a difference—it might make all the difference. The combustion of crude oil is responsible for 32 percent of global fossil energy greenhouse gas emissions[1] and thus contributes majorly to the climate crisis which might jeopardize safe and healthy living conditions for people on Earth. Processed into plastic, crude oil is responsible for 80 percent of marine debris polluting global oceans.[2] The onset of global oil use coincides with the beginning of the Anthropocene,[3] the geological era in which human societies have become a "force of nature," interfering with biogeochemical cycles visible in stratographic records. Originally existing in local deposits in specific areas, oil is one of the products most traded internationally. For all these reasons, oil has become a global substance, directly or indirectly affecting all humans, all non-human organisms, geological strata around the globe, as well as the atmosphere.

At the same time, however, the production and consumption of oil affect different actors differently, and thus have very localized, context-specific impacts. Fifty-two percent of global greenhouse gas emissions, for example, are caused by only ten percent of the global population, i.e., those with the highest incomes and the highest per-capita consumption.[4] At the same time, poor and vulnerable communities, who are responsible for very few emissions, as well as future generations, who have not caused any emissions at all, are, and will be, most affected by the impacts of the climate crisis. The consumption of oil rests upon visions of unlimited freedom and liberty, which are fueled by industries benefiting from growing sales of oil and oil products. On the other hand, lives and livelihoods are threatened by oil, either through the impacts of oil consumption, with the climate crisis degrading the health of ecosystems, or as a direct consequence of oil extraction in the sites affected.

The photograph *Christmas Tree* by George Osodi, taken in the Niger Delta in 2007,[5] visualizes many of the differences introduced by the substance: In the foreground,

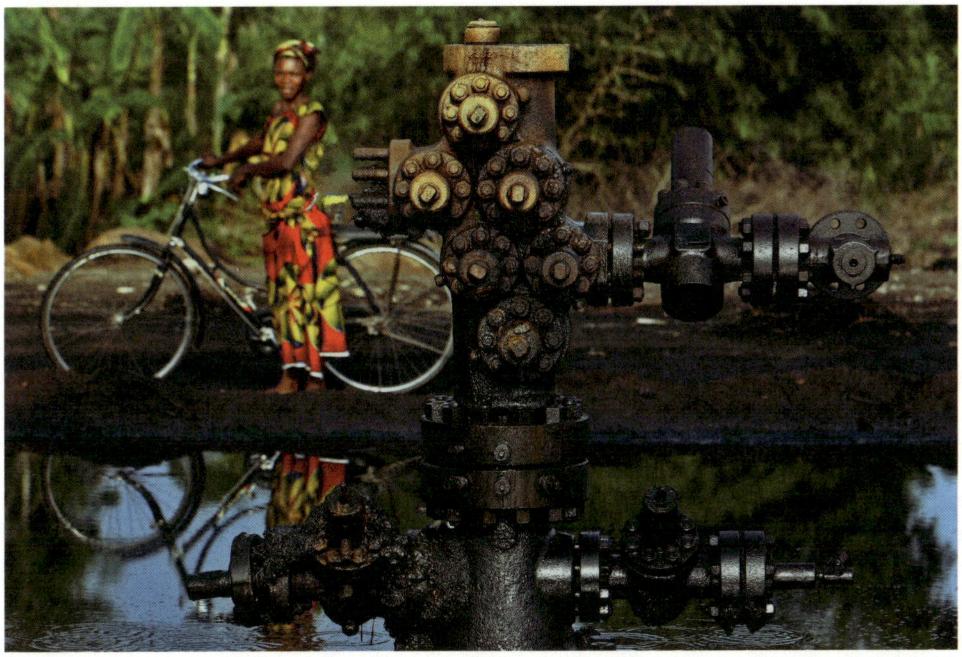

George Osodi
Christmas Tree, 2007

we see an oil pump which provided crude oil to European companies in the past, while the surrounding water is still black and shiny from continuous pollution through the exiting substance. In the background, a local woman dressed in clothes produced in Holland with a traditional Nigerian pattern holds a European bicycle. Even the title of the photograph represents the difference between contextualized and disconnected meaning: a Christmas tree, in the context of Nigerian oil exploitation, is not (only) an ornamented tree symbolic of a Christian holiday, but also the device closing an oil well after the end of its use. The photograph thus demonstrates how a global substance changes the real living conditions of people in an area of oil extraction, as well as the symbolic meaning of things in the local context.

Transitioning out of oil will require an unprecedented global effort.

While much of the debate in the past has focused on the technological challenges of such a transition, and potential technical solutions, now the political, social, and economic challenges are increasingly being addressed. A transition towards a global society which satisfies the needs of all people on Earth while not overusing global ecological capacities will involve no less than negotiating among different interest groups, developing new governance systems for common pool resources, and creating economies that support ecological health, among others. After all, the changes required to transition out of oil will need to be as dramatic as those that brought the world into the oil age: a post-oil future will differ from the present as much as the pre-oil past has differed from today.

1 Pierre Friedlingstein et al., "Global Carbon Budget 2020," in *Earth System Science Data 12*, no. 4 (2020): 3269–3340, https://doi.org/10.5194/essd-12-3269-2020.

2 International Union for the Conservation of Nature (IUCN), "Marine Plastic Pollution. Issues Brief," (2021), https://www.iucn.org/sites/default/files/202204/marine_plastic_pollution_issues_brief_nov21.pdf.

3 Simon L. Lewis and Mark A. Maslin, "Defining the Anthropocene," in *Nature* 519 (2015): 171–180, https://doi.org/10.1038/nature14258.

4 Intergovernmental Panel on Climate Change (IPCC), "Demand, services and social aspects of mitigation," in *Climate Change 2022: Mitigation of Climate Change. Contribution of Working Group III to the Sixth Assessment Report of the Intergovernmental Panel on Climate Change* (Cambridge, UK, and New York, USA: Cambridge University Press, 2022), 10.1017/9781009157926.007.

5 George Osodi, *Christmas Tree*, 2006, from the series *Oil Rich Niger Delta*.

—03/02.04

Oil—The Substance Lubricating a Society Thirsty for Change

David Misch

Niger Delta
crude oil
delta operator
geology
ecosystem
energy transition

The Niger Delta. An art piece of nature that, with its anastomosing riverbeds embedded into a bright green landscape prograding into the blue of the Atlantic Ocean, has an almost surreal beauty. On the other hand, as portrayed by photographer George Osodi under life-threatening conditions, an ecological catastrophe so gigantic and overwhelming that even the incorruptible camera lens seems hardly able to convey a dirty truth that words would not do justice. Millions of liters of oil spilled virtually everywhere. Almost as if an expanding black hole would suck the color out of each and every tree branch, stream, pebble, and grass root to feed its never-ending appetite. It's not that the oil's deep black coloration and silky shine wouldn't also inherit a certain beauty in themselves. But disconnecting its visual elegance—for lack of a better description of its intense visual presence—from the drastic consequences of its harmful appearance, is unthinkable. Adding animals to the picture—even humans, toddlers, elderly women baking traditional bread and cake over gas flares set up a long time ago by global players in the oil industry, young, apparently strong and healthy men working in rudimentary refineries and following the promise of long-desired wealth and social status—makes for the plot of a disaster movie way beyond Hollywoodesque exaggeration. And yet the pictures show nothing but the plain reality of a society addicted to turbo consumption. A reality in which we all play our part. A reality that seldomly becomes as graphically visible as in the Niger Delta, yet existing in similar ways all over the globe—besides the realms of those wealthy enough not to be held responsible for their

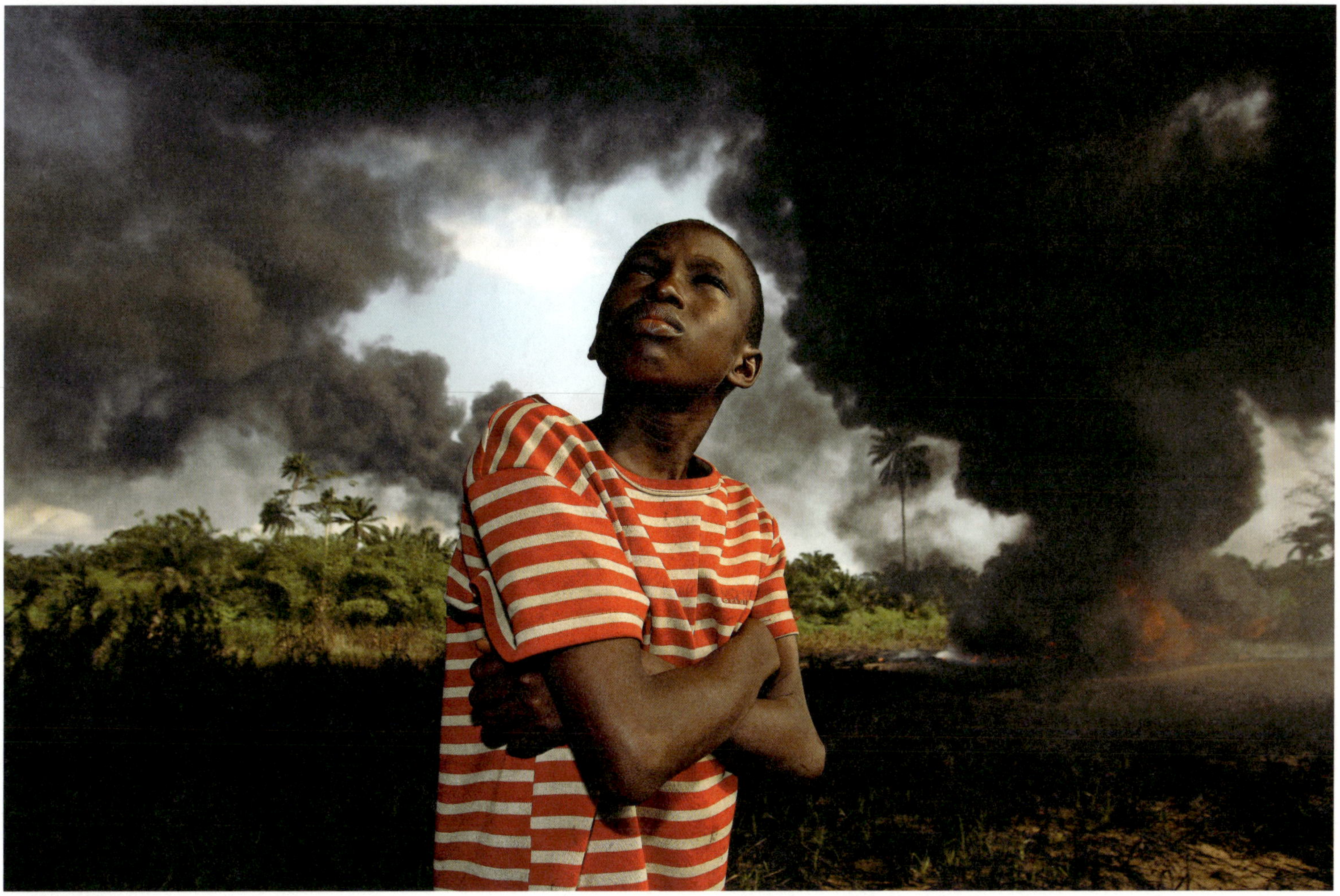

George Osodi
Ogoni Boy, 2007

actions. Could anybody look at these sceneries and not be embarrassed about the destructive power of industrialization—or whom- or whatever to blame?

The fluvial delta owes its name to the eponymous triangular-shaped Greek letter—an obvious geometric match when looking at the Nile Delta, which was first named accordingly. However, in technical language, the delta operator also means change. First introduced by the Swiss mathematician, physician, and astronomer Leonhard Euler,[1] the meaning of delta as a measure of property variations—for example a differential in temperature or pressure—is now one of the first things to be brainwashed into the heads of aspiring youngsters in technical universities. Delta means change. Full stop. Did Euler, who also had a profound interest in geography, see the less obvious connection between the delta operator and the fluvial delta—both being associated with constant change?

The not so simple truth about geographical deltas is that, by far, many of them do not actually resemble the Greek letter's

triangular shape. It is all down to the contrary forces of the fluvial system, transporting sediment from the continent and depositing them into the delta, and the open marine system, which tries to erode its way deeper into the delta plain during high tide or times of rising relative sea level.

Throwing coast-parallel wave activity in the mix, deltas may form all kinds of complex shapes beyond the overly simplified concepts of a basic geology class (or an enthusiastic climate movement, for that matter). Not only the forces of nature, also the uncountable variety of aqueous and terrestrial species claim their part of the diverse and sensible ecosystem that a delta represents, being fed by nutrients that are transported towards the delta by continental waters, laying foundations for growth of life, from microorganisms to large mammals. Last but not least, the delta is a place of oil. Rocks that are formed from the deposited sediments in deltas may be the source of oil (and, more frequently, gas), and, even more importantly, may also provide the subsurface reservoirs in which these natural substances are accumulated. In the Niger Delta, the oil is trapped very near the land surface, making it extraordinarily extractable—and, as evidenced by George Osodi's pieces *Black Gold*[2] and *Ogoni Boy*,[3] the region's omnipresent demon. Due to it being less dense than water, oil has an almost unstoppable physical tendency to force its way to the surface, which could almost be seen as metaphorical to Western societies' hunger to exploit it from the subsurface for constant growth. One could be tempted to find an excuse in its physical nature—as if oil would demand its constant consumption. For sure that would be a rather stupid argument—although not too far away from the perception of oil in an industrial era when the black gold was a symbol of success and stability. And for the wind of change.

Nowadays, the zeitgeist makes us believe that oil and gas are not part of us, or nature, but is rather the fuel for a cruel and immoral mafia of super-corporations so powerful that it may seem as if their acting would be completely decoupled from any democratic rationalities. That even the slightest doubt regarding the absolute evil of oil and its invisible sidecar CO2 is plain backwardness or driven by purely egoistic motives of those on the *winner's side*. And these prominent voices are not generally wrong—it could not be clearer that the lifestyle of a minority of Earth's human population, still a considerable number of people, is an ecological dead-end. Yet still we decide to buy our BMWs, MacBook Airs, and e-scooters—ok, sure, you are not a part of we, but obviously too many of us are. Because the world is not as black and white as these voices often tend to make us believe, but way more than fifty shades of grey. Yes, we will need a transition away from fossil fuels and more global social equality, but the truth is also that, as of today, there are no such concepts—real concepts, not simple wishful thinking—that do not come with a price that may or may not be equal to or higher than what has already been paid by the poor majority. Shutting down an oil well here and a tar sand extraction site there is a noteworthy achievement, but not a driver for global change, as getting rid of oil and gas will create a new delta. A gap that will not be filled solely by reducing energy consumption in rich societies or by counting on apparently cleaner technologies—or whatever may be on the wish list of those with a strong belief in clear visions and simple truths.

"In this bright future, you can't forget your past," sings Bob Marley in "No Woman, No Cry." May the future answer if "No Oil, No Cry" is a possibility, and at what price we can make it a desirable reality for the majority of us. For now, oil is still a neutral chemical substance composed of carbon, hydrogen, oxygen, and traces of a few other elements. For now, young men in Nigeria still seek their way into their bright future in the polluted streams of the Niger Delta.

For the slightest chance to change this status quo for the better, we will need to use all the tools and knowledge that only our surf on the oil wave could help us develop.

1 Leonhard Euler, *Institutiones calculi differentialis [Foundations Of Differential Calculus]*, vol. 1 (St. Petersburg: Academiae Imperialis Scientiarum Petropolitanae, 1755), 5.

2 George Osodi, *Black Gold*, 2015, from the series *New Niger Delta*.

3 George Osodi, *Ogoni Boy*, 2007, from the series *Oil Rich Niger Delta*.

—03/02.05

The Raw and the Refined

Benjamin Steininger

Niger Delta
crude oil
refinery
petromodernity
ecological damage
guerrilla chemistry
delta petro dollar

Although brightly lit 24/7, refineries are invisible. They subvert visual perception on several levels. For one thing, what goes on in their tube systems is far too small to be seen with the human eye. It involves the dissolving and connecting of hydrocarbon molecules, which play out on spatial scales of 10-10 meters. On a temporal scale, these elementary chemical acts occur in tiny periods of 10-12 to 10-15 seconds. At the other end of the scale, the kilometers-long process landscapes are far too large and complex to be grasped at a glance. But what truly escapes the senses, is the role of the refinery as the central transition point of petromodernity. It is here, where a more or less natural, pre-human, fossilized raw material is transformed into artificial materiality, technically designed down to the smallest molecular detail—“science-fashioned molecules,” as a 1946 advertisement once put it.[1]

So, to try to gain any meaningful understanding, one would have to follow oil’s entire route into the refinery, from reservoir rocks underground via drilling technologies, transportation, tankers, and pipelines, as well as every route out of the

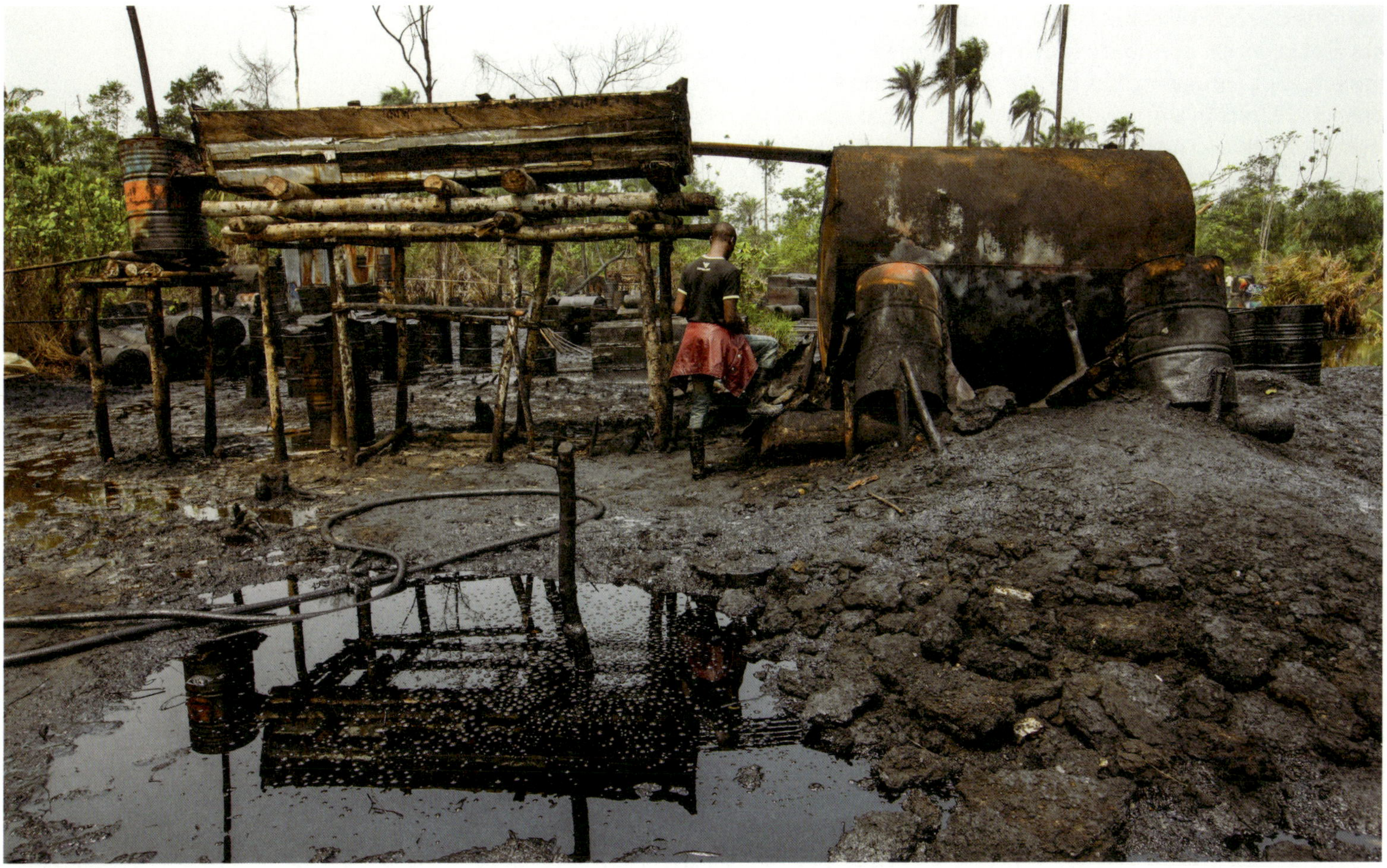

George Osodi
Illegal Oil Refinery, 2013

refinery, including all means of mobility, plastics production, pharmaceuticals, cosmetics, fertilizers—and thus into the bodies of animals and human beings.

From there, one has to deal with all kinds of causal relationships in the biosphere and the technosphere in order to make sense of the refinery as a core component in this journey. The fullest possible understanding of the refinery as a key element of actual "planetary technology" would include the fullest possible understanding of the planet. However, it is in fact only possible to interpret small parts of the entire route and certain exemplary geographies.[2]

The technology of the refinery shows that it is not black, natural crude oil that "makes history," but a set of chemically refined hydrocarbons that, in the range between kerosene, explosives, mascara, and superglue, drive a complex historical chain reaction with many feedbacks and resonances.[3] Indeed, the ecological impact of the globe's refinery-controlled manufactured products is much more drastic on a planetary level than any oil spill, no matter how severe.

Humans can collectively establish and describe these routes technically. But they are visible only in exemplary sections. These sensual obstacles seem all the more remarkable considering that, on many levels, "visibility" and "recognizability" cannot abstract in any way from the products that result from refineries. Currently, every science and media technology we have is simply inconceivable without the output of refineries. Neither the satellites, computers, and data networks of global communication, nor, at the other end of the technical scale, the simplest dyes that humans use for semiotic technology and optical systems of technology, would exist without refineries. Given the role of pharmacy and cosmetics, and that of individual transport, in producing the self-image of petromodern humans, in a broader sense, it would seem that "sensual activity" itself is connected to petrochemistry.

The fact that such gigantic process landscapes are clearly necessary, at least indirectly, for making fossilized "nature" available to the field of technology, and thus the history of mankind, gives an indication of the scale of what is being processed there. What is encountered at the refinery is indirectly, and beyond all immediate human standards of perception, an "aesthetics of the sublime"—the "industrial sublime," but which precisely in this conveys the "natural sublime" of the fossilized raw material and its planetary effect in an exemplary manner.

In contrast, the illegal refineries that George Osodi has photographed in the Niger Delta have a very visible, very tangible, frighteningly sensuous direct effect: we see brachial apparatuses made up of tanks and pipes, racks of wood, condensation lines, and barrels for raw materials and other goods erected in a clearing in the bush. The ground is black from crude oil. Here, sticky raw material is converted by distillation into marketable and motorable products. Although no molecule chains are chemically cracked—these types of plant are not suitable for that—a natural substance is also being transformed into a technical product. The presence of oil and its refining could not be more sensual.

But here, too, central parts of what happens undermine the level of the sensual—in terms of horror as well as in terms of empowerment and emancipation. The backdrop to these drastic bush refineries is not only the immediate, ecological horror of the Niger Delta, but also the economic-technical misery of a country plagued by colonial, but also national, corruption. One of the richest countries in Africa is only able to domestically refine and market a mere one percent of the oil it produces in official chemical refineries. Self-made bush refiners eagerly fill this gap. Bizarrely, in addition to causing further ecological damage to the delta, they also generate considerable wealth. What they also give rise to, in the midst of ecological horror in an exemplary sense, is a surprisingly self-determined coupling of the otherwise technically, geographically, and culturally separate realms of "upstream" and "downstream."

What shapes the global regimes of extractivism and exploitation is a more or less strict geographic separation of extraction, refining, and consumption. A separation that is somehow united in this type of guerrilla chemistry.

"Wrong life cannot be lived rightly," so says Theodor W. Adorno's famous dictum from *Minima Moralia*.[4] But as a form of coping with a "damaged planet"[5]—to quote the famous book title by Anna Tsing and others—the guerrilla chemistry that is carried out by the young people of the Niger Delta is exemplary and points in a promising direction. In physics, measuring the difference between two values—for example, "delta T" or "ΔT" for time—can be used to extrapolate further values, as long as a well-known dynamics allows for this extrapolation. In other disciplines, such as in historiography, extrapolation from a measured delta is less promising—at least if one expects an exact prognosis. Still, the production of guerrilla fuels in an extraction country operates with a very specific difference: it touches upon the crucial tension and difference between extraction and refining. In this sense, the bush refineries of the Niger Delta decisively truncate a structural factor, what we might call and measure as "Δ$" (delta petrodollar). This techno-economic difference-operator could not only serve to measure neutral economic differences, but also the tension between the horrors of extraction and the anonymous value creation of refining and consumption. The creation of maximal wealth by maximal horror would approximate Δ$ to zero.

To catch up with the so-called Global North, using this type of guerrilla appropriation of petrochemistry and petrocapital, would mean that acts of respective appropriation would have to follow. These might include guerrilla mines and guerrilla spills in the midst of the glittering and alienated centers of the West, in order to drastically bring extractivism, which invisibly powers Western life, into the full view of the West.

1 *The Inside Story of Modern Gasoline: Science-Fashioned Molecules For Top Performance*, a "Leadership Through Science" film presented by the Standard Oil Company of Indiana (Jerry Fairbanks Productions Inc., 1946), https://archive.org/details/0320_Inside_Story_of_Modern_Gasoline_The_21_01_00_00.

2 See, as one exemplary analysis, Benjamin Steininger, "Ammonia synthesis on the banks of the Mississippi: A molecular-planetary technology," in *The Anthropocene Review* 8, no. 3 (2021), 262–279. See, as a collection, Benjamin Steininger and Alexander Klose, *Erdöl: Ein Atlas der Petromoderne* (Berlin: Matthes & Seitz Verlag, 2020). English translation by Ayça Türkoğlu: *Crude: Atlas of Petromodernity* (Santa Barbara: Punctum Books, 2023).

3 See, as an interpretation of the history of the technology of catalysis in the context of the refinery, Benjamin Steininger, "Refinery and Catalysis," in *Textures of the Anthropocene: Grain/Vapor/Ray*, ed. Kathrin Klingan et al. (Boston: MIT Press, 2014), 105–118.

4 Theodor W. Adorno, *Minima Moralia: Reflections from Damaged Life*, trans. Edmund F.N. Jephcott (London, England; New York: Verso, 2006), 39. (Original work published in 1951).

5 Anna Lowenhaupt Tsing et al., eds., *Arts of Living on a Damaged Planet: Ghosts and Monsters of the Anthropocene* (Minneapolis: University of Minnesota Press, 2017).

—03/02.06

A Journey Through Oil's Space

Reflections on Oil, Architecture, and Text

Arianna Mondin

Niger Delta
crude oil
Petrolio
abyss
architecture
infrastructure
greek letter delta
oil space

In quest'opera il punto di vista è sempre al vertice. Le cose sono colte in un loro momento di attualità così estrema da presentarsi come cristallizzate o pietrificate. [...]. Tuttavia questo punto di vista culminante non disdegna di prendere in considerazione di tanto in tanto (anzi, per la verità piuttosto spesso) le profondità dei baratri; non solo, ma addirittura di osservare come le cose, formando laggiù nei baratri, salgano lentamente di quota, fino a emergere e a cristallizzarsi nei vertici: a coglierle addirittura, in somma, nel loro moto, nella loro evoluzione, nella loro storia. Ma–tra vertici e baratri–c'è una terza alternativa: ossia la 'mezza-costa'.[...]. Se il grafico dell'opera è costituito da una serie di 'salti' tra vertici e baratri è costituito anche—e con una certa continuità—da una linea regolare, che è appunto quella della mezzacosta.

In this work the point of view is always at the peak. Things are caught at a moment of actuality so extreme that they appear crystallized or petrified [...]. Yet this heightened point of view does not disdain to consider from time to time (quite often, in fact) the depths of the abyss; not only that but, indeed, to observe how things formed down in the abyss slowly rise up until they emerge and are crystallized into peaks; in sum, to capture them exactly in their movement, in their evolution, in their history. But—between the peak and the abyss—there is still a third alternative; that is, the "middle road".[...]. If a diagram of the work consists of a series of "leaps" between peaks and abysses, it also—and with some continuity—consists of a regular line, which is precisely that of the middle road.

Pier Paolo Pasolini, *Petrolio*.
Note 43. Flashes of light on *Linkskommunismus*

A massive mountain-shaped white house appears in George Osodi's photo. It has pseudo-classical columns and corner solutions with approximate ashlar decorating the building, its high walls punctuated by other white columns.

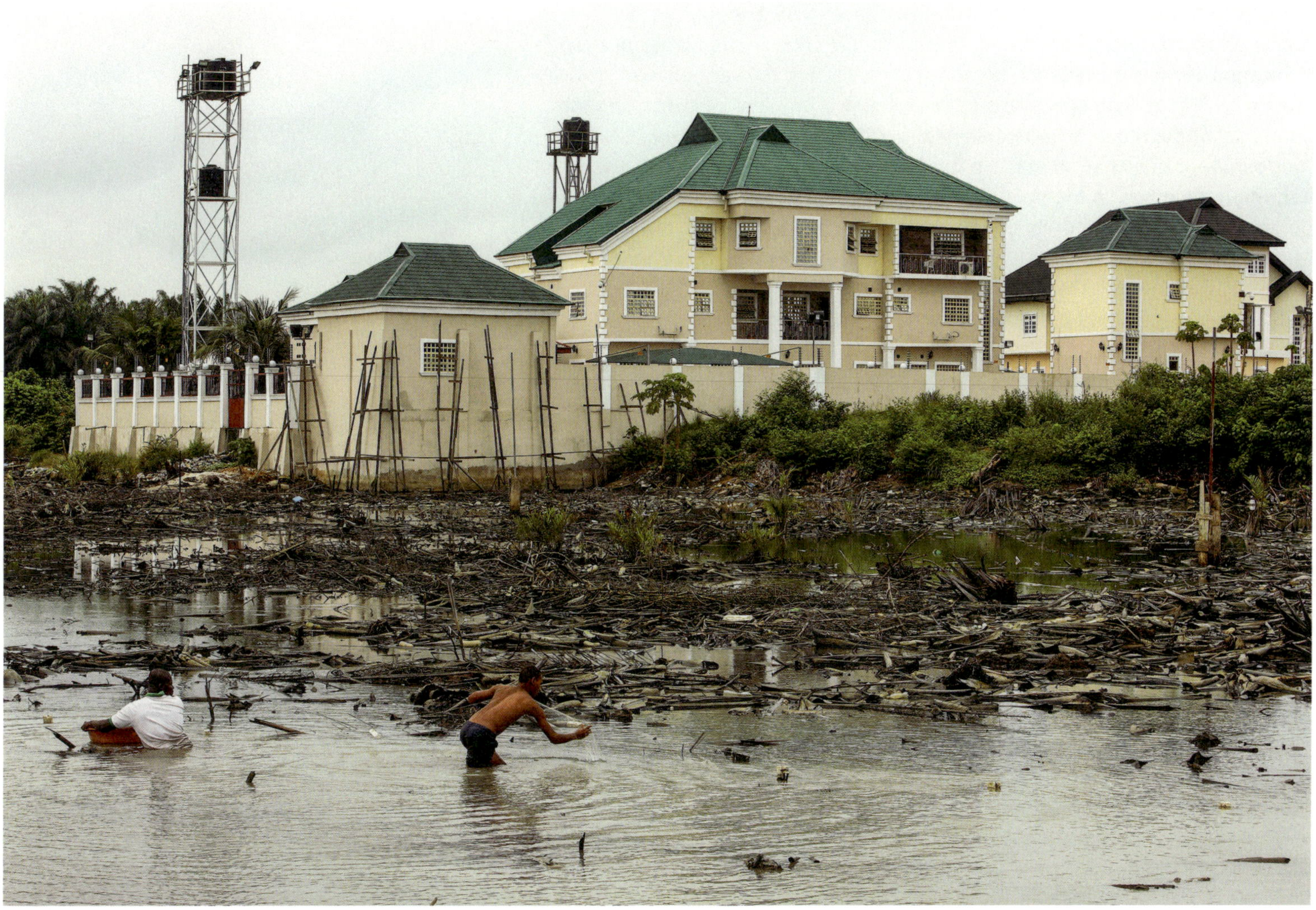

George Osodi
Ogu, 2013

All the white-cream colors of the building and its elements easily liquefy in the black oily water that occupies the bottom of the photo. This white mountain that emerges from the dark water full of oil of the Niger Delta is the realization of the dream of illegal refinery owners who, once they become wealthy enough, can finally build a house that's "a bit neo-classical, a bit modernist, a bit enriched West's periphery." At this scale, we can observe the contradictions and complexities of oil and its reflections on space. White architecture emerges from the abysses of the black water and from the earth where crude oil "slowly rises up"[1] to be transformed. We can consider this photo as a diagram that allows us to see how oil shapes our planet.

Oil is space and oil is language. It is the language and the space of our contemporary world, of capitalistic society. It is our blood with which we write our history and give shape to our cultural artefacts.

Despite its ubiquity—"everything is mapped (above all, because of Oil)"[2]—it is "doomed to blindness," according to Bertolucci in his film *La via del petrolio*.[3] Oil pumps life in our existence by acting on the sharp border between visibility and invisibility, in both space and language: it is a physical infrastructure that connects, finds, but also separates and, quoting Reza Negarestani, it is the "undercurrent of all narrations."[4] In this blurred border, we read and hear about it through the news, in the political, economic, ecological, and social discourse, but we easily forget about its constant presence in our daily life, our everyday "encounters" with it, as Jordan B. Kinder writes in his essay. We don't easily see its travels through the Earth, but we recognize its "bad" consequences as its spills and leaks—the black liquid surface in ecological disasters.

As space and language, Pasolini wrote *Petrolio*, his last unfinished novel he started writing in 1972 and that was abruptly interrupted by his homicide on the night between November 1 and 2, 1975, at Ostia's seaplane base. The book is an architecture made of text—an attempt to unveil the backstage of our world by letting the readers move through the spaces of the novel and, in this way, experience oil and its structure. The constructive element of *Petrolio's* architecture is the note (*appunto*). The notes (*appunti*) also determine the work's rhythm, unity, and fragmentation. They build a space that develops both vertically and horizontally, as the quote that introduces this text explains.

Oil is the *topos* of power, we can read our society through its structure. And the same is true of the architecture of Pasolini's book: something is hidden, and something emerges in "crystalized forms" from the deep abysses. Vertical and horizontal means putting the network and the hierarchy together and this is exactly how power and oil work: "networks are generally nested in hierarchies, nomads stick to riding camels and raiding, and the war machines run on coal and petrol."[5] Moreover, the language power uses is, apparently, multiple and diversified, and in fact, according to the original project, *Petrolio* was to have been made not just of notes, but also of letters, newspaper articles, interviews, songs, and illustrations.[6]

Many languages are necessary in order to grasp the complexity of oil; similar to Pasolini's project, in this group's contributions, the ambiguous condition of visibility and invisibility of oil is expressed through the point of view of different disciplines and practices, and so, by using several forms of texts and contents. Various languages and contents build a space where the reader can travel from the abysses of oil to its peaks, but they might also find the "middle road," where the texts connect like pipelines in the desert or the steppe. As in the work of Pasolini, where "the fragmentary character of the whole book ensures that, for example, certain 'narrative pieces' are in themselves complete,"[7] the contributions build a space by themselves but, at the same time, they are linked together creating a movement that makes it pulse like magma. It is a structure that allows this section of the book to keep together a plurality of individual contributions, their *differences*—because oil "makes all the difference" as Simone Gingrich writes—but also the connections between them, or the "middle road." The symbol that connects and at the same time differentiates all contributions is Δ, the delta. It means, indeed, difference and change. Moreover, delta is a triangle, geographically identified in the Niger Delta—effectively illustrated by George Osodi's photos—and it is symbolically related to vertical and horizontal movements, a "constant change," that is physical, chemical, biological, and geographical like the one David Misch narrates.

The delta, Δ, is an architectural diagram that also represents the "peaks" and the "abysses," the building that emerges from the oil depths.

The journey through the architecture of this section goes inside the Earth, in the abysses where oil reservoirs are, and it arrives at its summits, where oil comes out and is transformed, thanks to the extracting technologies.

It finds its built forms in the various scales of the refineries, because "the fullest possible understanding of the refinery would include the fullest possible understanding of the planet," as Benjamin Steininger writes in his text. Oil runs around the world within its transportation, follows its transformation, and becomes the fuel that builds the spaces we live in. Oil expresses our world in all scales, for this reason, the micro-scale of oil movements inside rocks, its compositions and behaviors, helps us to understand our society and environment as from the refinery to the planet, from oil micro-flows inside rocks to big rivers. As Pit Arnold explains: "The flow in porous media is contingent on its topology and can only be accurately modelled with three-dimensional information. As in a river, there are faster and slower flow paths, introducing intricacies to the transport dynamics."

Oil runs through all the scales of our existence, from the air we breathe to cities and space projects. To capture it in a single image is impossible; many voices and viewpoints are needed to understand it, voices that are both equal and contradictory, like oil itself.

Pit Arnold writes that "each variant of crude oil has a unique composition and physical properties, making it a fascinating and complex substance," and so are the contributions in this section: Reflections on Oil. Each contribution produces its own reflections, the journey through them is like a walk through the rooms of a building, each one with its own peculiarities and all together building the space of the palace.

1 Pier Paolo Pasolini, *Petrolio* (Turin: Einaudi, 1992).

2 Pasolini, *Petrolio*.

3 *La via del petrolio* [The Path of Oil], directed by Bernardo Bertolucci, 1967.

4 Reza Negarestani, *Cyclonopedia: complicity with anonymous materials* (Melbourne: re.press, 2008).

5 Paul Hirst, *Space and Power: Politics, War and Architecture* (Oxford: Polity Press, 2005).

6 Pasolini, *Petrolio*.

7 Pasolini, *Petrolio*.

—03/03

The Becoming of a Graphic Novel: Teresa

Olaf Osten, Ulrike Payerhofer

workshop
energy transition
interdisciplinarity
speculative thinking
imagination
graphic novel

The following text summarizes the most important moments, considerations, and processes that took place during the "becoming of" our graphic novel *Teresa*. In the summer of 2021, we were given a clear brief: to develop a graphic novel with a group of participants from a range of disciplines that would address the much-needed energy transition away from fossil fuels. As a team, we had one year to produce the novel collaboratively, together with six experts selected from the arts, scientific research, and activism. We were allocated six double-page spreads in a future publication, as well as several preparatory online meetings, before coming together to attend, in June 2022, an intensive two-day workshop at the University of Applied Arts Vienna to develop the storyboard and main narrative.

As group moderators and an artists, we knew that before a rigid timeline with fixed milestones could be set up to guide the team we had to allow members of the group to get to know each other and become familiarized with the diversity of expertise and knowledge that each participant would bring to the project. Only then could we establish a context for possible content creation. As such, art historian **Amanda Boetzkes** from the University of Guelph outlined her research on the aesthetics of plastic that is informed by contemporary art history and theory. **Kinga Kiełczyńska**, a multidisciplinary artist based in Warsaw, introduced her work on forests, sustainability, and considerations of the human-nature relationship. Reservoir engineer and head of the Department Petroleum Engineering at the University of Leoben, **Holger Ott**, shared his research on current technical developments and geological aspects of green energy technology. **Cleo Reece**, an environmental activist, filmmaker, and member of the Fort McMurry 468 First Nation based in Alberta, Canada, provided insights into her experience of the reality of Indigenous communities living in tar extraction zones. Researcher **Johannes Schmidt**, who focuses on sustainable economic development, presented his expertise on the transitions towards renewable energy systems in Latin America and their impacts on land use. And finally, **Janet Stewart**, a sociologist with expertise

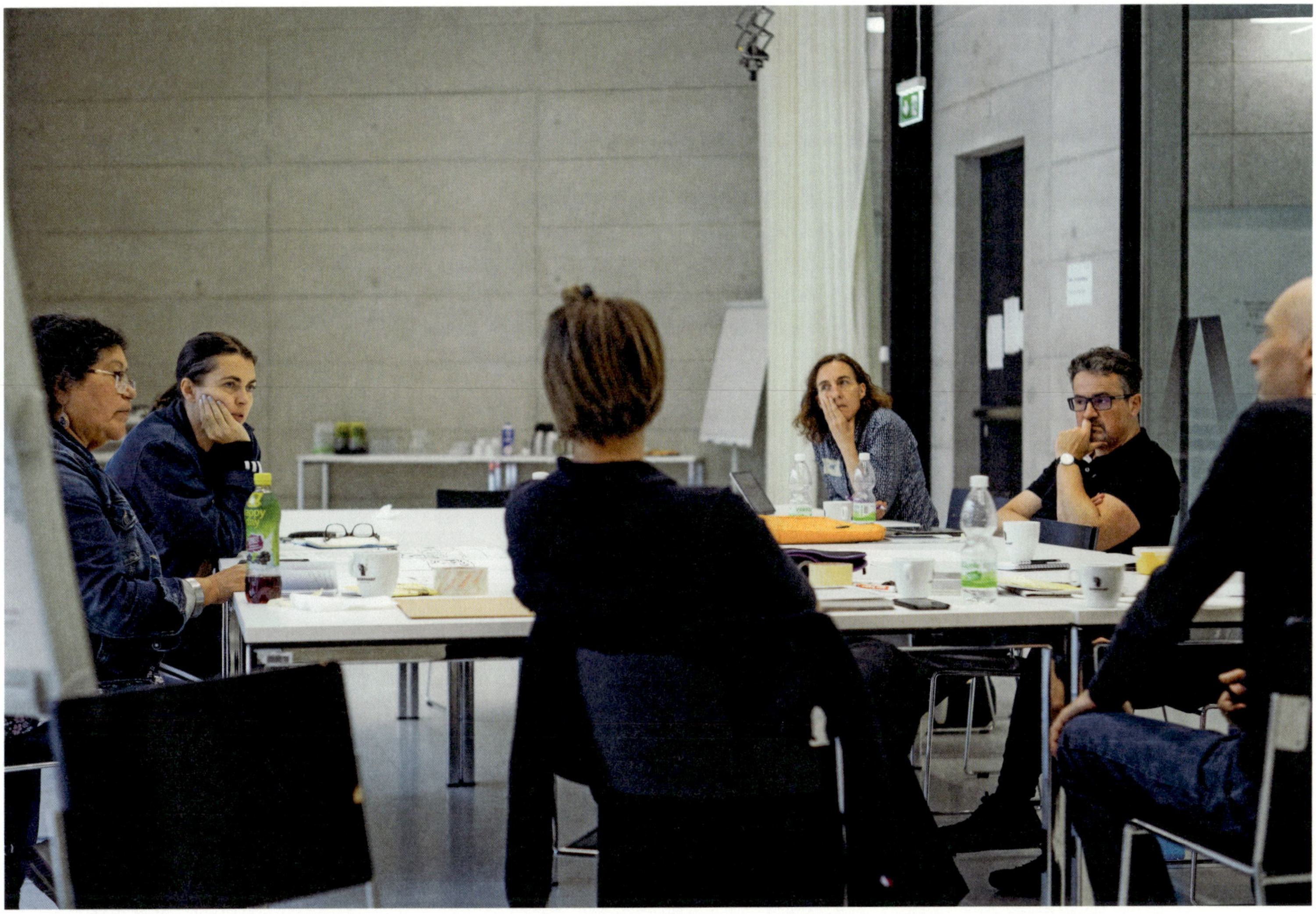

Working group 3, discussion on main narrative and story board, Reflecting Oil Colloquium, University of Applied Arts Vienna, 2022

on visual culture, modernity, and the history of petroleum, introduced the group to historical narratives of human life entangled with petroleum.

From the fertile ground of differing perspectives, there emerged the first connections, questions, and contradictions between the participants and their various fields of knowledge. Indeed, it soon became clear that "productive tensions" would lead to fruitful conversations. After the initial presentations and discussions, a critical shift in terms of facilitating the group towards the graphic novel was instigated.

We felt it crucial to encourage participants to move away from disciplinary-bound expertise and initiate a phase of free speculative thinking and creative imagination. We did this in two stages. First, we opened up a free associative discussion on the dimension of time, connecting it to processes of transition and guiding it by asking questions such as "When did the transition happen and how long did it take?" and "What was the transition like for so-and-so…?"

Key associations thrown up by this conversation were used to build the framework of the graphic novel. In a moderated discussion round, we explored the story's possible timeframe, whether it should take place in some distant future, say 200 years from now, or within a period of time that is closer to today. To set an approachable tone, the group felt the story should cover the lifespan of a human being and, given the novel's six-page format, that it should be structured roughly by decade. With this timespan in mind, the group then navigated questions like "What might or can happen within decades?" and "What are our assumptions about fiction, speculation, and reality?"

To bring these meta-discussions to a more concrete level, the next phase involved asking the participants to choose from a list of possible characters. These included a blogger, Marie Curie, a virus, a General Secretary, a Shell CEO, Greta Thunberg, a divine figure, a cyclist, an eight-year-old child, love, a dragonfly, an O molecule, Mark Zuckerberg's daughter, a plastic cup, a guardian, a Nobel Prize winner, and a tree. The idea was for participants to use these tangible, if fictive, figures to free up their imaginations and further enhance their speculative thinking. As future protagonists in the graphic novel, the characters allowed members of the group to dive deeper into the subject matter and to connect it to their respective fields of interest or specialisms. Once selected, the participants were asked to endow these characters with traits.

In preparation for the two-day workshop in the framework of the colloquium, we accompanied the group members in developing their characters, asking them to sketch out some initial ideas about their chosen element's qualities and the potential contexts they might appear in. Kinga Kielczynska explored the characteristics of the oxygen molecule, emphasizing its centrality to life as well as its ability to merge with and shift between other molecules. Holger Ott chose the plastic cup as an object derived from crude oil. He imagined its life in the headquarters of an oil company—a life hovering between deep depression and fleeting usefulness. Amanda Boetzkes picked the virus as a symbol and a force that is strongly intertwined with our lives and for its ability to create great structural change to our social fabric. Johannes Schmidt chose the eight-year-old child and brought his daughter on board to help amplify the character. Together they came up with a school girl named Teresa who lives in a rural part of Brazil and has three cats. Janet Stewart delved into the historical meanings and connotations of trees and their existence as centuries-old witnesses to life on Earth. Cleo Reece, for her part, picked the trickster figure Weesageechak as her protagonist, highlighting the ambivalent nature of this being, between faithful companion and protector, trickster and opportunist.

Equipped with all possible—and impossible—lines of thought and imaginings, we facilitated June's two-day workshop with the goal of collectively producing a storyboard for the graphic novel. We chose a chronological narrative structure that begins, on page one, with six individual storylines (one for each character) that run in parallel to each other; these start to merge as the tale progresses until they are all combined in a single image that appears on the novel's last page—the story gradually developing from today's political problems to a potential hopeful future that speculates on the knowledge and wisdom that is yet to come.

The graphic novel is a fictional biography about the girl Teresa and her involvement with the other five characters. Told in six stages of her life, we see Teresa being confronted with complex challenges faced by society and deciding to be part of the solution. She becomes an activist and a scientist in order to help tackle these problems. Through knowledge and experience, she brings all the elements that appear in the story together, revealing their contexts, which finally leads to her thinking of the world as an interconnected whole. By taking responsibility and through effective communication, Teresa fights for change and publishes her ideas on the future of energy politics. The story dares to end with the optimism that we might just find a way to make things better. Although we cannot know what the world will look like in 50 years, it is the Teresas of today who give us hope and remind us that we should all act to be part of the solution.

The way in which the different elements interact in this novel demonstrates that it is not only scientific knowledge but also emotional and psychological qualities that allow us to define and reach goals. The drawings convey this by depicting a range of imagery and atmospheres, from statistical diagrams to sequences that are almost surreal, yet somehow remain concrete.

However, the storyline is kept ambiguous as it progresses, allowing for individual associations and narratives to develop.

The gaps that have intentionally been left, between the characters, the narrative combination, and the indeterminate chronological sequences, give the reader a lot of freedom to fill in, construct, and interpret the story for themselves. Consequently, readers take on the role of co-authors and contribute significantly to the story's "completion."

As an artistic medium, graphic novels are a type of "comic," but rather than being oriented towards comics they make direct reference to the "novel." The word "novel," which the Cambridge Dictionary defines as "a long printed story about imaginary characters and events," also implies a certain seriousness, scope, and narrative depth.

A central aspect and challenge of the entire graphic novel-making process was to ensure that both the content produced by the participants and its formal design were considered together. This was in order to create a sequence of images and a narrative that hovers between the concrete and the ambiguous—a condition that mirrors the current state of developments towards a green energy transition.

Teresa

a fiction on a not-so-deep
future of energy

in the following story
you are going to meet

- a plastic cup
- an "oxygen" molecule
- a trickster
- Teresa
- a virus
- a tree

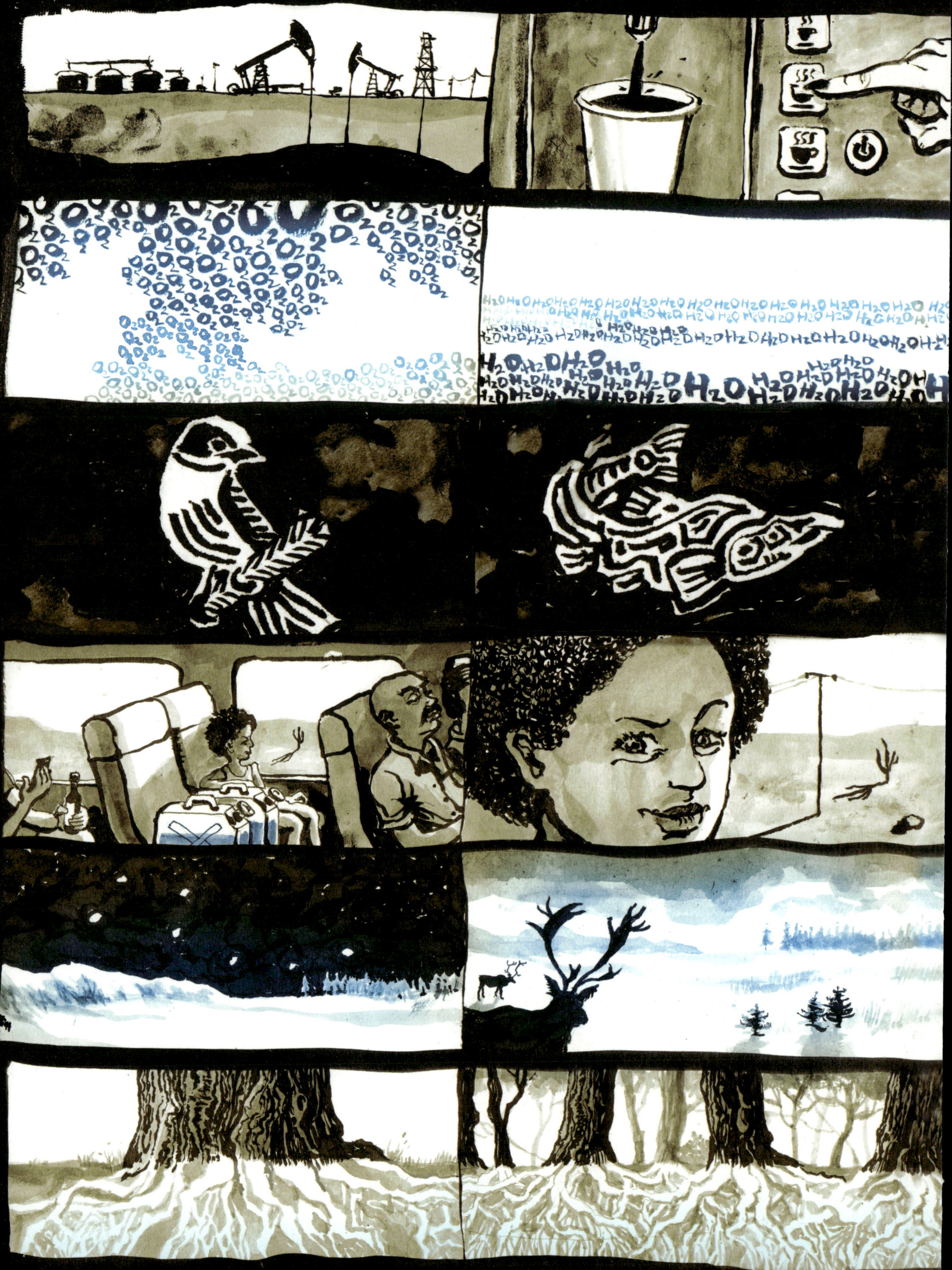

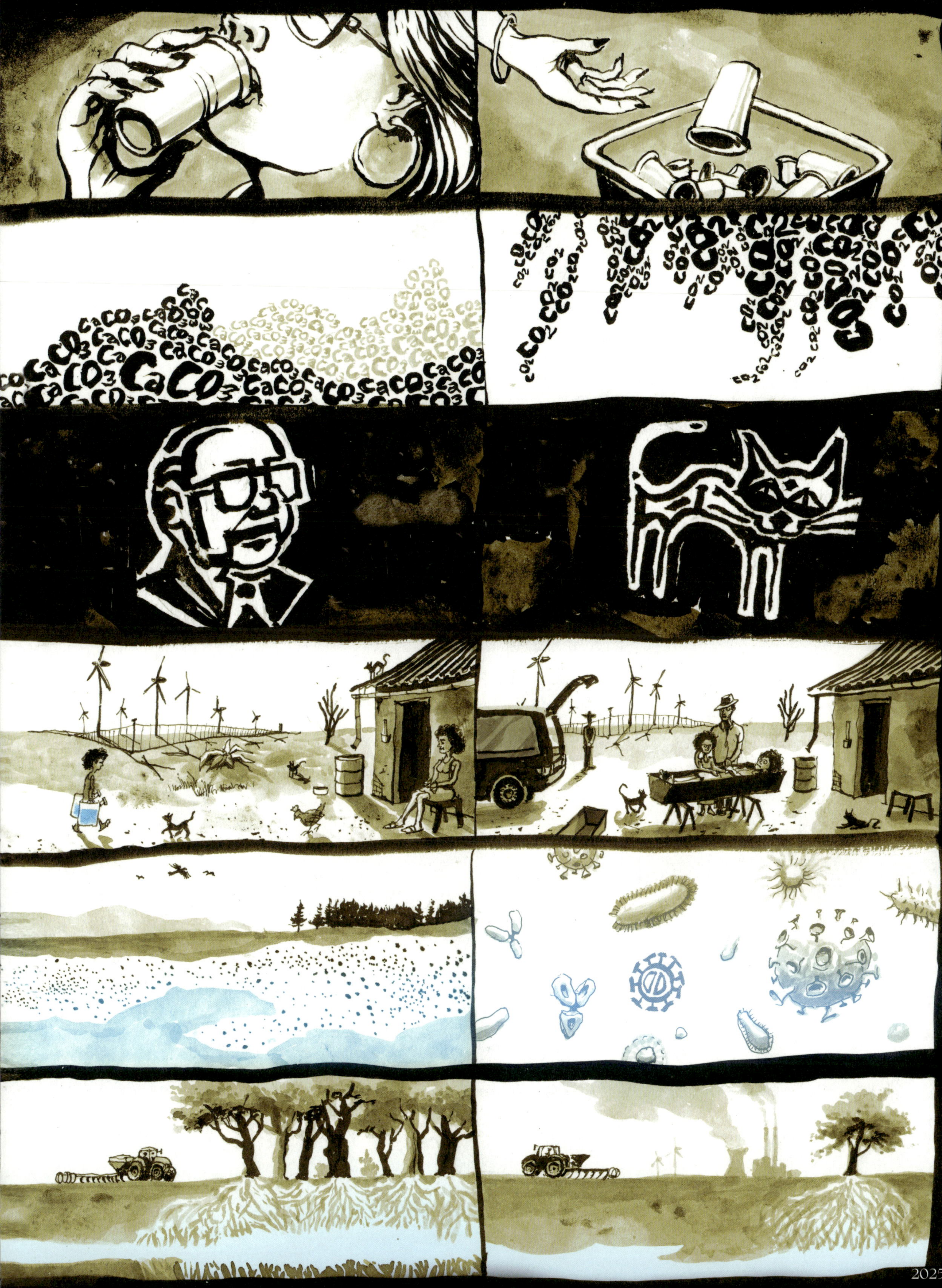

2025

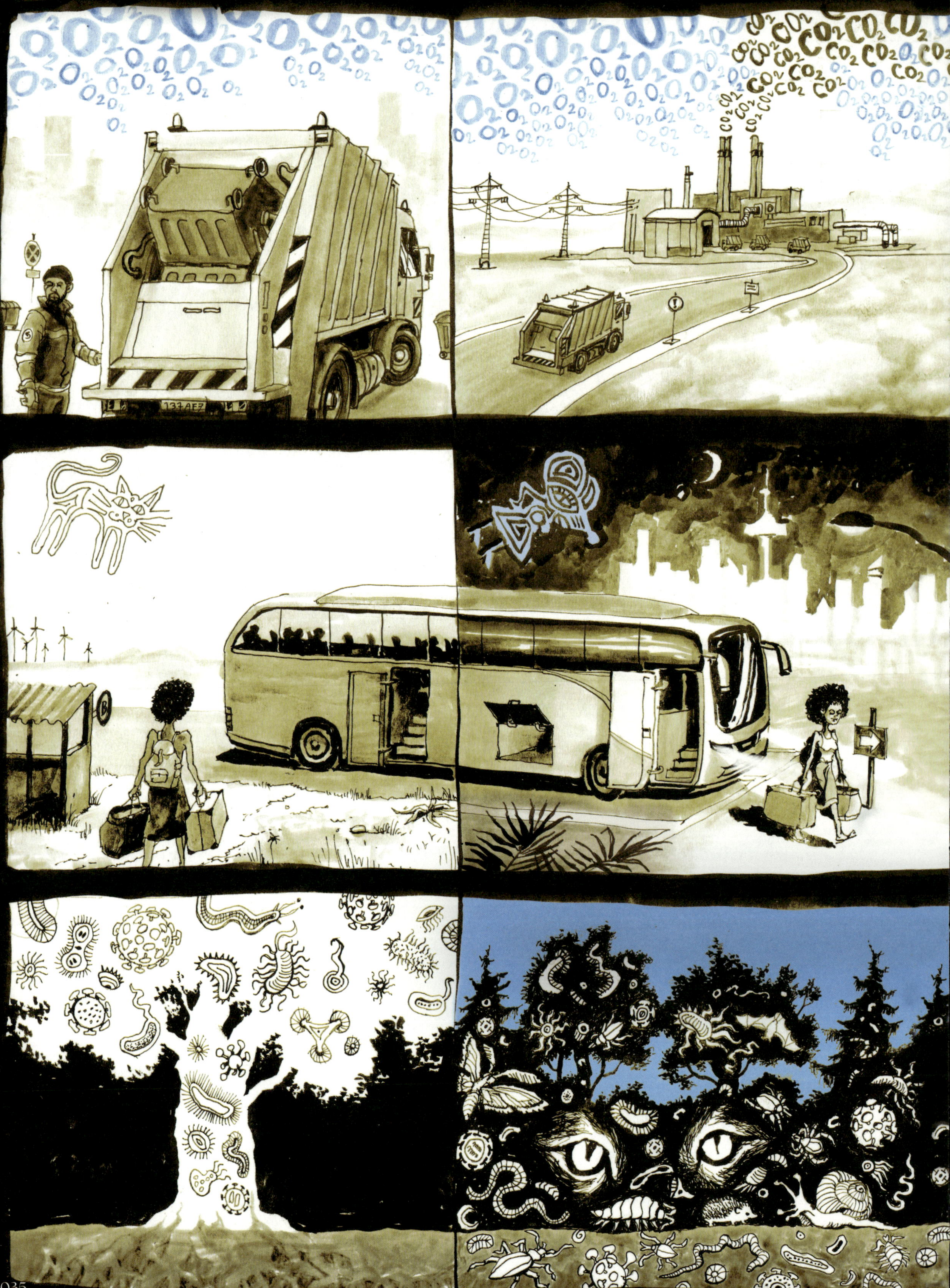

2035

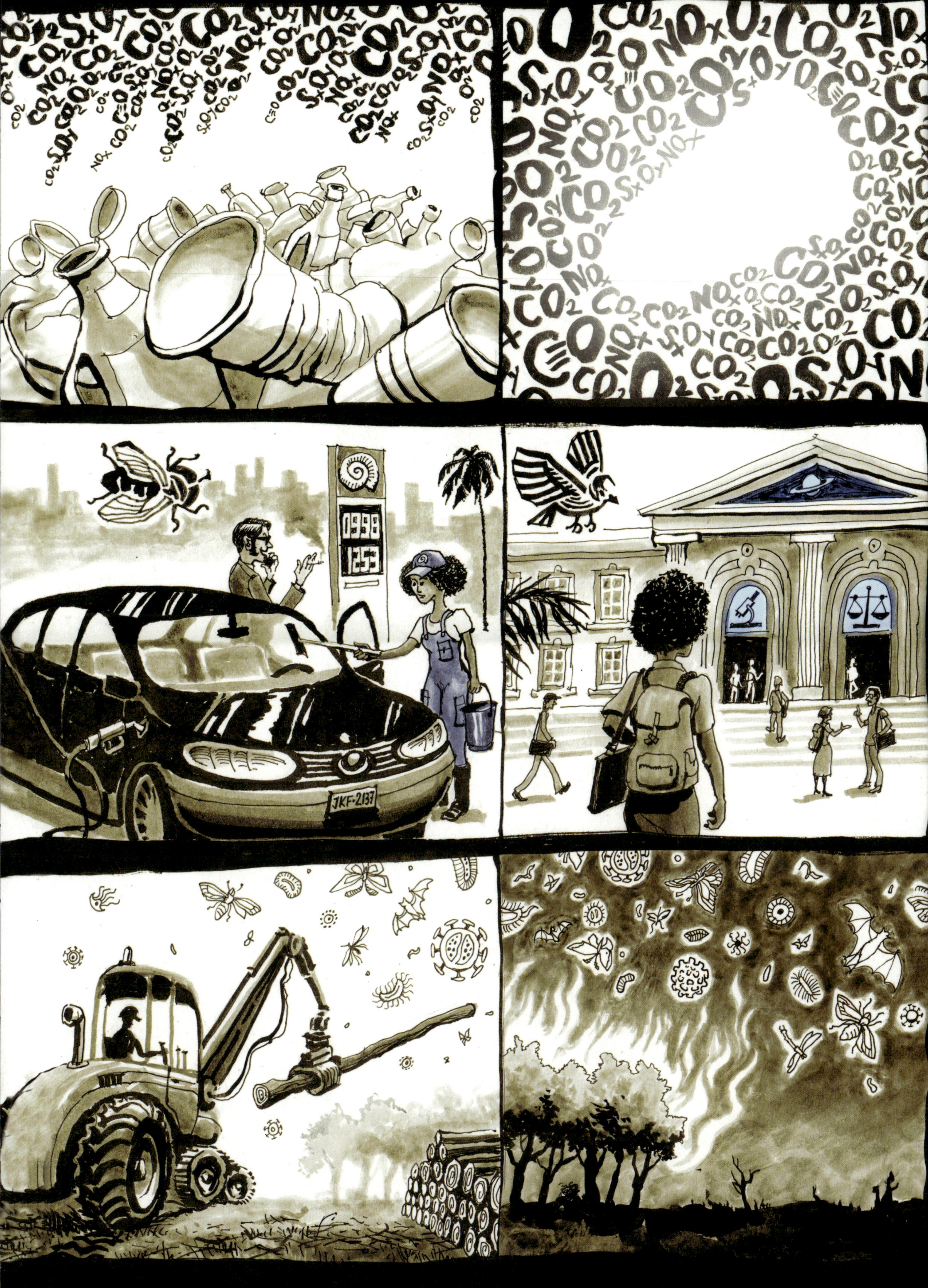
0998
1253
JKF-2137

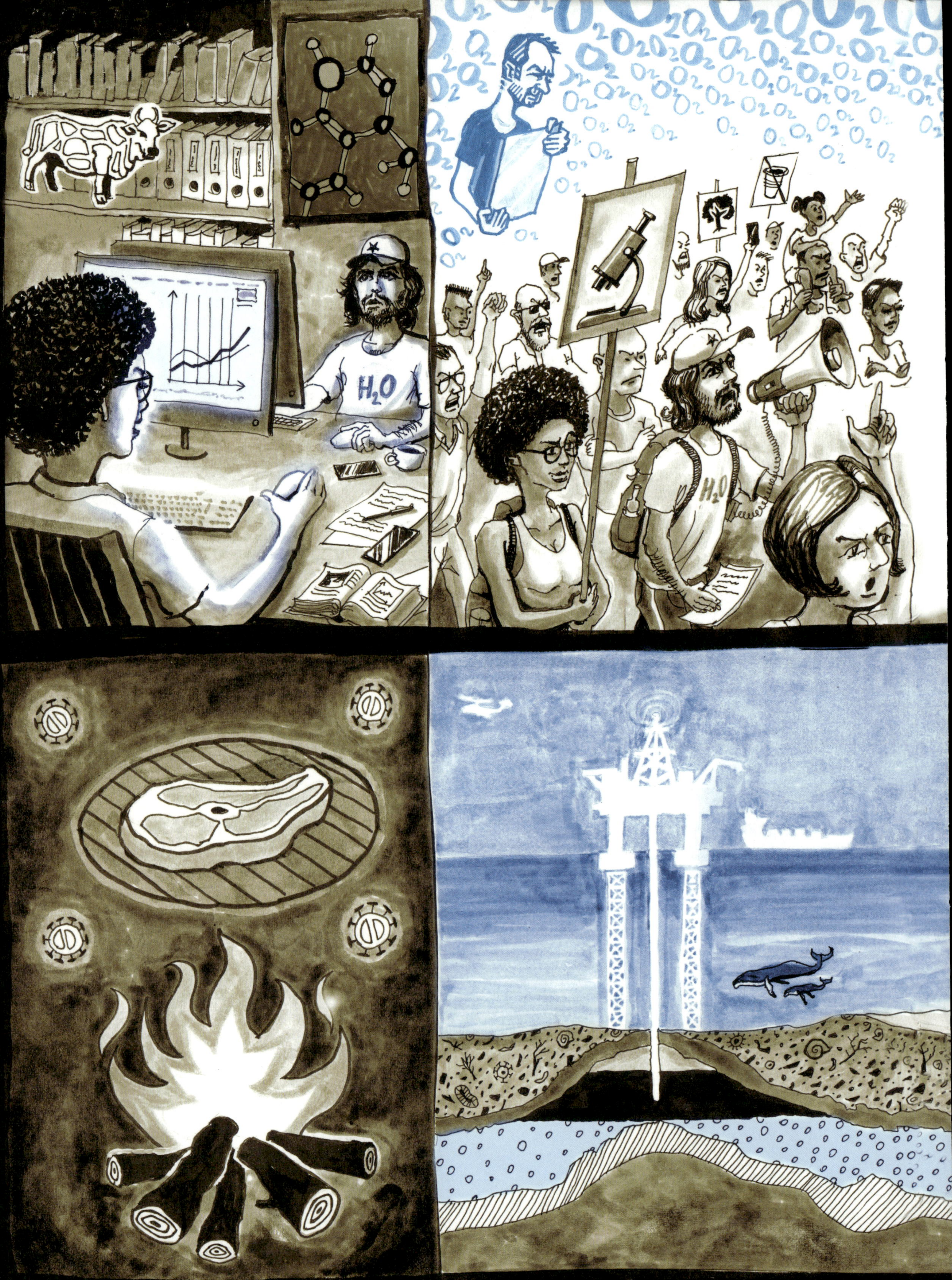
H2O
H2O

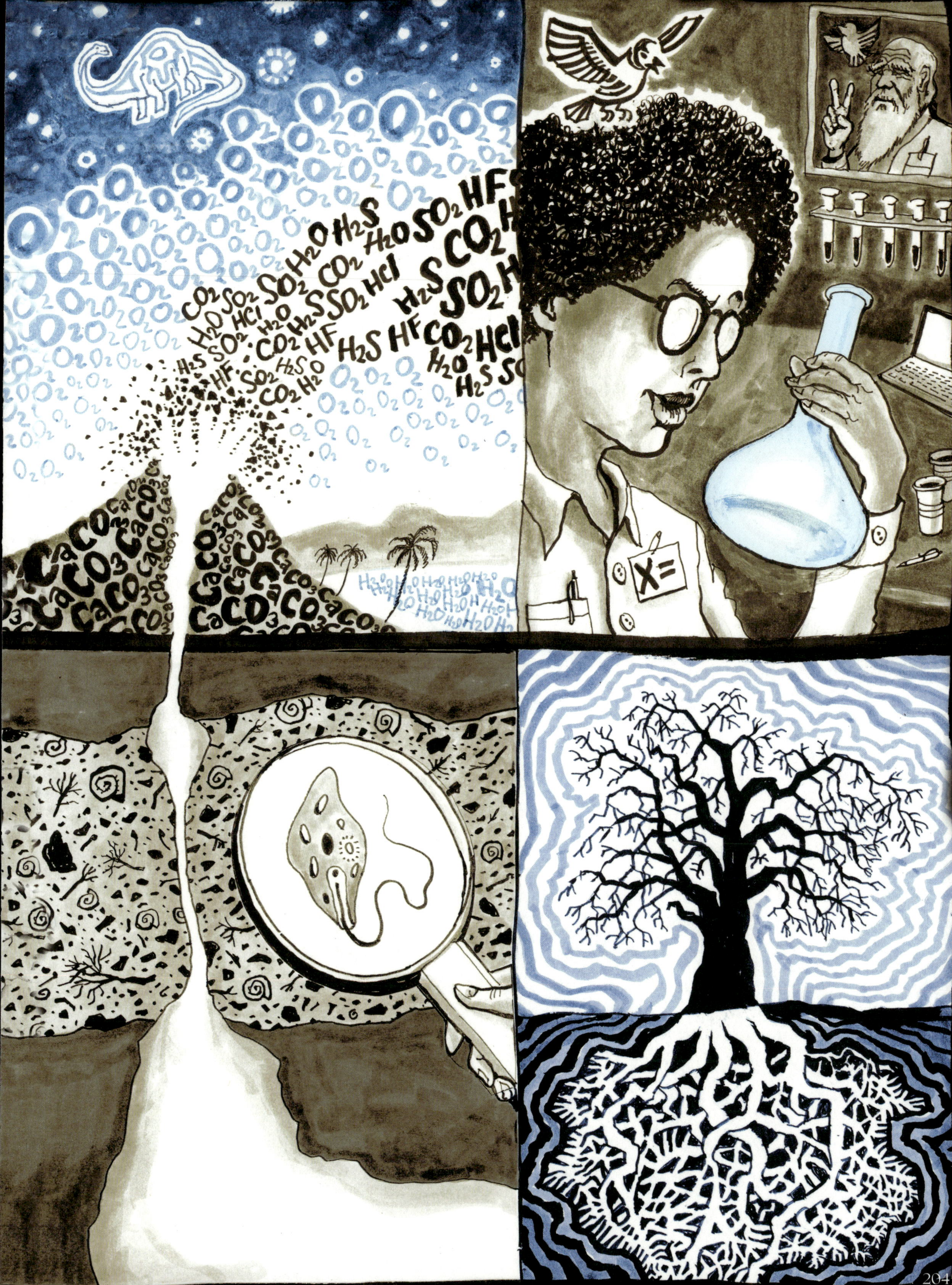
H_2O H_2S H_2O SO_2 HF
CO_2 SO_2 SO_2 H_2O CO_2 H_2S SO_2 HCl H_2S SO_2
CO_2 HF H_2S HF CO_2 HCl
X=

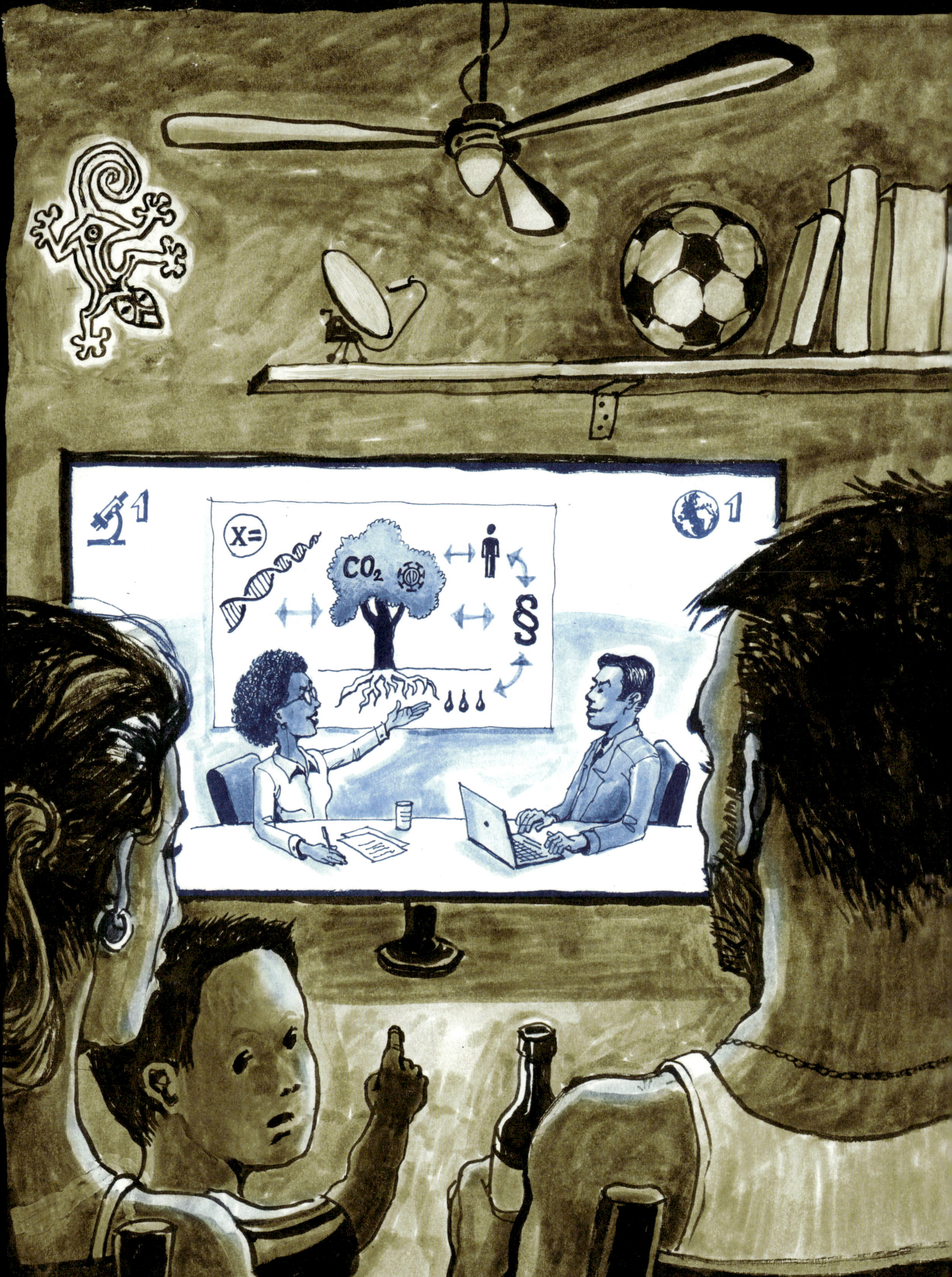

2055

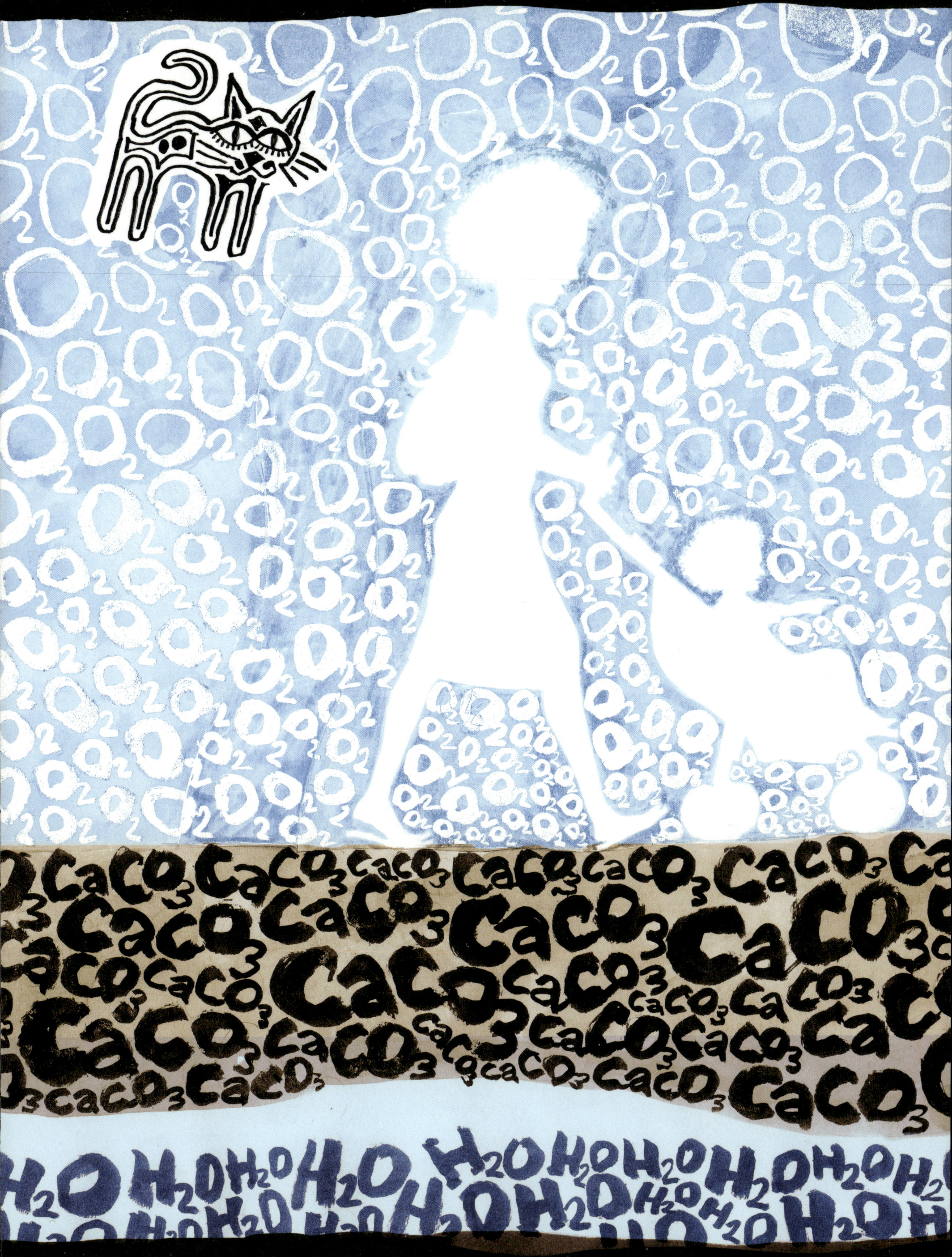

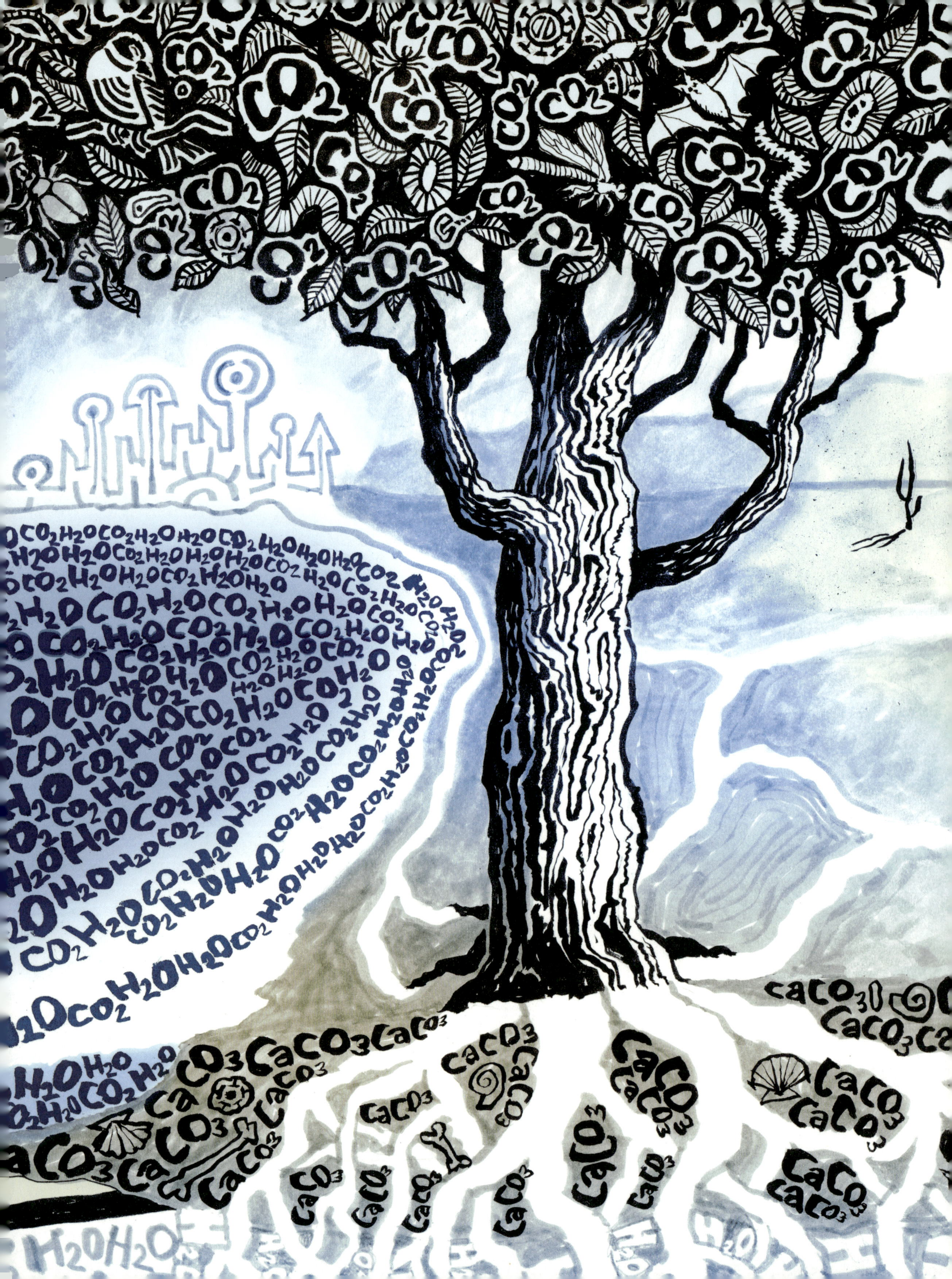

CO_2
H_2O
$CaCO_3$

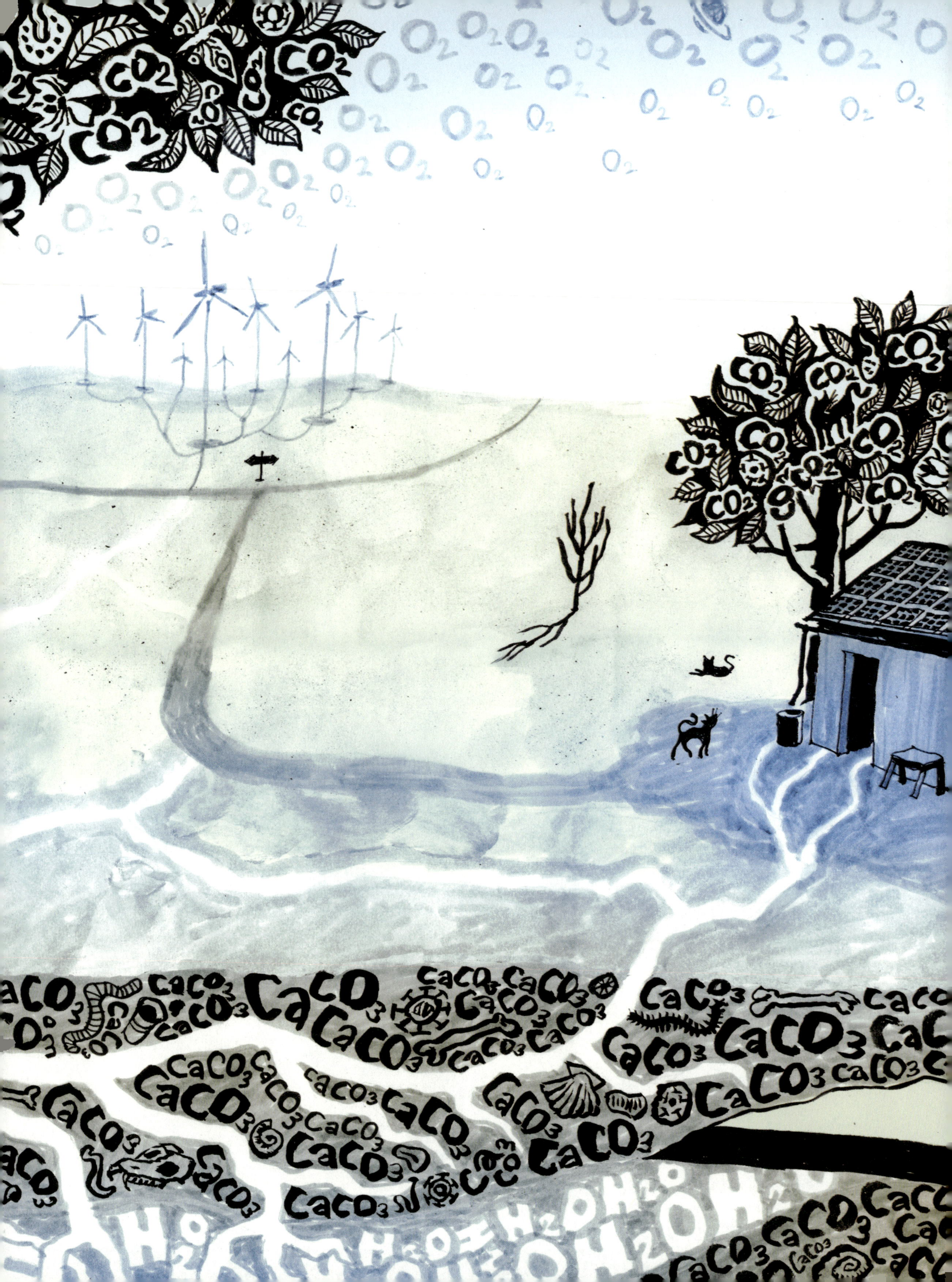

CO_2
O_2
$CaCO_3$
H_2O

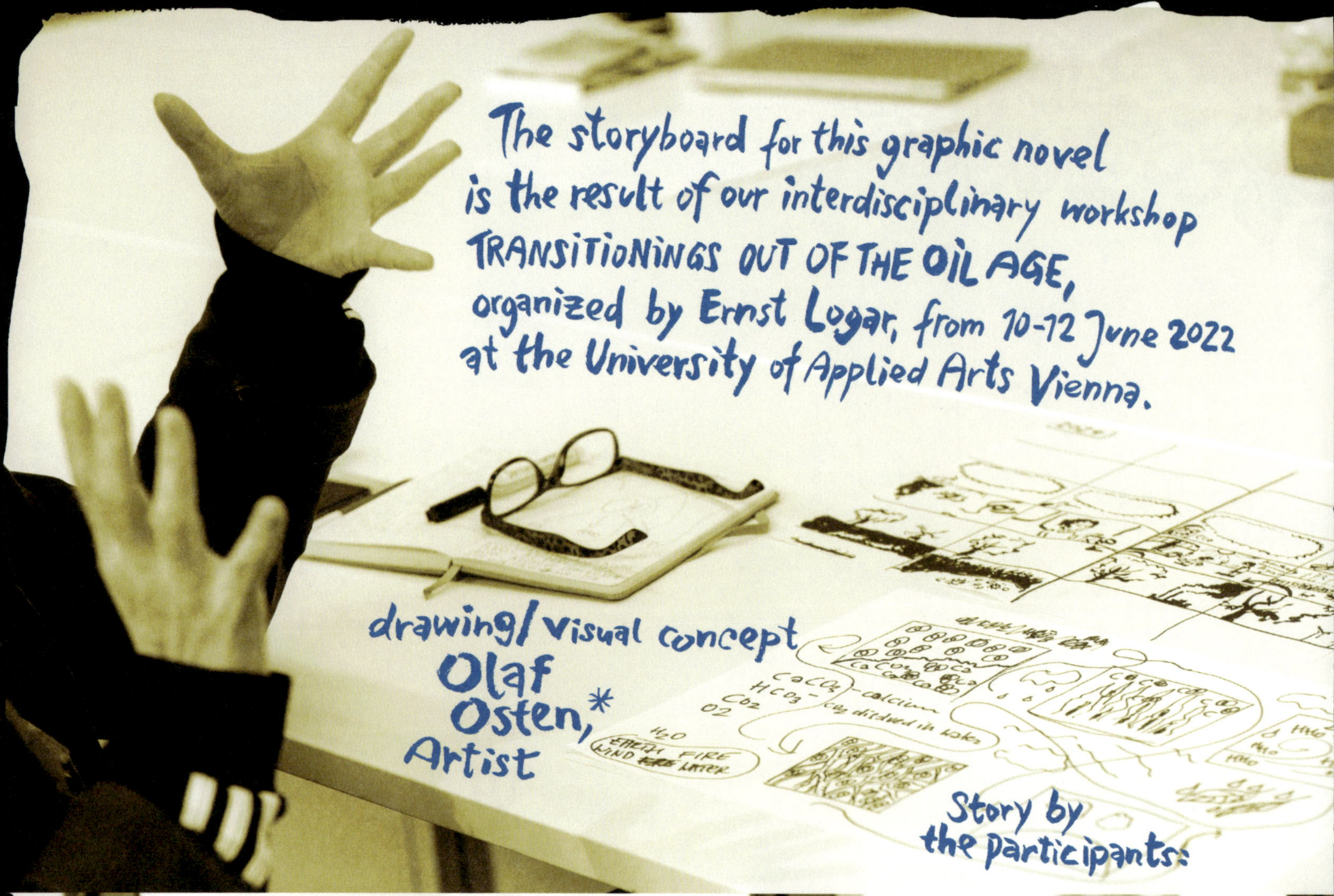

The storyboard for this graphic novel is the result of our interdisciplinary workshop TRANSITIONINGS OUT OF THE OIL AGE, organized by Ernst Logar, from 10-12 June 2022 at the University of Applied Arts Vienna.

drawing/visual concept
Olaf Osten,*
Artist

Story by the participants:

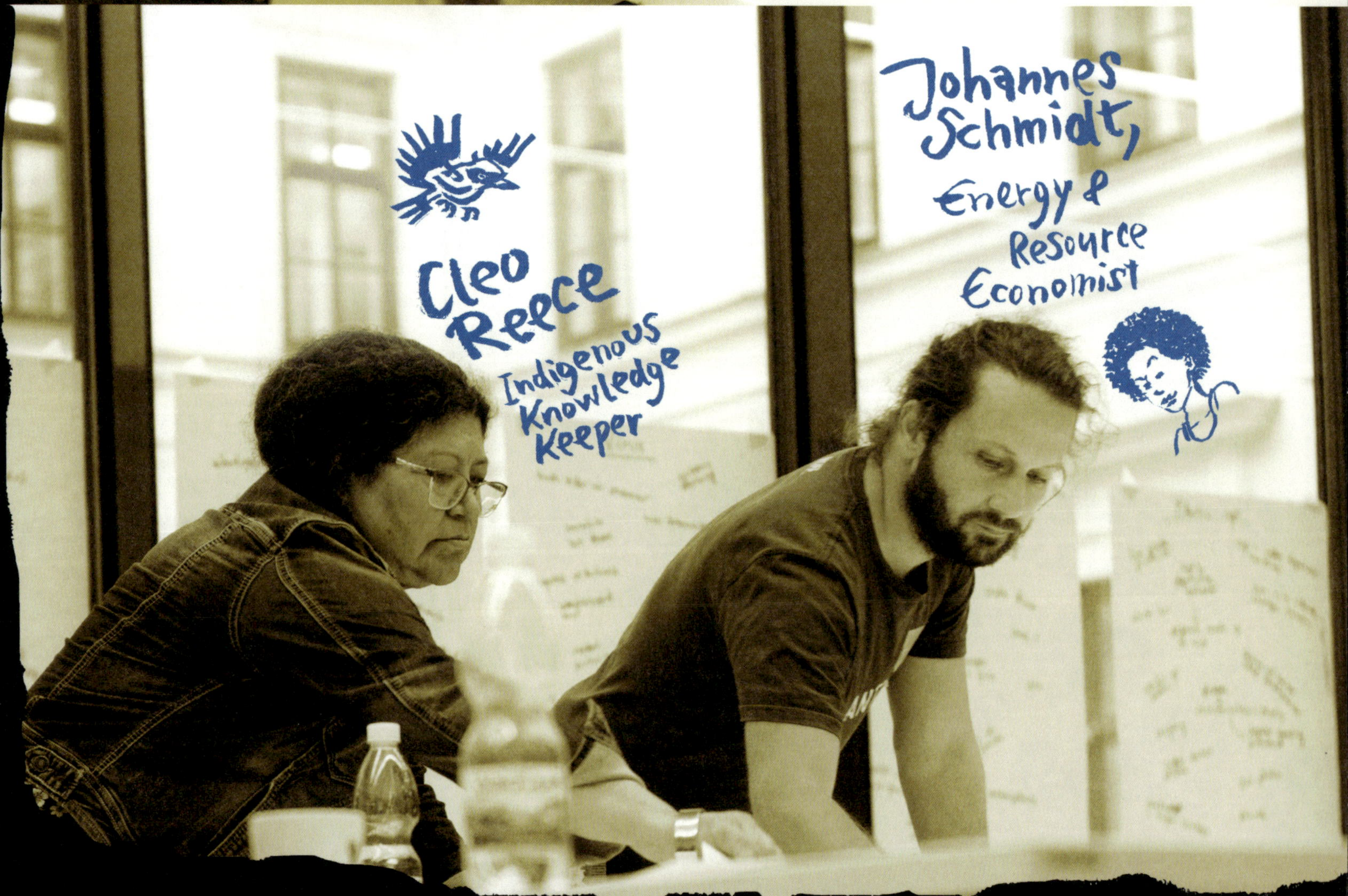

Cleo Reece
Indigenous Knowledge Keeper

Johannes Schmidt,
Energy & Resource Economist

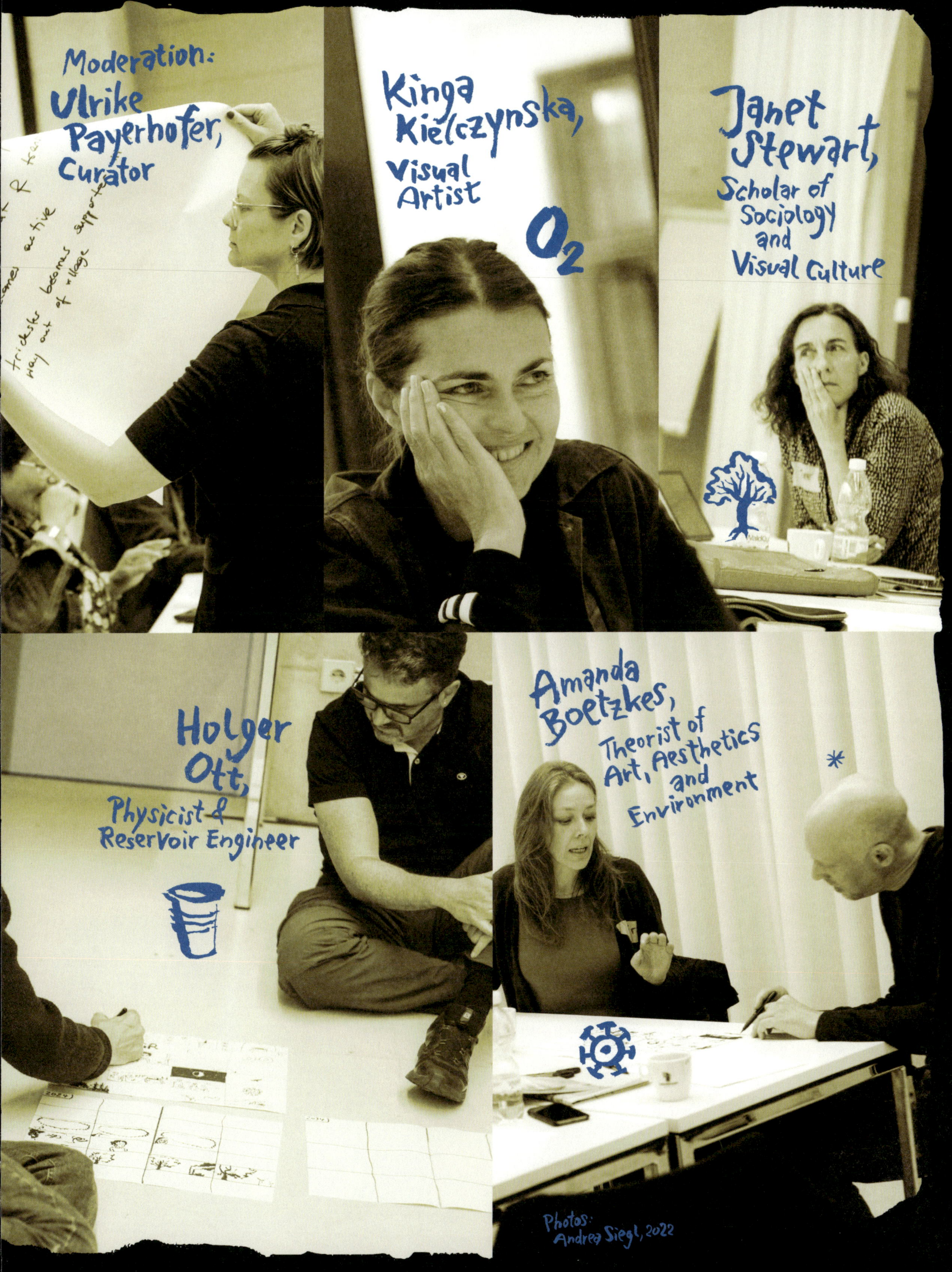
Moderation:
Ulrike Payerhofer,
Curator
Kinga Kielczynska,
Visual Artist
O2
Janet Stewart,
Scholar of Sociology and Visual Culture
Holger Ott,
Physicist & Reservoir Engineer
Amanda Boetzkes,
Theorist of Art, Aesthetics and Environment
Photos: Andrea Siegl, 2022

—04

A Crude Encounter

Learning with Art to Say Farewell to the Petro-Energy Regime

Raphaelle Occhietti

exhibition
Angewandte Interdisciplinary Lab
artworks
crude oil
blood
experiments
petromodernity
sensorial encounter
aesthetic experience
fossil-fueled capitalism
energy regime
oil relationships

— *"We thought it was oil!"*
— *"but it was blood!"*
Nnimmo Bassey[1]

"The alarms are loud and clear: we must reclaim the means of our reproduction—our homes, the land we live on, the energies supporting our mutual dependency, and the capacity to decide the kinds of human beings we want to be."
Rosemary Hennessy[2]

"Everybody knows, everybody knows
That's how it goes
Everybody knows"
Leonard Cohen[3]

Crude Oil as ~~Society's~~ the Artist's Blood

The sudden roaring sound of a starting engine breaks the business-as-usual convenient silence surrounding crude oil, both metaphorically and physically, and draws visitors into Ernst Logar's *Reflecting Oil* exhibition.[4] The familiar noise of the air-fuel mixture of an engine's ignition accompanies most people's everyday routine exponentially since the start of the motorized transport through combustion motors. But this recording is more than a soundscape designed for visitors to conjure up images of the overwhelming transport reality that is still mostly sustained today through gasoline, one of the many products obtained by the refining of crude oil and undoubtedly one of the main symbols of "petromodernity."[5] Logar's artwork goes a step further. As visitors seek and find the source of the recording, they are suddenly hit visually by what is occurring in a glass cube strategically positioned on a steel pedestal: in the artwork titled *Good Vibes*, as the soundtrack of a starting and running Harley Davidson motorcycle is transferred from the MP3 device to a speaker lying face up at the bottom of the cube, the speaker's diaphragm vibrates energetically, causing brownish liquid to splash dirtily onto the glass walls of the

Ernst Logar*
Good Vibes, 2024
Loudspeaker, crude oil, amplifier, mp3 player, steel tub on steel pedestal, glass cover

*All artworks in this article are by Ernst Logar, exceptions are cited

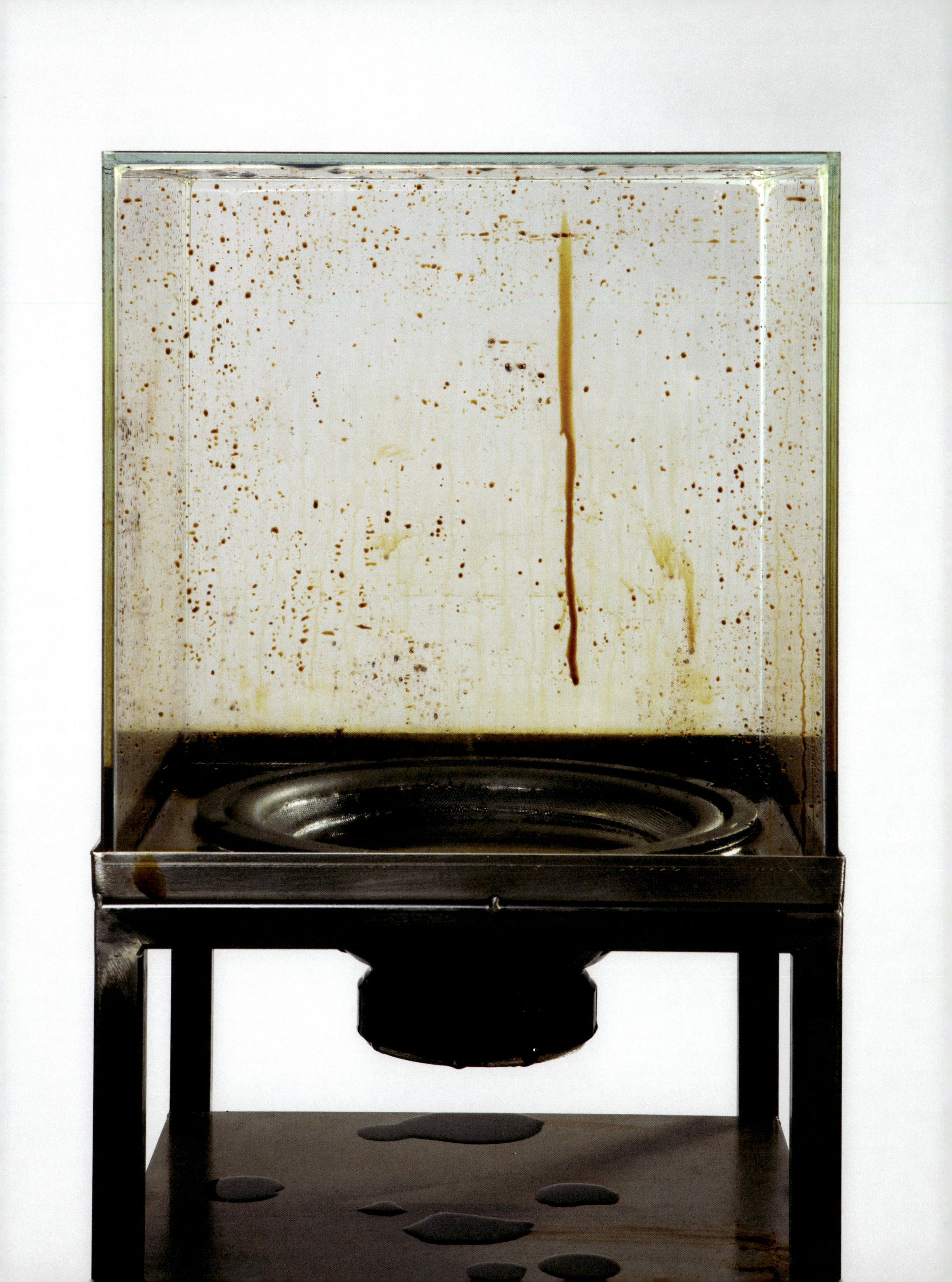

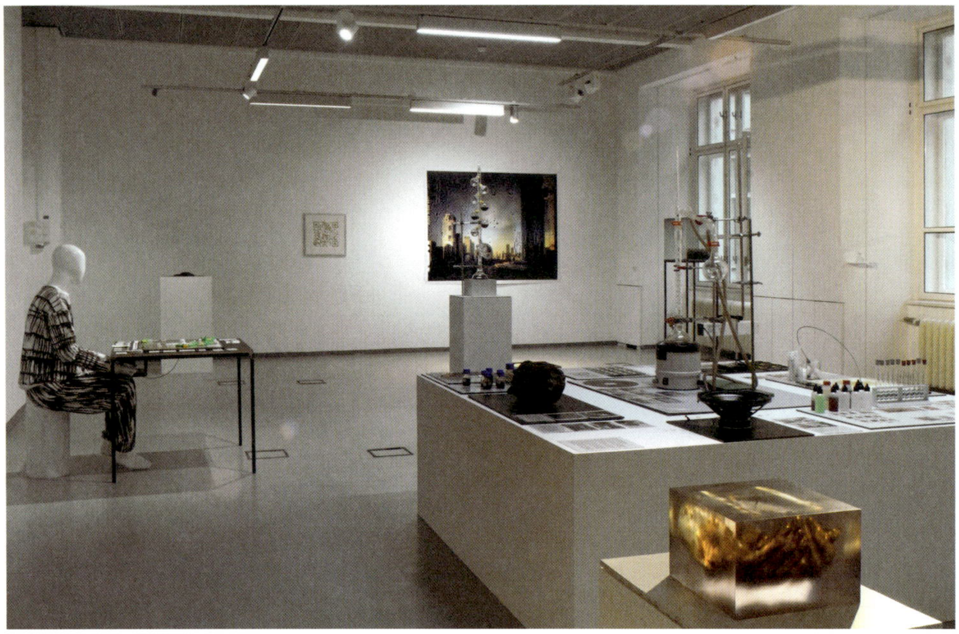

Reflecting Oil—Petroculture in Transformation
exhibition view, Angewandte Interdisciplinary Lab (AIL), 2024

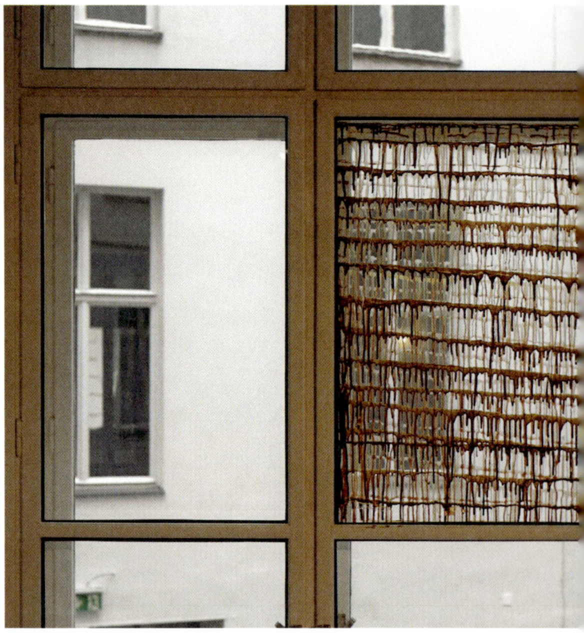

Oil and Blood, 2024
Glass sheet, crude oil, blood

cube. The combination of the paradigmatic sound of a motor ignition with the splattering of crude oil that comes to resemble splashes of blood is telling. The sculpture ingeniously uses a familiar sound to reverse and complicate its seemingly innocent or, at least, trivial meaning. Here, the banal mechanical technology that powers our everyday travels has the visual effect of a massacre. With *Good Vibes*, Logar points to the impossibility of ignoring how industrial exploitation of crude oil is inevitably riddled with lethal consequences.

Crude oil as the "blood" of society is one of the most recurrent metaphors used to convey the critical importance of this substance for almost every aspect of modern life as we know it, both at a physical and a symbolic level.[6] In the *Reflecting Oil* exhibition, Ernst Logar takes this metaphor quite literally. Crude oil resembles or can even be briefly mistaken for blood, like in *Good Vibes*. But in other artworks the artist stages an actual encounter between blood and crude oil, thus moving towards the concretization of the metaphor. In *Oil and Blood*, a glass sheet displaying horizontal stripes of an almost regular pattern of slightly overlapping dark red and light orange-brown lines is installed in lieu of one of the exhibition space's windows. The same gruesome aesthetic as *Good Vibes* is here transferred into a coagulated form, with crude oil and blood trickling down at a regular pace. It is a clever artwork that embeds the question of society's overreliance on oil into the very fabric of the architectural setting, forcing visitors to look at "life" outside the window through crude oil and blood. And as the exhibition makes clear, it becomes pressing that one should use this combined oil and blood filter to look at pretty much every aspect of life, as unpleasant as the exercise may be. As crude oil and blood drip with a similar viscosity, what is there to be learned by their overlapping materialities?

One shouldn't mistake these sensorially striking artworks for a simple gory equation between oil and death/violence/bad. Both sculptures must be considered as part of an exploration of crude oil as a substance in itself, with for once no direct application other than getting to know it for its own sake and in relation to sensorial human experiences. In fact, one of the major feelings that emerges through *Reflecting Oil* is that data on pollution, extraction sites, and corruption surrounding crude oil can empower some of us but will fail to mobilize at a large scale, whereas a sensorial encounter with oil could at least spark a profound inquiry,[7] almost a schism: where does one stand in regard to this peculiar substance?

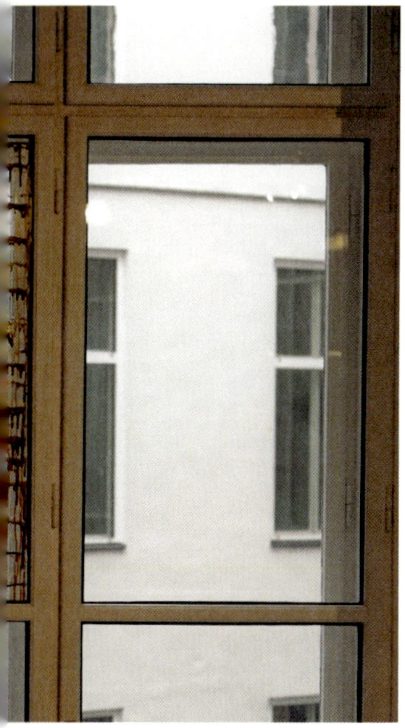

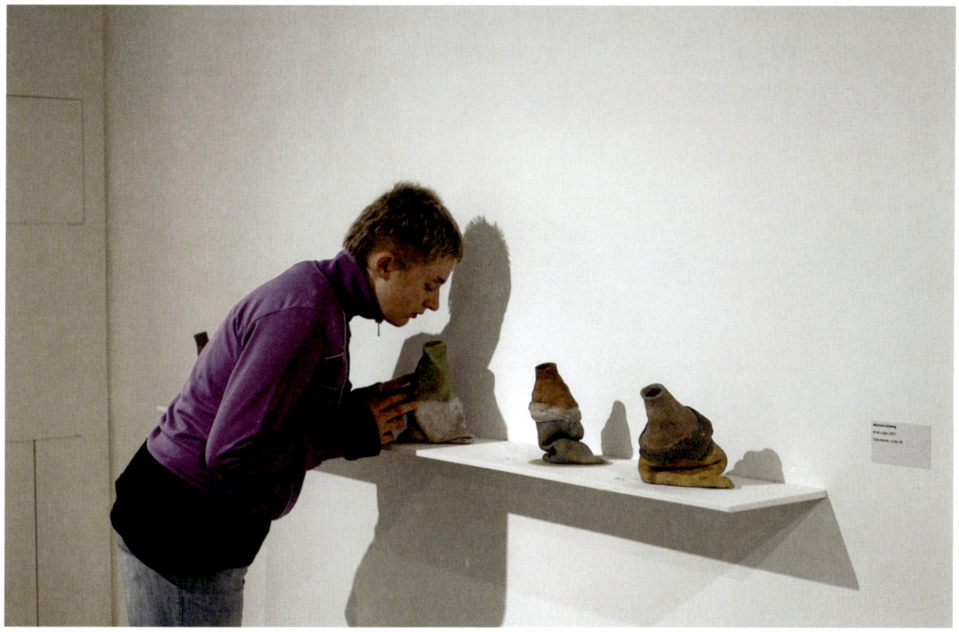

Abstract inhaling, 2024
Clay objects, different crude oils

Of course, we are not all equally affected by the risks posed by direct contact with crude oil. As Nigerian scholar Philip Aghoghovwia deplores, research about oil often "[...] elides a fundamental aspect of the oil encounter: the lived experience of local inhabitants at the sites of extraction," as "[m]uch of the existing scholarship operates at a level of social scientific abstraction."[8] Communities that live close to extraction sites and workers in charge of the most heavy duties are routinely exposed to oil in unfair conditions that threaten their health and life, not to mention the devastation of the surrounding ecosystems and habitats. But considering that many people don't live in the vicinity of extractive facilities, can a tangible encounter still take place? *Reflecting Oil* as an interdisciplinary exhibition precisely manages to bridge the irreducible unknowingness of the reality of crude oil extraction common to many of the visitors and citizens, with a controlled yet entirely creative encounter with oil anchored in the emulation of its physical presence.

In one of the many experiments that Logar and his colleagues conducted with the the University of Leoben team is the Fingerprints Experiments, where participants touched different crude oil samples and imprinted on paper their own fingers drenched with the otherwise forbidden toxic substance. Through various other scientific or artistic sensorial encounters with crude oil—with its colors, its textures, and its smells—the artist brings forth a potent message: to resist a total ignorance or indifference towards crude oil as well as to rebut an outright apology of industrial societies' uses of oil, one avenue is to become acquainted with the materiality of the substance. In fact, crude oil is quite fascinating, not at all monotonous in appearance nor homogeneous in composition.[9] In the effective *Abstract Inhaling* display, different crude oil samples are showcased in terracotta vessels that one can actually smell. Samples come from diverse places such as Austria, Scotland, Norway, Kazakhstan, or Egypt, and each of them has indeed a very distinctive aroma, pungent or almost pleasant, rich or invasive. At first sight the terracotta devices through which visitors encounter the samples' scents look like melting bottles, but they are, as a matter of fact, a translation in clay of the shapes of plastic bags used for abusing inhalants (i.e. "huffing paint"). Hence, the artist tricks the visitors through their olfactory curiosity into a posture of addiction. The artist thus forces the visitors to acknowledge their dependence on oil and petroleum-based products by forcing an encounter into the very intimacy of their pulmonary cells, making the compounds of crude oils travel through the visitor's bloodstream.

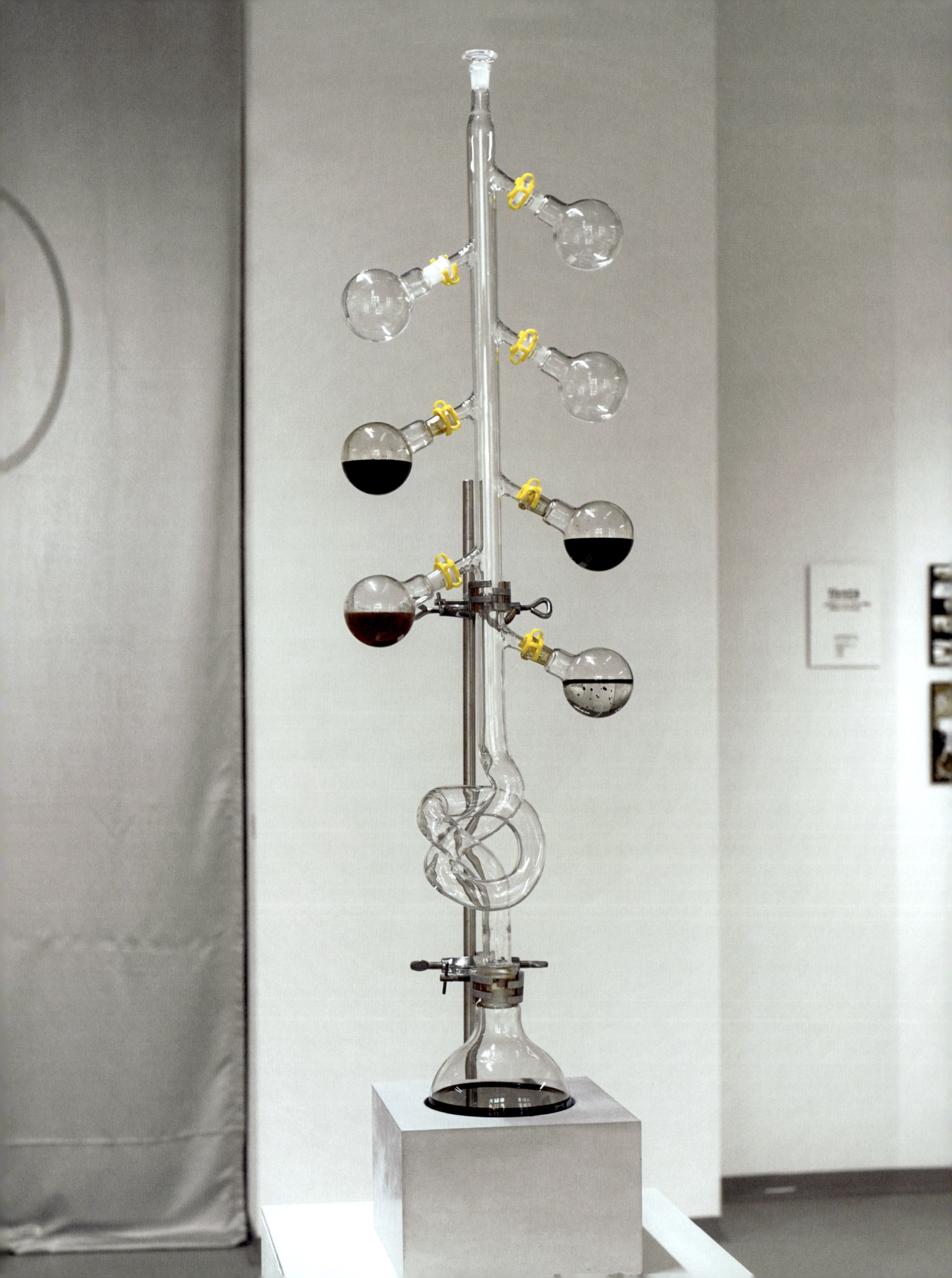

Ernst Logar's artworks create close proximity with oil, demanding a sensuous and consciously intimate encounter with oil's material qualities, highlighted by the rarity of such encounters even with other materials, let alone this potentially toxic substance. But this embrace seems to arrive precisely at a moment when we are saying our goodbyes to the petroleum industry. Most like what Amanda Boetzkes and Andrew Pendakis[10] wrote about oil's hyper visibility coming right at the time of its foreseen shortage, this renewed sensorial encounter with oil seems, too, to come about exactly at the moment of its predicted demise. However, as the artist makes apparent, even if there is a transition towards sustainability we will still have to deal with the far-reaching consequences of fossil-fueled capitalism in the future. In *Refined* for example, round flasks attached to a glass column typically used in labs for distillation are filled with different liquids whose somber colors or turbid aspect do not bode well. Distillation is an important step in crude oil refining, hence the title of the artwork. Here, however, the artist deviates the purpose of the industrial process and instead explores the mixing of different fluids with oil. We find actual blood again, but also oil-contaminated water and even tailing pond liquid, the latter being a particularly meaningful addition to the artwork considering that "[t]ar sands mining operations have generated over 250 billion gallons of toxic tailings—a poisonous brew of water, sand, silt, heavy metals and other petrochemical waste products—which they store in toxic lakes that cover an area greater than Manhattan and Boston combined."[11] Urged to view these mixtures of liquids up close, visitors get a sense of a profound and totalizing heaviness. Lying at the bottom of these tiny and crystalline flasks like poisonous potions, and somehow disturbingly protected by the purity of the laboratory equipment compartmentalization, are these terrifying liquid mixtures that hint at the pervasive consequences of the oil industry.

Oil as the *blood of society*; oil as *the blood of the Earth*.[12] And is oil our blood too? Discreetly positioned on a lateral wall, right beneath the striking oil and blood window and thus easily missed, is an elegant glass vial with its cap. Titled *Human Blood—Crude Oil Distillate*, it is the only artwork in the exhibition actually featuring the artist's own blood. The composition is unassuming yet thoroughly effective in its poetic gesture. At the bottom of the vial lies a transparent liquid, while at the surface floats a slightly more distinguishable yellow-white colored liquid. Even though the artist mixed approximately 150 ml of his own blood with 300 ml of crude oil, and then made one single distillation, the result is two visibly distinct distillates that are immiscible. For visitors, it is not that easy to know which of the two liquids is the crude oil distillate or the blood distillate. Yet their transparent quality creates a seeming fusion. One might be surprised to learn that the yellower liquid is the oil distillate, as one can feel its life potential almost throbbing in comparison to the immaculate, inert transparency of the blood distillate. Particularly interesting is the artist's choice to thwart the critique of oil based on crude oil's sole aspect and color by underscoring the many guises in which oil can present itself. That the artist's blood comes in closer contact with petroleum derivatives' physical properties, and thus with crude oil's identity, is both slightly upsetting and strangely moving. It acts like an offering, materializing the now irreducible bond between petroleum substances and human blood. With this simple vial and its peculiar content, the artist signals his support to those who are forced to spill their blood so that others may continue to live in oil's bounty. As such, the artist asks anyone profiting from the oil economy to risk their own blood as well, for the sake of, well, everything that truly matters.

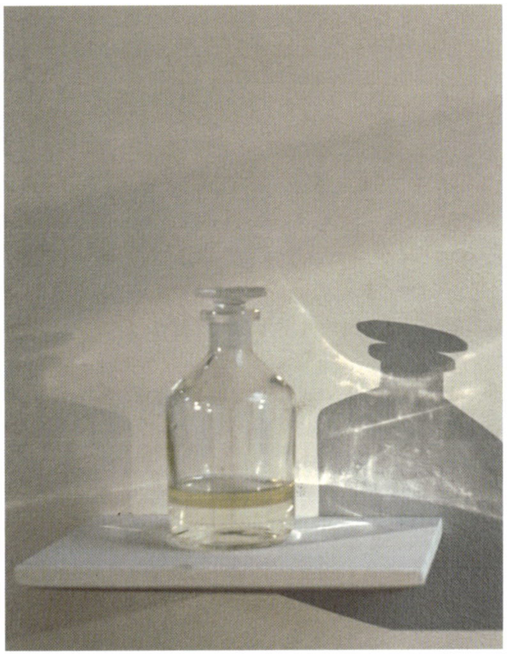

Human blood—crude oil destillate, 2024
Laboratory bottle, crude oil–blood distillate

Refined, 2024
Glass column, round-bottomed flasks, concrete, steel, crude oil, various types of fluids (blood, honey, oil contaminated water, tar sands tailings pond water, flood water sample)

Moving Deeper into "Crude Capitalism"[13] Through Recursive Spectatorship

The exciting aspect of Ernst Logar's exhibition is that the more visitors interact with the artworks, with the accounts of the experiments, and with the 2022 *Reflecting Oil Colloquium* outputs, the more the interrelation between the body of works becomes striking, and the more the nesting of crude oil in every corner of our minds and bodies becomes apparent. In a way, the exhibition invites spectators to adopt a form of scientific standpoint that emulates the protocols of the scientific experiments that have formed the core of the artistic research project *Reflecting Oil* as a whole. One must lay foundations for the procedures, test different combinations of variables, observe the results, and...start over. So, let's start again. Before the visitor is aware that the exhibition has even begun, an LED panel subliminally displays what at first sight appears to be random words. Placed in the liminal zone between the former cashier hall of the Austrian Postal Savings Bank (the Postsparkasse designed by Viennese Secession architect Otto Wagner) and the actual entrance of the exhibition space in the Angewandte Interdisciplinary Lab, the LED panel displaying red-lettered words scrolling unhurriedly from right to left acts like the pediment of a temple. The words are a list of 1200 objects used in everyday life that are made of petroleum-derived materials. There is everything, from dialysis machines to hair curlers, and binder clips to face masks. The LED display marks the place where visitors will enter a form of initiation to crude oil, and where they must commit to the content of the exhibition. The quantity of the objects listed also means that it is mostly improbable for any visitor to be able to witness each and every word appear on the LED display, thus alerting the spectator to the immensity of what crude oil is and means, and to the fact that one can never completely fathom its extent, though it is still worth a try.

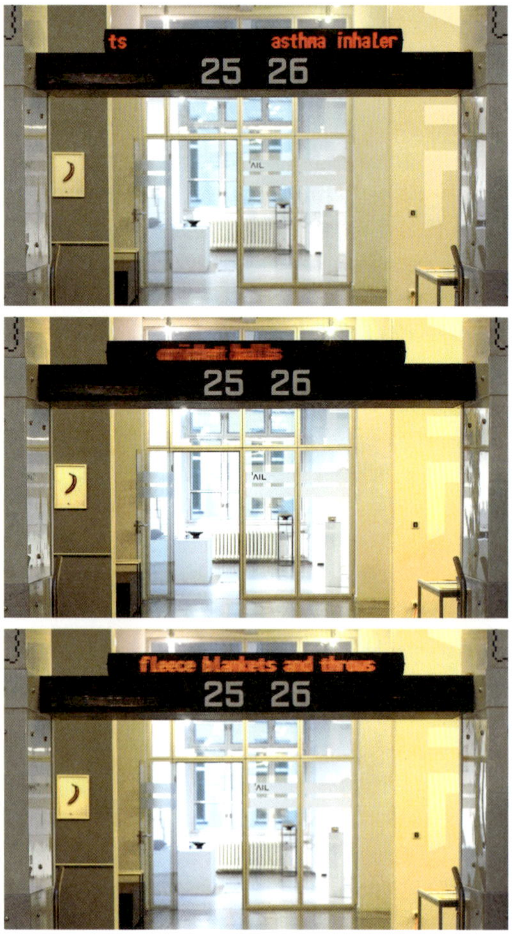

Made Of, 2024
Dataset of consumer goods based on oil, scrolling text display

Another easily overlooked artwork placed at the onset of the exhibition is an inkjet print of a banana covered with oil. The effect is stunning. The profanation of the substance and essence of the banana by the brownish-reddish-darkish glaze is oddly mesmerizing as the sleek surface becomes enticing in a twisted alluring way. The unnatural overlapping of materialities seems to convey the idea that petroleum is everywhere, and we might as well just pour it on our food. The banana is one of the materialities confronted and coalesced with crude oil during the exhibition, like wood in the tree slice covered in bitumen, or honey that we find contaminated with crude oil in a hula hoop hung on the wall.[14] But first the artist gives another word of caution. In the photograph *The Beauty of Oil*, green tree branches are reflected in a puddle. The water looks as though contaminated by gasoline, as shown by the characteristic iridescent halo, but in fact it is the artist himself who poured crude oil in order to replicate the phenomenon of daily small-scale pollution. As visitors are just about to enter the main space of the exhibition, it looks like this image is there to warn of the potentially hypnotic presence of oil. Oil can be sexy; oil can be desirable; we love oil because we cover ourselves with it. *The Beauty of Oil* is also a perfect compendium of what the *Reflecting Oil* exhibition is about: seeing everything reflected through the prism of oil because our world is built on the largely unacknowledged filter of petroleum.

When visitors enter the main exhibition space, they immediately face a stand where the experiment's paraphernalia and visual outputs have been gathered, which gives a fascinating account of the many material explorations the Vienna team has developed in collaboration with the University of Leoben team. Furthermore, this stand of experiments presents a legend of sorts enabling visitors to decipher the rest of the exhibition and appreciate the amount of work involved in materializing the art objects directly involving substances as crude oil, bitumen, or naphtha. Visitors can thus move like butterflies between the experiments table and the artworks, and with each visit complement and nourish their understanding of the body of works. It is especially relevant that this stand should be placed in the middle because in a sense it represents the heart of the very original and brave process that has brought

Untitled, 2024
Inkjet print

Pages 130–131
The Beauty of Oil, 2024
Inkjet print

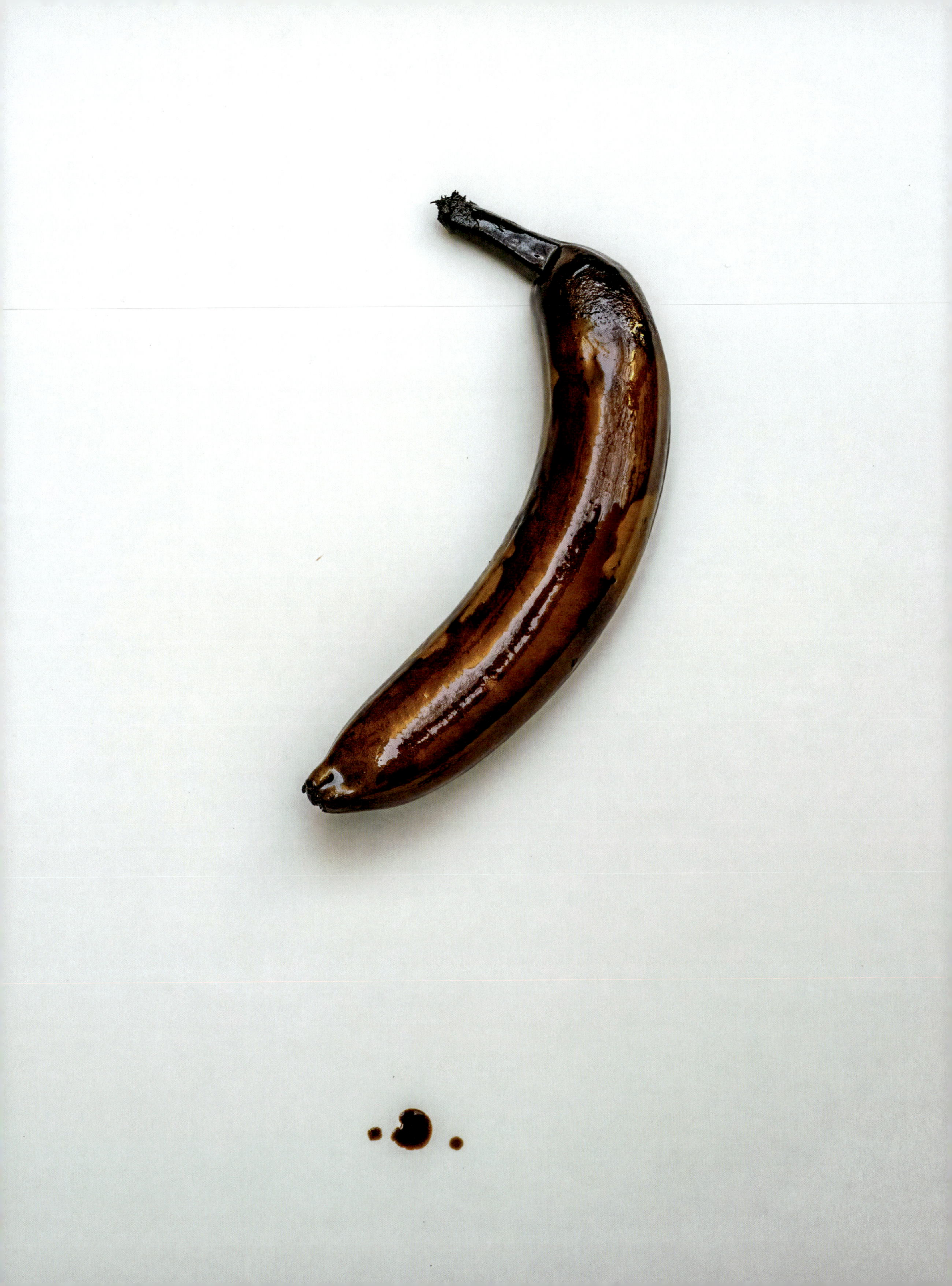

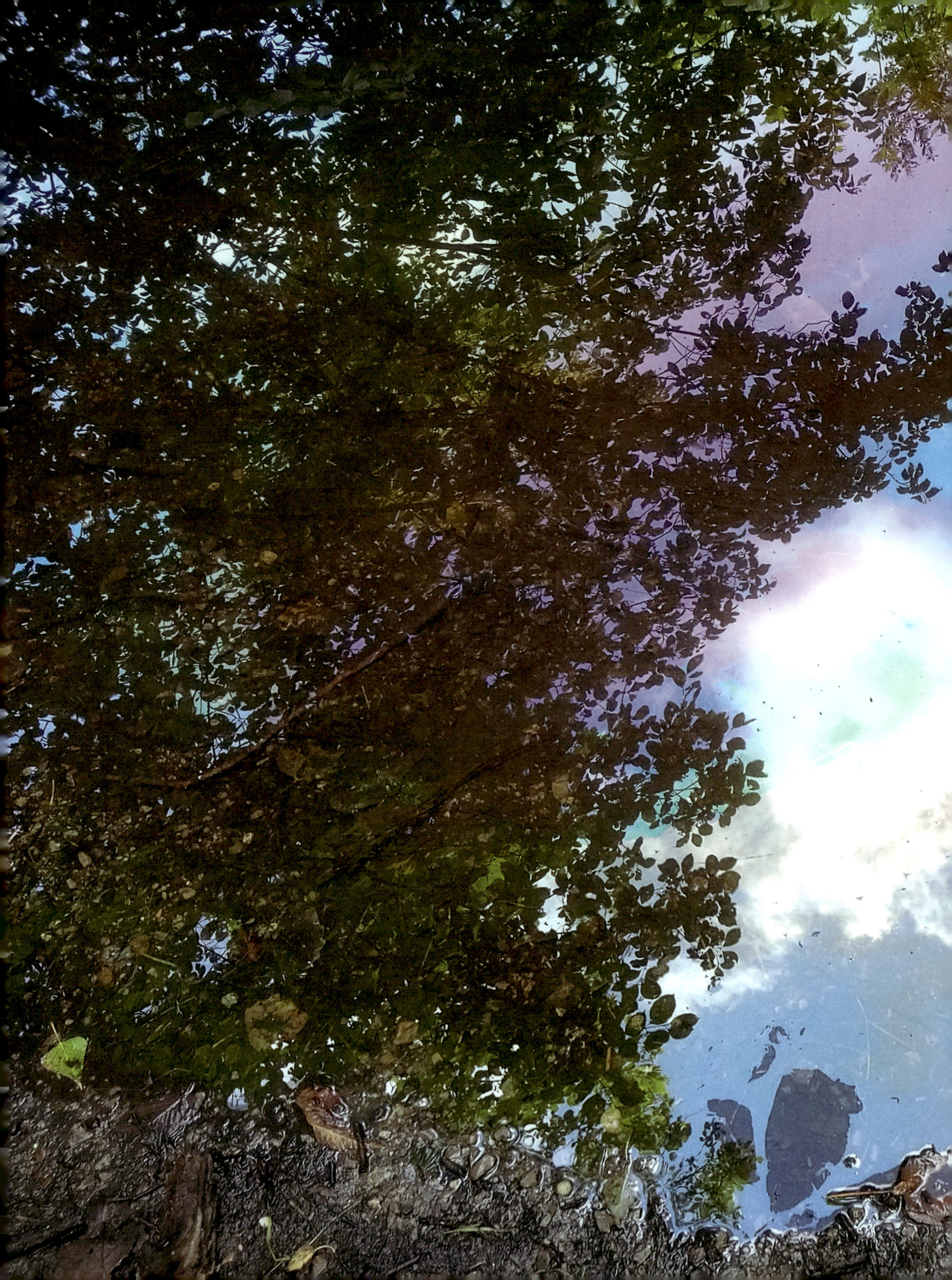

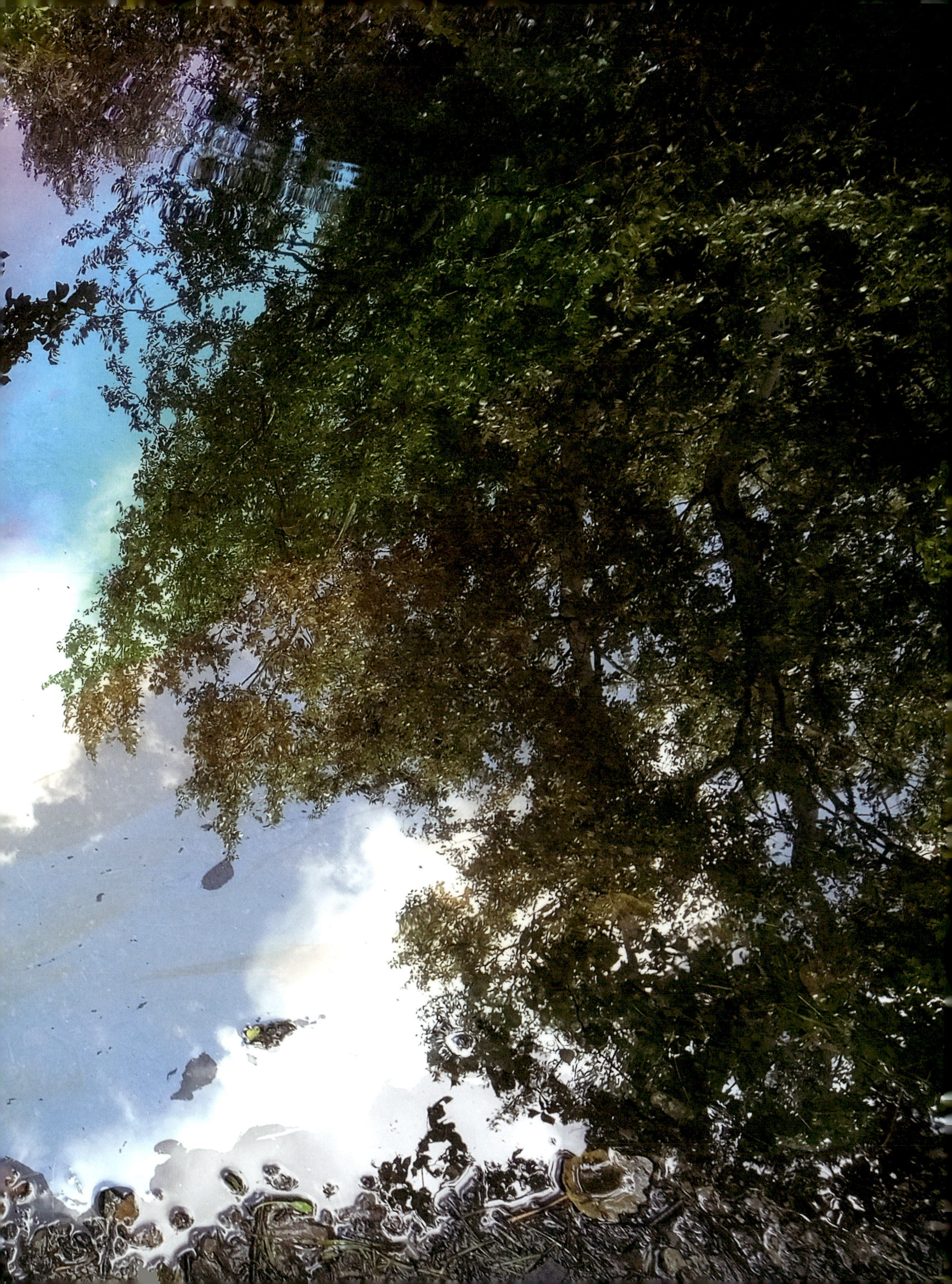

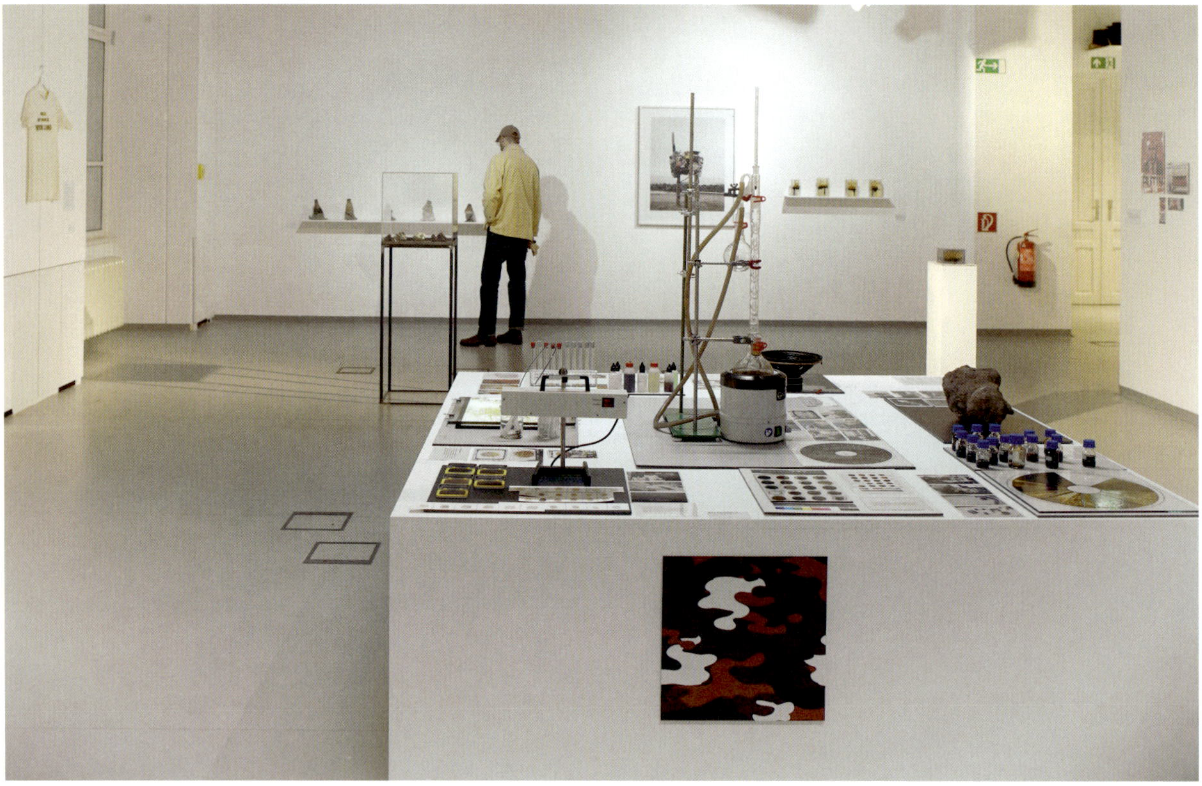

Reflecting Oil—Petroculture in Transformation exhibition view, AIL, 2024

science in close dialogue with art. In fact, one of the most revolutionary aspects of this exhibition might well be the amount of work invested by the petroleum engineers, the artists, the activists, and the humanities scholars to get to know and understand each other. Crude oil and the petro-energy regime have been created and enacted by human groups; as such, they are our creatures. The artist encapsulates this appropriative approach to fossil fuels in the *Oil Formation* composition featured in a smaller adjacent room. Comprising a tray displaying glasses for different types of beverages—cocktails and beer—the artwork departs from reality in the composition of the drinks. In fact, real plankton and algae have been placed inside the beverage glasses, in habitats meant to recall the environments where fossil fuels were generated after millions and millions of years. Visitors are given the opportunity to contemplate the origin of this story, with a zest of self-mockery or even outright sarcasm in the mundane presentation of past ecosystems as cocktails. It is precisely this sort of humor that can help deflate the tension between opposing views and relationships to oil. The artwork is ideally placed in dialogue with two of the visual outputs of the 2022 *Reflecting Oil Colloquium*, one video and one photograph, that both present stunning scientific imagery. Both *Primordial Soup: Dance of Exchange Systems and Variables*—the video created by reservoir engineer Patrick Jasek and artist Herwig Turk, and the text and photographs[15] of *Oil Dialogue* between drilling engineer Karez Abdulhameed and artist Mari Fraga, feature scientific procedures magnifying the reactions of crude oil to other materialities like salt or iodine. These images are useful for the visitor because, with the experiments table in the middle of the main room, they bridge the gap of scientific illiteracy surrounding oil. The documents are also proof that the *Reflecting Oil* project provided a safe space for scientists and especially engineers to find a renewed sense of marvel about oil that deviates from its mere industrial exploitation.

Oil Formation, 2024
Glasses, stainless steel tray, water, plankton, algae, plants, clay

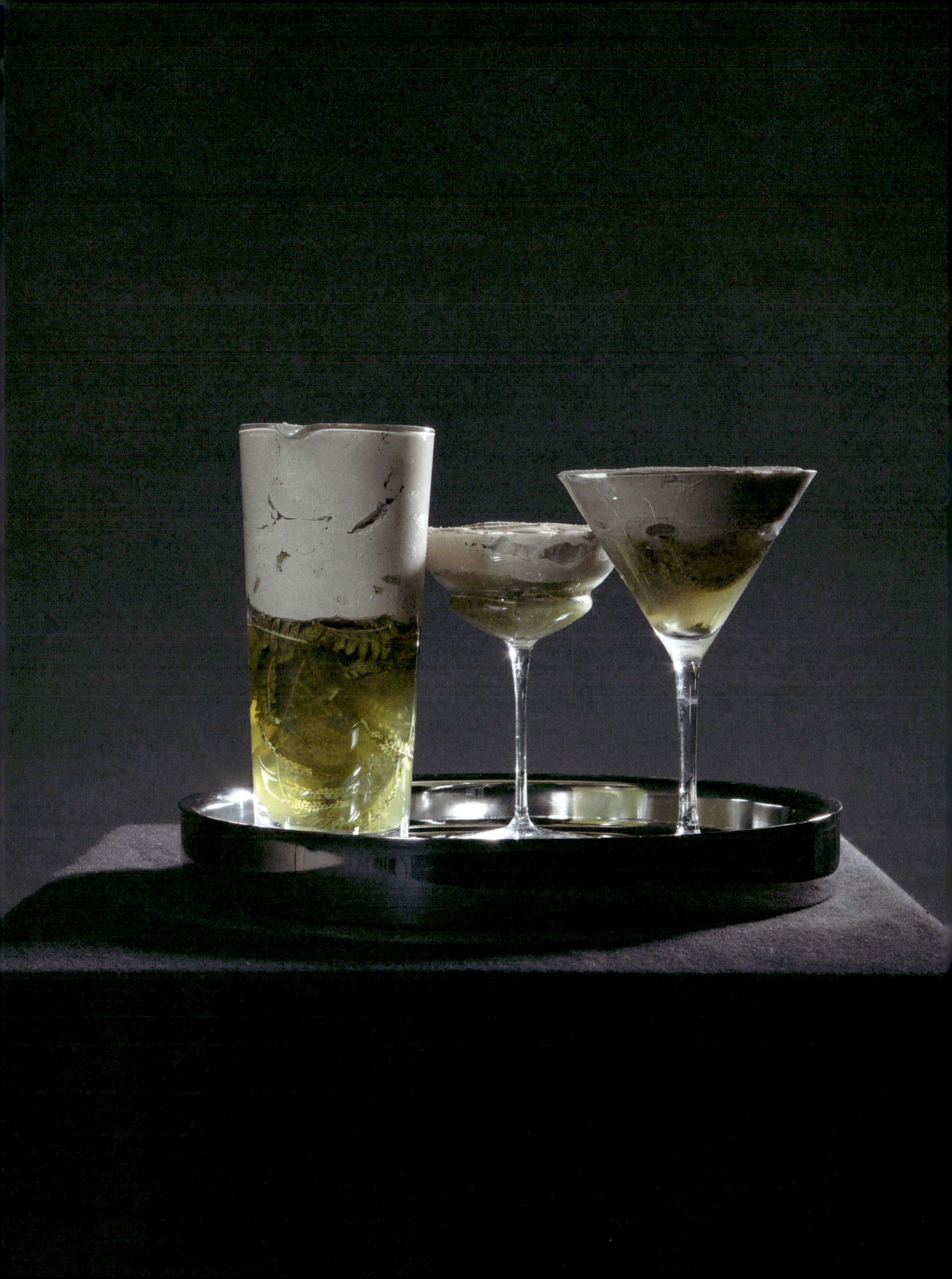

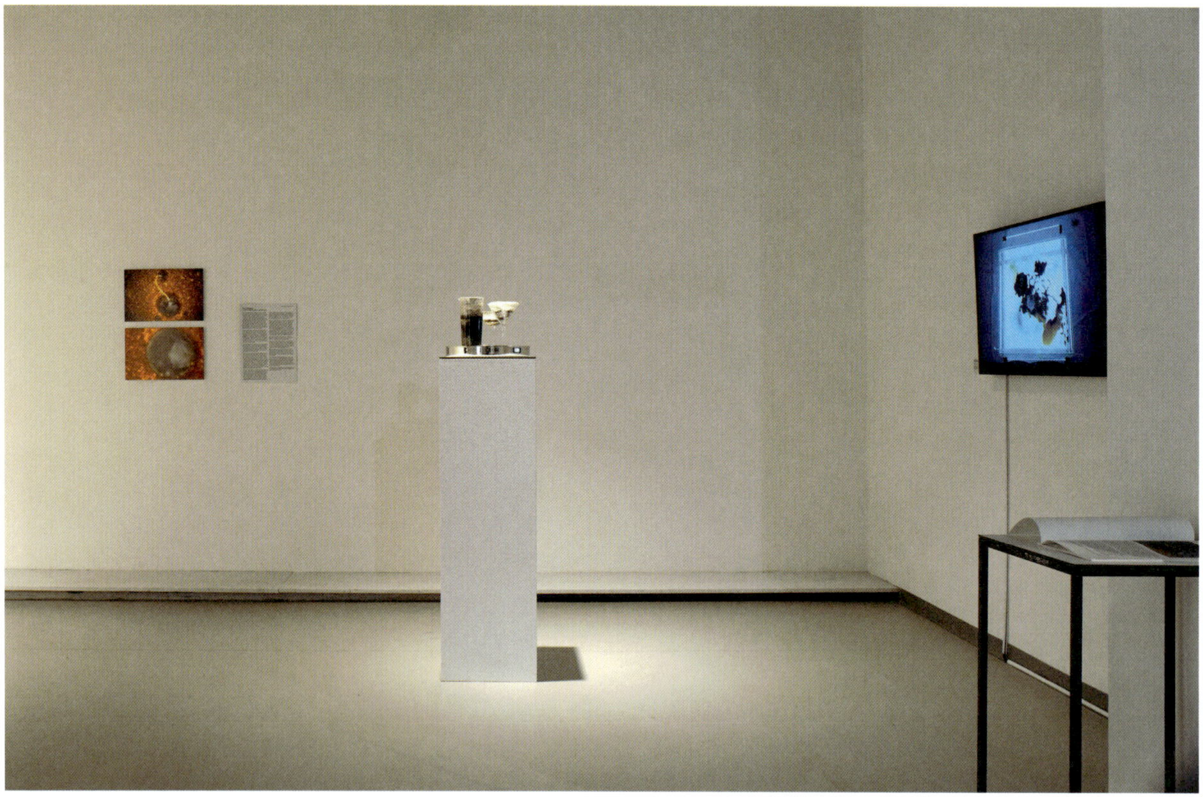

Reflecting Oil—Petroculture in Transformation exhibition view, AIL, 2024

The last element completing this room departs from the strictly speaking scientific side of the other accompanying contributions housed within. Yet this last artwork of the adjacent room presents a form of circularity in the process too, this time in Logar's journey with oil. In *Smashed*, pieces of a broken mirror lie pathetically on the ground. Instead of the traditionally used materials of glass and aluminum or silver, these pieces are actually made of bitumen—not simply covered with, but made of bitumen. The mirror theme is important of course in relation to the main title of the exhibition, but also has deeper roots. As part of an earlier project titled *Invisible Oil*—developed in and about the city of Aberdeen in Scotland to explore its links to the oil industry—Logar ended the 2008 exhibition of the same name held at the Peacock Visual Arts Centre in Aberdeen with one last artwork that consisted of a plexiglass box filled with oil. The artwork's title, *Reflecting Oil*, would eventually come to designate Logar's new research project developed from 2019 and culminating with the 2024 exhibition of the same name. In the 2008 artwork, despite the illusion of stillness of the mirroring surface, oil was continuously pumped and circulated through the box. It thus highlighted the importance of movement for the petroleum industry, as explained by specialist in film and visual culture Alejandra Rodríguez-Remedi:

"Millions of barrels are pumped through pipelines every day to make our lifestyles possible. Logar challenges us to discover how we see ourselves in a mirror which brings together the political, economic and social implications of this movement. [...] The notion of movement conveyed by 'Reflecting Oil' gives a distinctive dynamism to the entire exhibition, in the sense that all the processes Logar unveils depend upon it."[16]

With the 2008 artwork, Logar magnificently complicated oil's reflective properties. Avoiding any grand gesture that would only distance oil into a sublime landscape, the artist displayed the oil for visitors to probe the depths of their own entanglement with it. In this new 2024 exhibition, the artist goes even a step further, literally

Pages 136–137
Reflecting Oil—Petroculture in Transformation
exhibition view, AIL, 2024

Left
Enjoy, 2024
QR code, crude oil on paper,
mp4 video (42 sec)

Center above
Oil Soaked—Dubai, 2021
Experimental photography,
crude oil on glass filter

Center below
Untitled, 2024
Wood, bitumen, steel tub

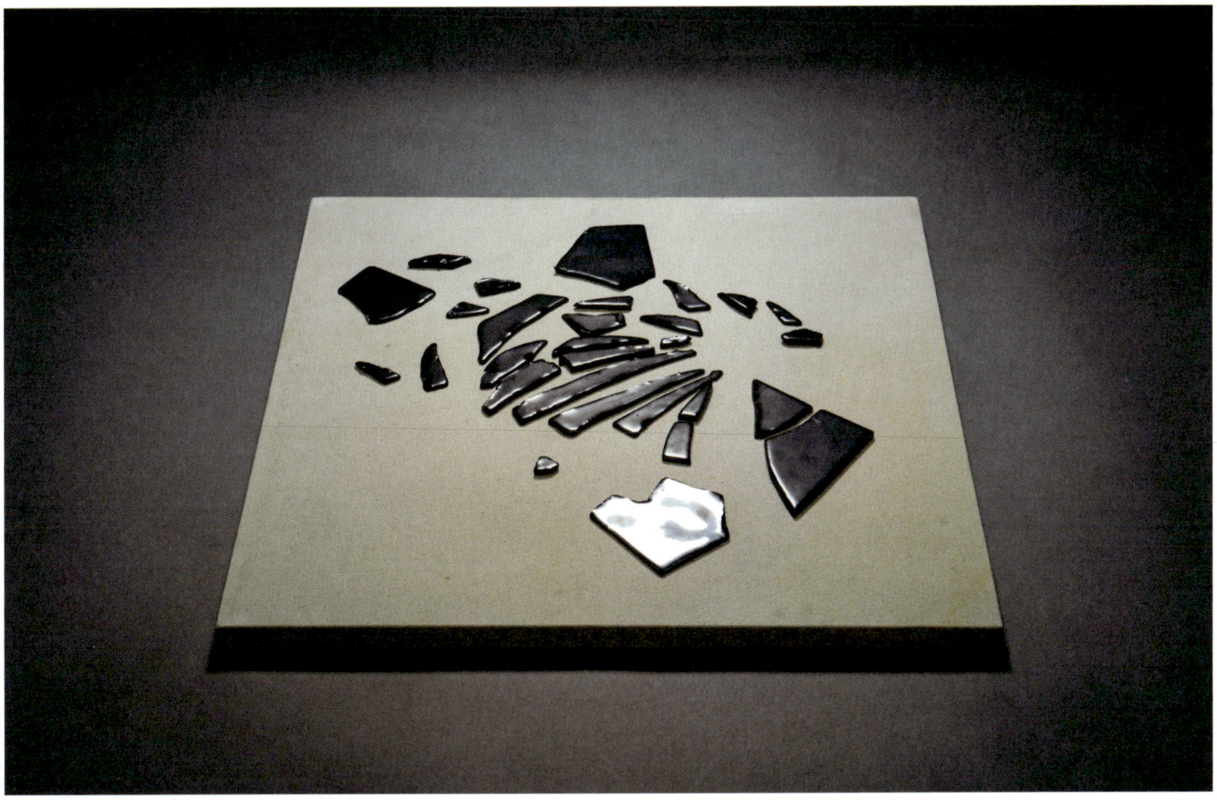

Smashed, 2024
Bitumen, sandstone

shattering the idea that we will know oil through a simple mirroring effect. The term "reflection" acquires a deeper, wider meaning that engages much more than just the visual sense. And so, with *Smashed*, the once-flowing oil is now congealed, like in millions of lives, commodities, infrastructures,[17] and plastics.[18] But strangely enough, presenting oil in this chemical state allows the artist to break the spell and finally crush the omnipotent substance.

Petromodernity, Which Way Out?

The truth however is that we can't get rid of oil that easily, not as long as the very essence of the principles orienting policies, the economy, politics, and everyday life continue to spring from oil's very own energetic and plastic properties.[19] And since there is no easy solution to this predicament, tangled as we are into this "Oleoviathan,"[20] then one way to start a profound reprogramming of dominant societies' use and abuse of oil could in fact be to come into closer contact with this omnipresent and omnipotent substance. This is why Logar's *Reflecting Oil* exhibition is a real *tour de force* because it builds an array of aesthetic experiences that gradually come to signify the petroleum phenomena as a whole, while simultaneously placing the spectator in an active role where each encounter with an artwork is reinforced and expanded by the next. The exhibition first succeeds in disclosing the extent of oil's hold on cultural frameworks, which in itself is no mean feat. For example, in an evocative inkjet print titled *Six oils—Beryl oil, Draugen oil, GA-086 oil, OMV-Gas condensate, RAG oil, Tordis Vigdis oil*, the artist has arranged the different color palette of six crude oils from around the world in an imitation of a military camouflage pattern. The print highlights how the petro-system connects geographies and military complexes, often under abstract modalities. But the artist grounds the oil economy in precise territories too. In a photograph called *Oil Soaked—Dubai*, a cityscape of the star city of the United Arab Emirates is textured and almost parasitized by bacteria- and cell-shaped forms as though seen through a microscope. The analog photograph is not photoshopped, and the artist

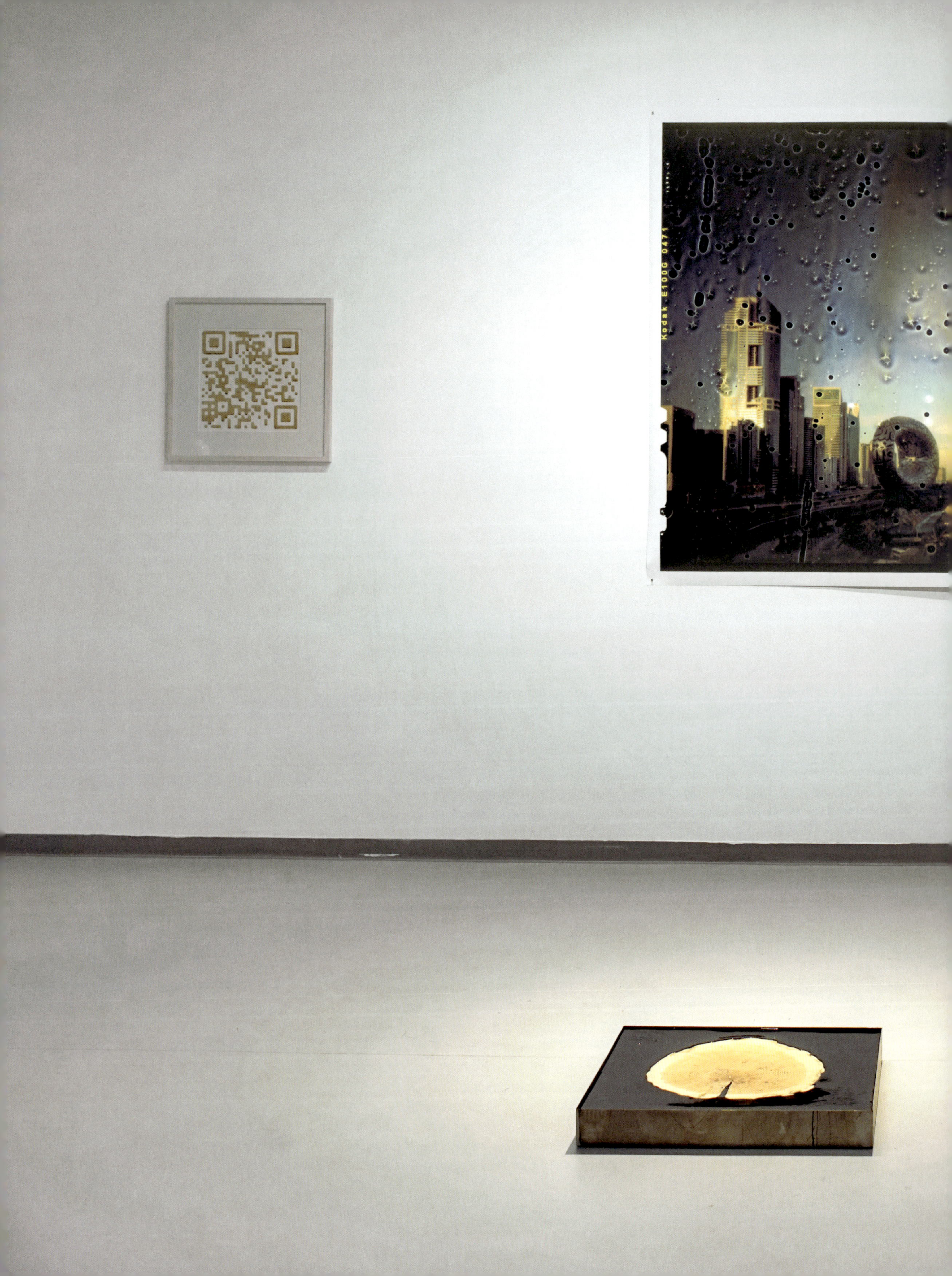
Kodak E100G 0471

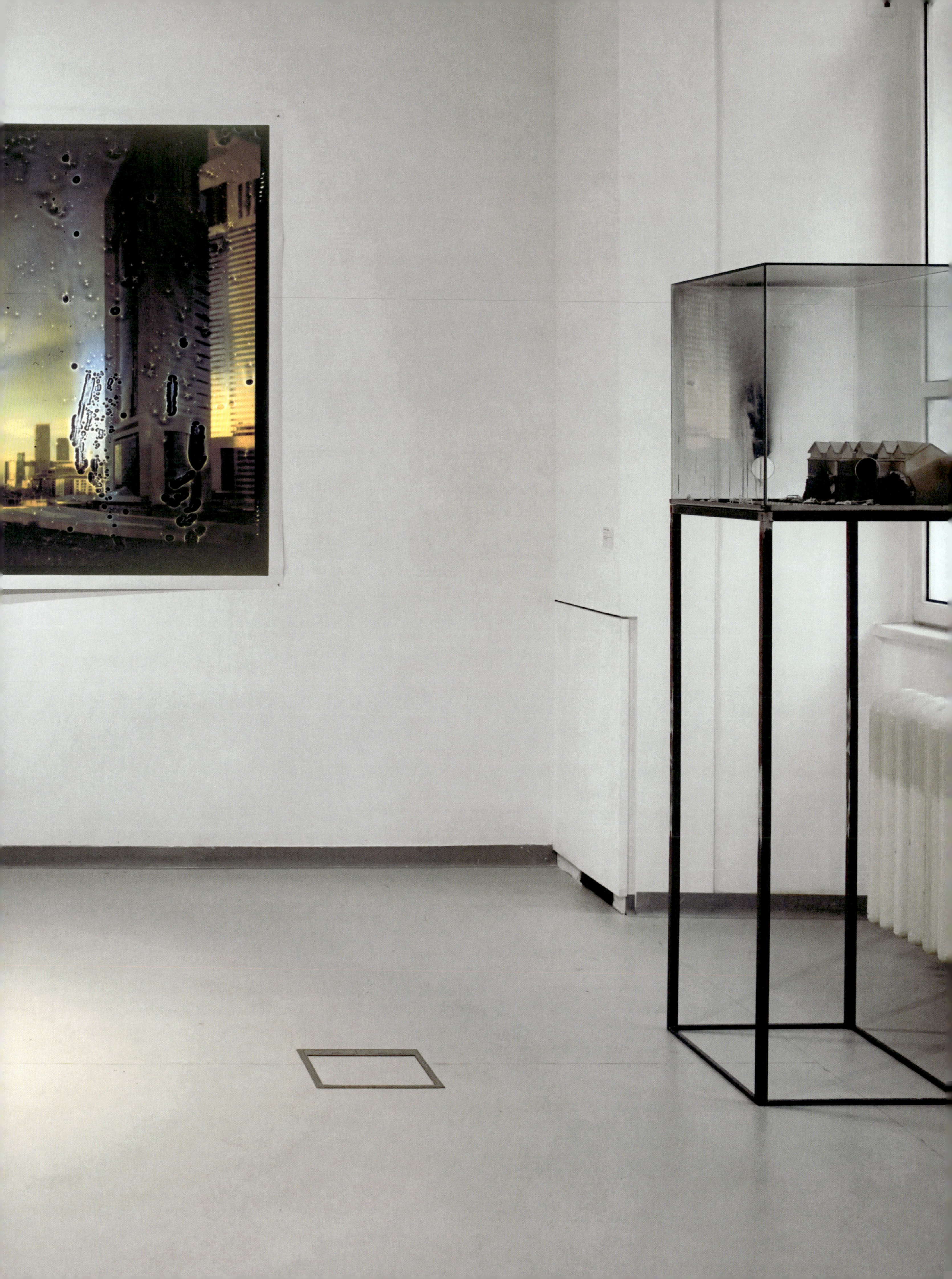

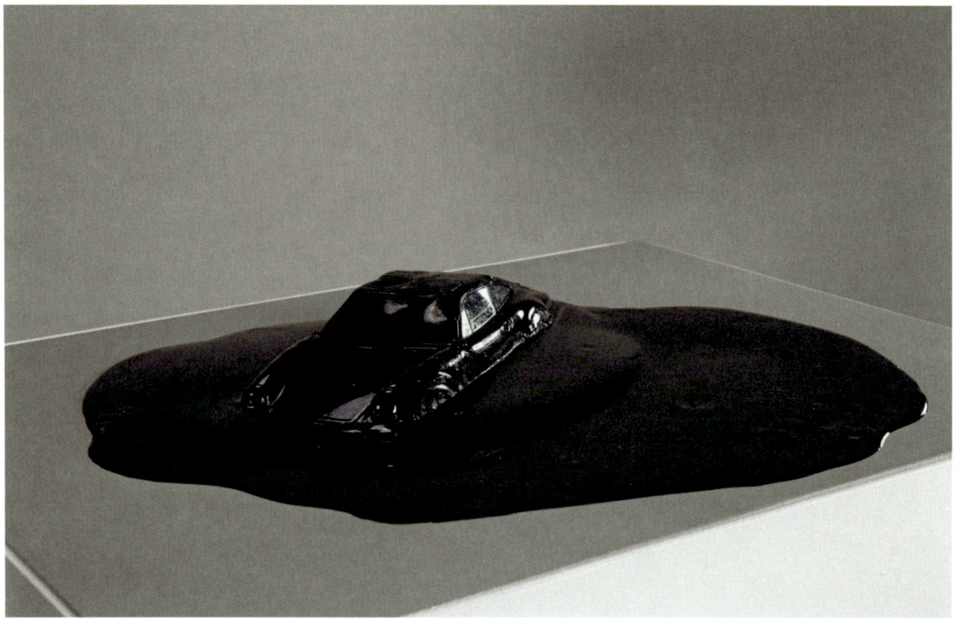

Melting away—Bitumen Porsche, 2024
Bitumen on anodized aluminum plate

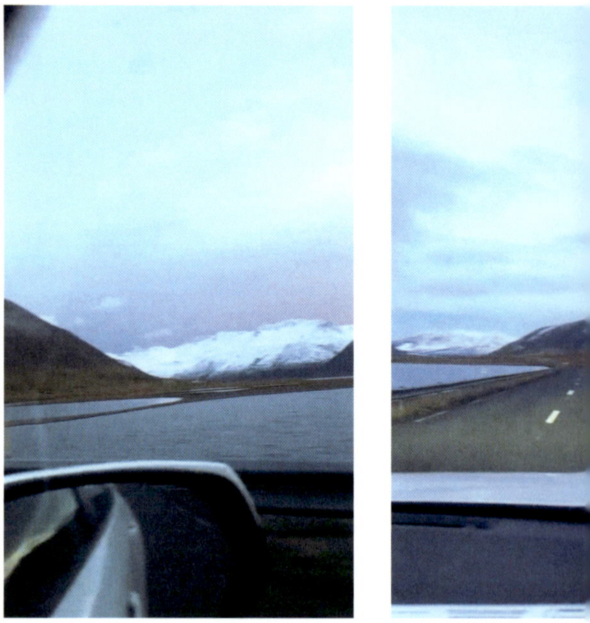

Enjoy, 2024
Videostills, *Iceland,* 2024, Margit Tesar
QR-code, Crude oil on paper, mp4 video (42 sec)

has used crude oil as an actual lens through which to look at this urban symbol of oil civilization.[21] Hanging on the wall in perfect symmetry on the other side of the exhibition space is another photograph, titled *Northfield—Aberdeen*, showing what at first glance looks like a harmless sculpture made of found objects on the beach, but which turns out to be an amalgam of plastic refuse that compose the distinctive silhouette of the oil rigs used for offshore drilling constellating the North Sea around Aberdeen. In both photographs, the very substance extracted helps materialize the community space built around oil extraction. Instead of distancing visitors from these places, these photographs highlight that "[...] we can and should ask how community is affectively and culturally produced in sites of oil production. Doing so might also foreground the social reproductive activities of extractive capitalist accumulation."[22] Though these two locations may appear distant for the public, the artist makes sure that exhibition visitors will still be involved in crude oil geographies. In *Enjoy*, visitors are made to scan a large-scale hand-made QR code painted with crude oil that leads to an online video displaying a tourist's recording of Iceland's landscapes through a moving car window. Tourism, global mobility, and the imminent witnessing of the consequences of global warming due in part to CO2 emissions, shown in the receding glaciers, are bound together with the energy consumption of our electronic devices. By obliging visitors to participate via activating the QR code, the artwork highlights how each of us reifies daily the fuel-based economy, albeit unknowingly or unconsciously.

"Resources are embedded in habits of mind as much as in earthly habitats,"[23] and it is this important constant dialogue, from extraction to consumption, lifestyles, and expectations that the exhibition foregrounds and interweaves. And so, how are we to radically transform these dominant mind frames concerning resources and crude oil in particular? In *Melting Away—Bitumen Porsche*, Logar chooses an interesting path of simultaneous creation and destruction. Instead of a real car trapped in asphalt like in another European fellow artist's practice,[24] Logar has first recreated a toy car in bitumen and subsequently melted it. The process is not so much a profanation of the substance as a playful experimentation with bitumen's plastic properties when heated. By modeling a car out of the substance on which it runs—this convenient, cheap, toxic road surfacing that quite literally greases the wheels of modern mobility—the sculpture reveals the concatenation

Pages 140–141
Burning Bedrock Experiment, 2024
Cardboard, plastic, crude oil, steel tub on steel pedestal, glass cover

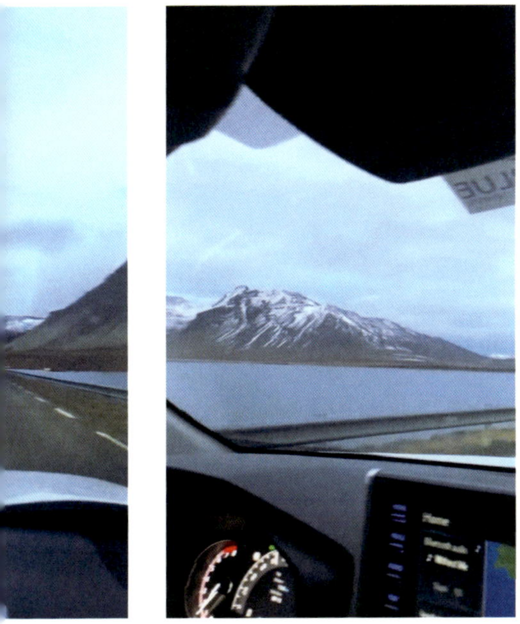

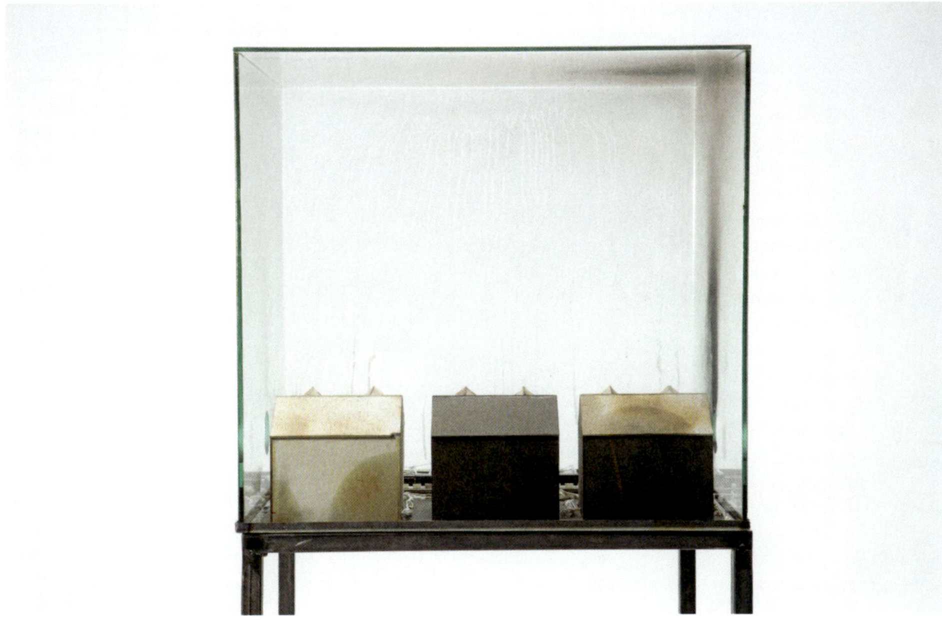

Burning Bedrock Experiment, 2024
Cardboard, plastic, crude oil, steel tub on steel pedestal, glass cover

between consumer choices and worldwide pollution and global warming. And the diminutive luxury car rightly points at the necessary transformation in the use and distribution of resources. The artist is thus preemptively “melting away” the absurd standards of wealth. In another artwork titled *Burning Bedrock Experiment,* the artist ignites another set of modern life standards and the “way of life” built on oil consumption.[25] This time, a suburban neighborhood—a miniaturized emblem of modern life *par excellence*—is challenged through oil’s flammable properties. The neighborhood architectural model is set in a glass box with two lateral holes, and the cardboard houses lie on a pool of crude oil. The artist has applied his knowledge of flash point parameters of samples of oil that he previously tested with the University of Leoben team, by heating the oil base which catches fire at a certain temperature. The result is a truly grim scene, as the houses are disfigured, and the small-scale plastic fences have melted and now resemble deformed skeletons. The title is meaningful, “bedrock” being a solid geologic formation, and seems to beg the question of what the bedrock of industrial-modern-capitalist civilizations is. Are we really sure we want crude oil, this hazardous substance, to keep being the foundation of social relations? By setting fire to the pool of oil onto which the suburban architecture lies, the artist burns down the precarious dreams embedded in petromodernity. The glass box creates a contained atmosphere where before our very eyes unfold the results of a “Western”-made, human-accelerated global warming and the consequences on Earth’s future climate. It is frightful.

Oil fuels a socio-economic system. It allows for social reproduction and social differentiation (who gets to travel, buy new clothes, go to university, procreate, work in finance or art history or politics or accounting, etc.). The entangled presence of crude oil is wired through every cell of our bodies, every fiber of our clothing, every wall of our homes, and every dream of our future lives. This all-encompassing yet often unacknowledged stranglehold is ripped open in *The Revised Game of Life*, a variant of a famous board game first created in the United States in the nineteenth century.[26] A jest about the normative progression that measures a “successful” life, the revised board game smartly incorporates counterpart consequences, in terms of oil extraction or pollution, for every daily activity. When these activities reach an energetic tipping point, a pump serves to inject crude oil directly on the gameboard itself (protected by a sheet of glass), de facto covering in oil the once oblivious

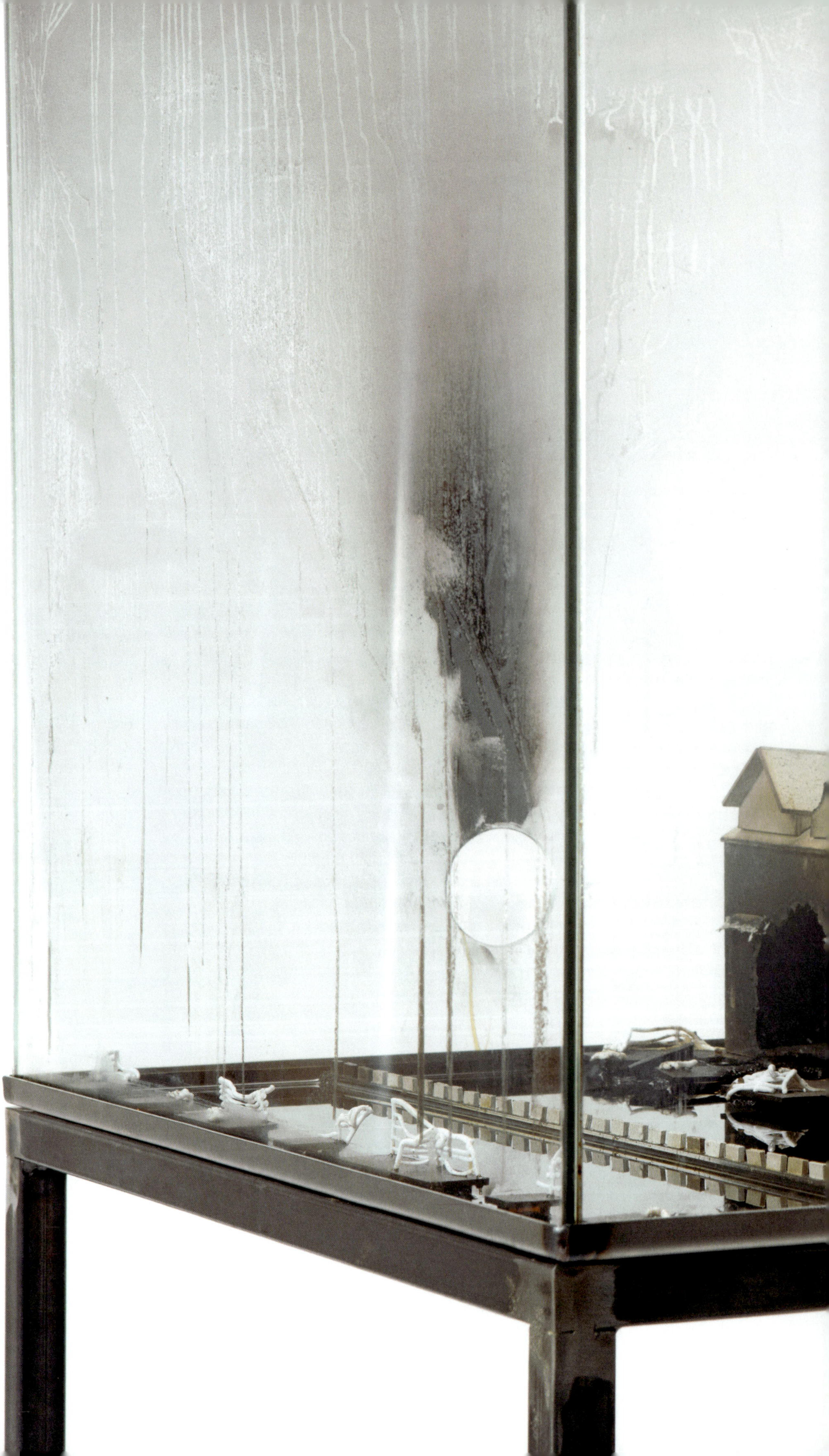

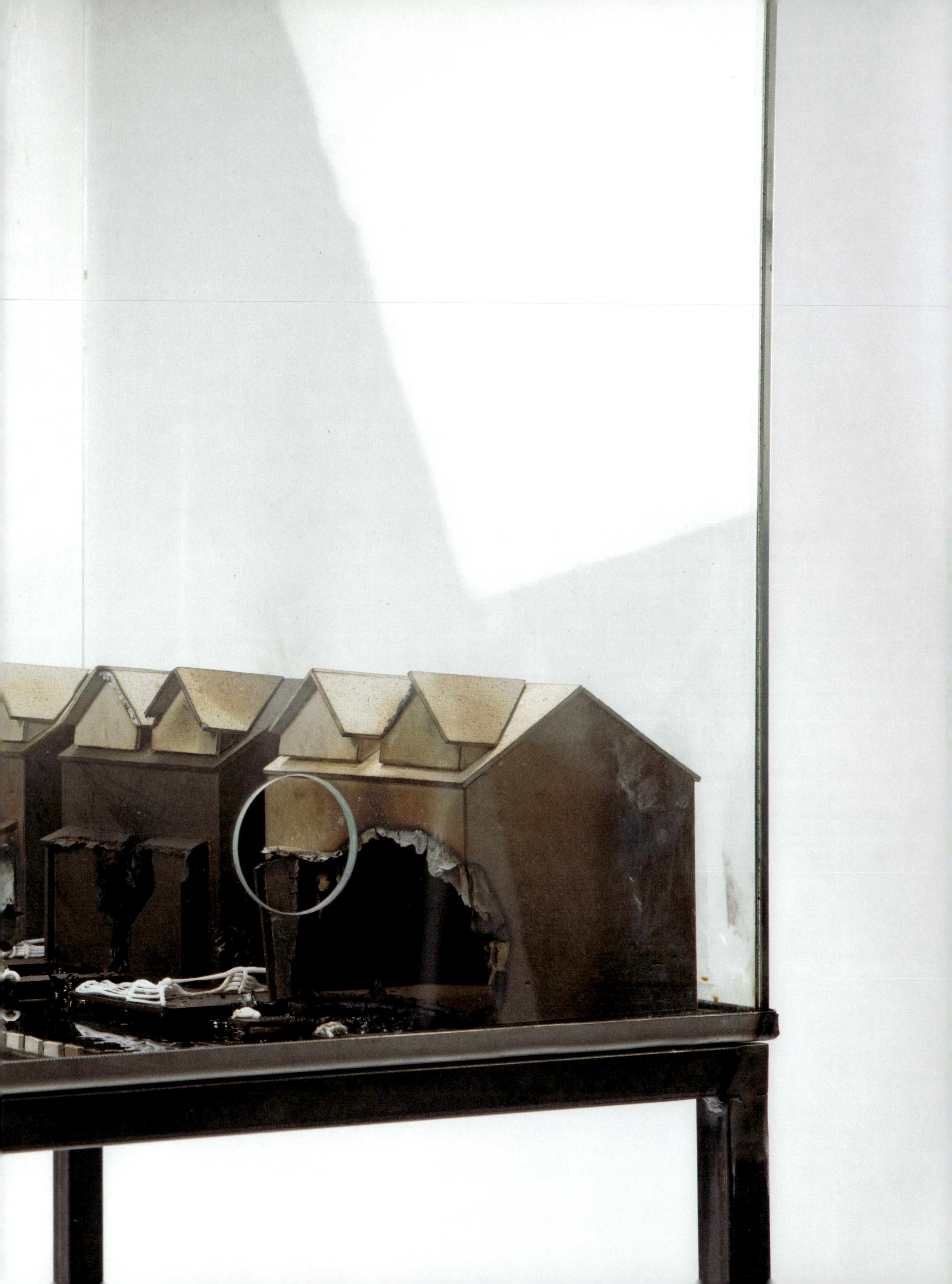

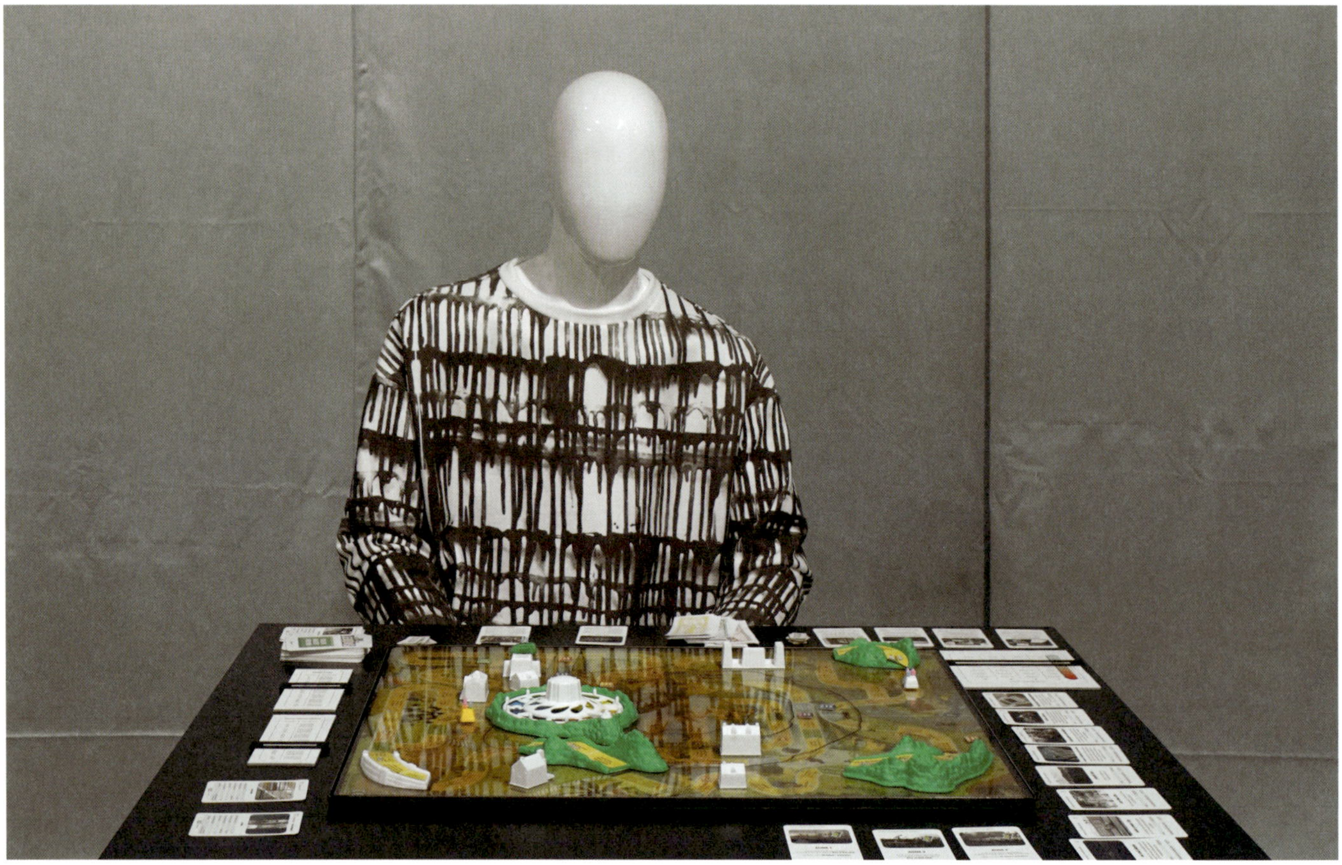

Ernst Logar and the *Reflecting Oil* team, *The Revised Game of Life*, 2024
Boardgame, steel pan, glass sheets, syringe pump, crude oil
Parasitic Pattern, 2024
Silkscreen print on cotton, dummy

and joyful life routes. The artwork is a truly brilliant way of interweaving individual and subjective experiences of modern life with the broader meaning of living in a society in which every step of life, from birth to death, is wrapped in oil. Presiding over the board game is *Parasitic Pattern*, a mannequin dressed in a sweatshirt and sweatpants displaying a crude oil printed pattern echoing the *Oil and Blood* window. In fact, the mannequin is facing this precise window at some distance, and the symmetrical placement between the two artworks reinforces the uncanny presence of the faceless mannequin with its clothes ominously "bleeding" oil. Even the most alluring perspectives of a sustainable transition seem improbable in view of the Western, energy-intensive way of life that *The Revised Game of Life* so judiciously displays. Alluding to this desired pathway out of oil is *Solarity*, an LED display of photovoltaic cells showing the word "solarity," more or less visible depending on the intensity of solar energy outside the exhibition space. A nod to the fragile promises of a sustainable transition out of the oil economy, the artwork sends but a flimsy image that questions what the alternative energy technology can actually achieve, echoing Andreas Malm's skeptical question on what the capitalist system is prepared or not to lose: "Can capital survive if fettered to the places and hours where the sun happens to shine and the wind to blow?"[27] Furthermore, inconspicuously placing the feeble word "solarity" in the *Reflecting Oil* exhibition hints at the dependence not yet overcome of renewable energies on fossil fuels. Capitalism is characterized by the interlocking of energy regimes, and "[a]fter two centuries of 'energy transitions', humanity has never burned so much oil and gas, so much coal and so much wood."[28] After all we have learned in the exhibition, one gets the clear picture that getting rid of oil won't happen magically. And do we really want to transition from one regime to the other without fully acknowledging the extent of some countries' and their industrial-financial groups' culpability in the climate crisis? As scholar Carolina G. Gonzalez sums up in her book chapter titled "The Sacrifice Zones of

Crude Oil Sculpture #1, 2021
Acrylic resin, crude oil

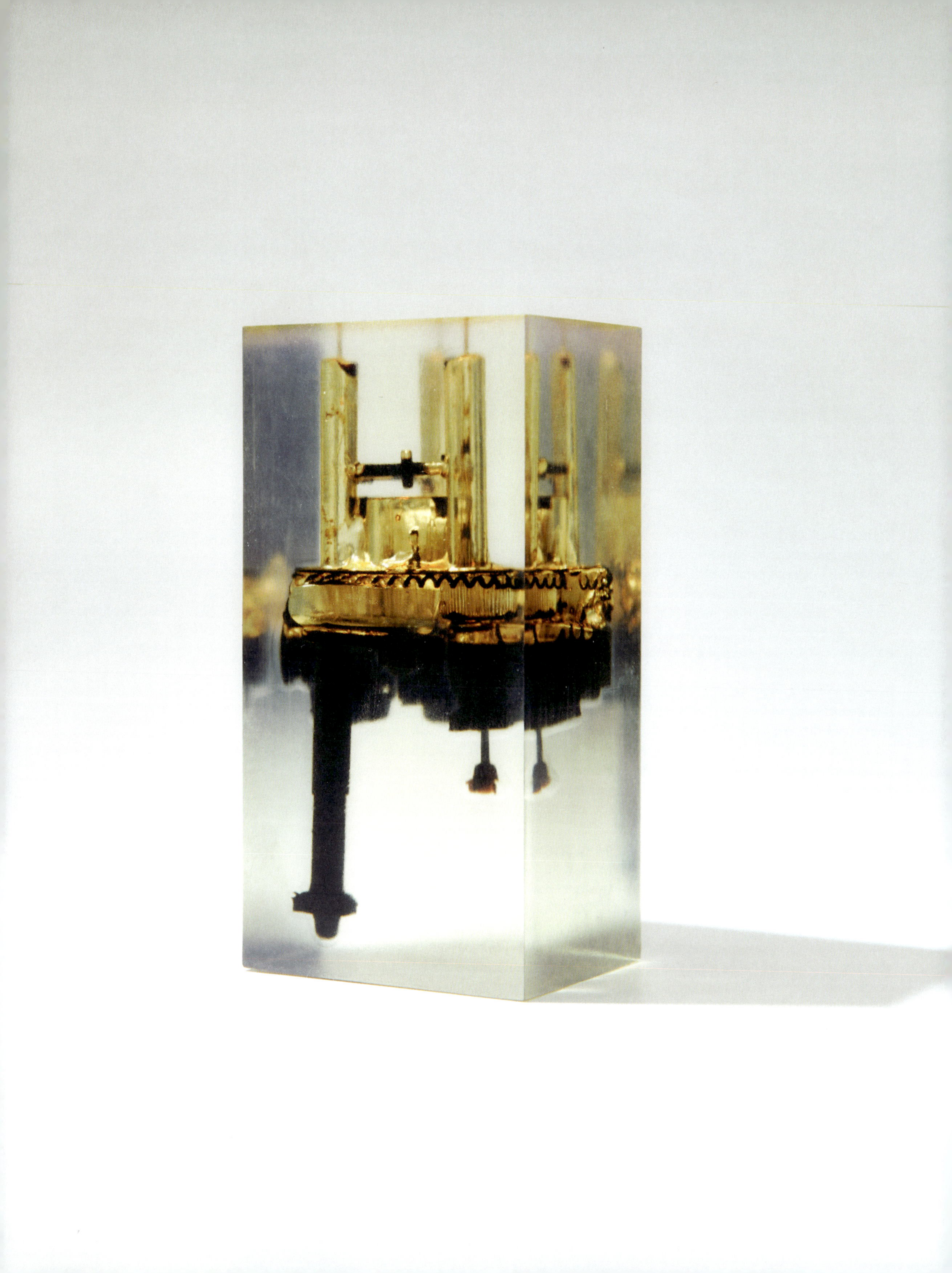

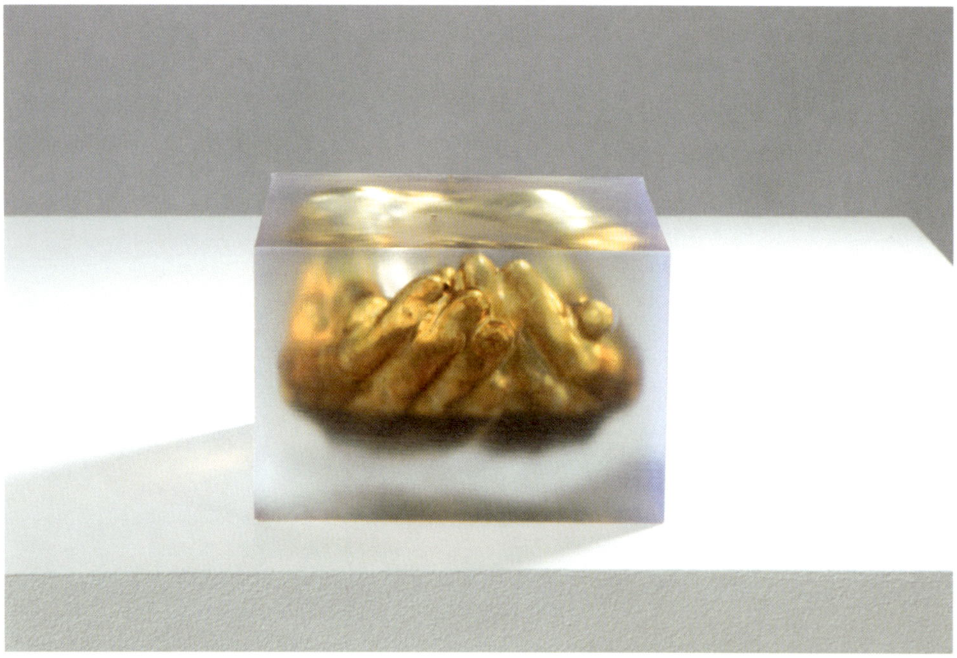
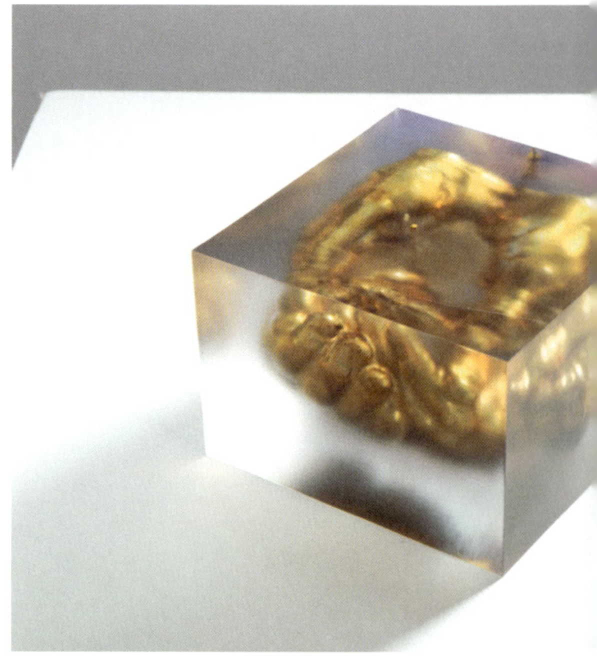

Holding Forming Structure, 2024
Acrylic resin, crude oil

Carbon Capitalism":[29] "The North's persistent evasion of its common but differentiated responsibility for loss and damage is breathtaking, but not surprising."[30] The specter of nuclear power, which seems as though it will inevitably accompany solar energy, looms on the horizon, as reminded by scholar Amanda Boetzkes to the audience of the panel discussion "Oil, Petroculture and the Transition out of the Oil Age."[31] But as is heavily apparent in the *Reflecting Oil* exhibition, we don't seem to be out of the petro-system just yet. So, how are we to frame the transition?

In a series of stunning acrylic resin sculptures, Ernst Logar ingeniously forges a compact rendition of petro-societies' ethos. Molded into oil rig shapes, these sculptures present what the artist calls a "negative space" that is filled with crude oil. In *Crude Oil Sculptures #1, #3, #4, #5,* the overall shape of offshore platforms for the drilling of oil is easily recognizable. But upon closer inspection, these oil rigs are composed of discarded pieces of trivial small objects: a blister pack voided of its pill, a plastic leg from a dismembered toy, plastic fusible beads, barrels of ballpoint pens, etc. Like in *Melting Away–Bitumen Porsche*, the rendition of a diminutive infrastructure is a way of grasping and appropriating oneself of the material reality of the drilling industry that is otherwise elusive precisely because it is gigantic. The minutia with which the shape of offshore oil rigs has been assembled by the artist is impressive. The lower part of the sculptures, corresponding to the drill below the sea level, is replete with oil. Designed around a void, the sculptures, when shaken, allow for oil to travel through all the pieces composing the overall shape of the oil rigs. Thus, both the submerged and unsubmerged parts of the sculptures communicate through oil. The higher parts of the sculptures, designed to recall the hoisting system and cranes, retain some traces of the dark substance, but still present a stark contrast with the lower parts drenched in oil. These sculptures are brilliant because of the compact manner in which, through oil and petroleum products, they render visible the autofueling cycle upon which capitalism is predicated. The way the artist has devised these miniature oil rigs around an empty space filled by crude oil is highly penetrating and seems to raise the question of what kind of space—physical and mental—is left by the petro-energy regime. If we go back to the exhibition theme, is the question of the mental reflection in a global socio-economic system dominated by oil necessarily reduced to this "negative

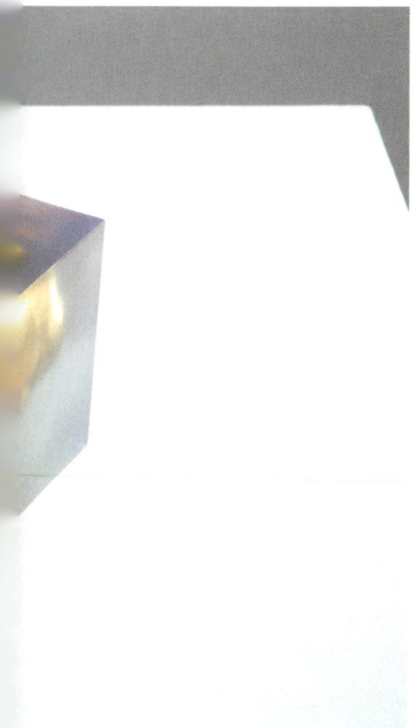

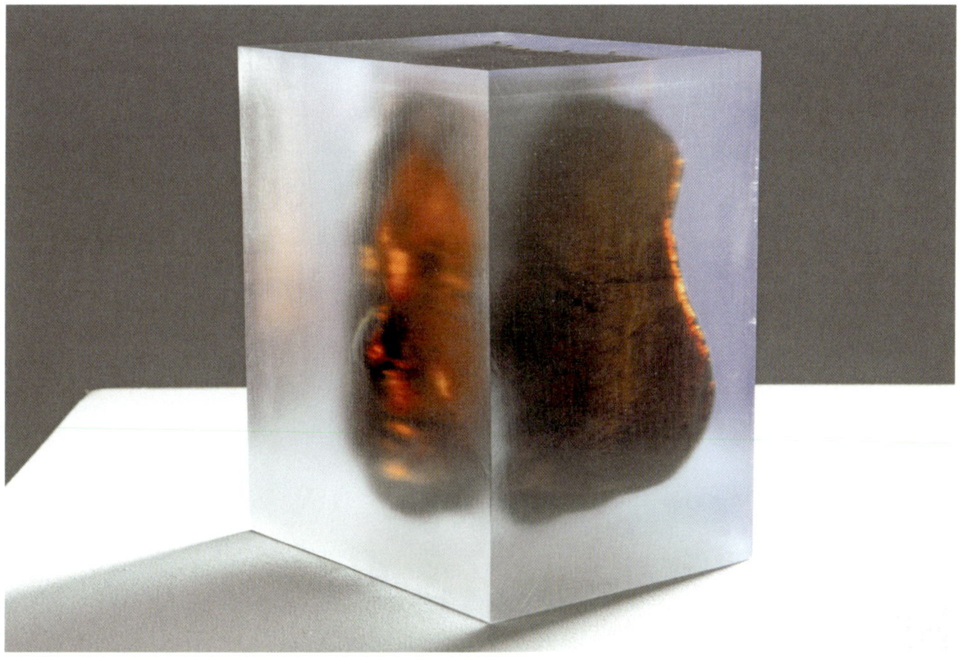

Formed Structure of Feelings, 2024
Acrylic resin, crude oil

space," a mental space that we just keep filling with oil without being able to extricate ourselves from it? What would dwelling in this "negative" space mean?

If the oil rig-shaped sculptures tapped into the essence of oil's iterative and expansionary cycle of extraction, consumption, amplification, and again extraction, two other acrylic resin sculptures using the same conformation of a "negative space" filled with crude oil present a valuable alternative experience of petroleum. In *Formed Structure of Feelings* and *Holding Forming Structure*, the sculptures are made from casts of the artist's head and the artist's hands respectively. That the artist fills his head with oil is yet another testimony, like the mixing of crude oil with his own blood, of his intense involvement with the substance over the last years. Close in visual aspect to a mortuary mask, the sculpture nonetheless conveys a lively and serene presence as the artist's features appear through the warm, coppery, and golden colors of the liquid. The artist's audaciousness in publicly acknowledging his own entanglement with the substance is inspiring. Presiding over the whole exhibition which highlights our own entanglements with petroleum, *Formed Structure of Feelings* is a mask that each of the visitors can feel they are wearing. Carrying on this responsibility of situating petroleum closer to each and every one of us is *Holding Forming Structure*. In this sculpture, ideally placed to be seen while entering as well as exiting the exhibition space, the artist's hands are placed so as to be holding a certain amount of crude oil in the palms. It is a provocative gesture, one that could easily be mistaken for an uncritical tribute to the power of this fossil substance. However, this sculpture is first and foremost a potent offering. The hands thus placed and thus filled condense the meaning of the extraordinary gift that the artist and each of the collaborators and participants of the *Reflecting Oil* project as a whole are offering to the spectators. By staging such a direct encounter with oil, Logar's artworks demand an unconditional willingness from visitors not only to engage with the substance instead of conveniently ignoring it, but also to admit their complicity in a fuel-based economy, thus sparking a serious reflection on how to step out into a truly different energy and cultural regime. Ultimately, and despite oil's many blessings, we will have to operate a physical separation from oil's multi-scalar materialities (consumer goods, fuels, chemical compounds, etc.) as well as an emotional detachment from the kind of life it made

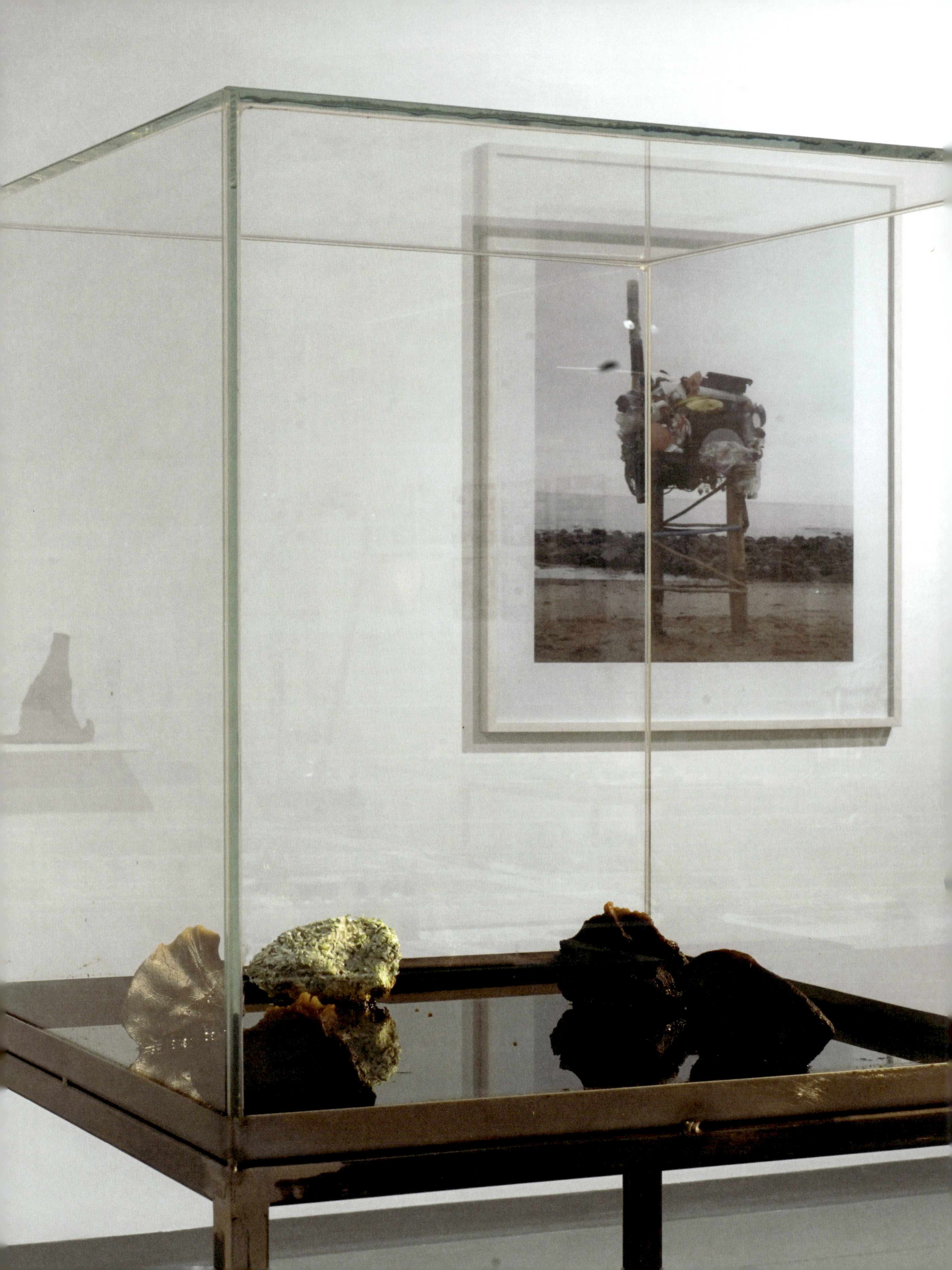

possible, however difficult it may be to relinquish. But as one needs solvents made of transformed crude oil (or other fossil fuels) in order to clean crude oil from the equipment used during scientific experiments, so one may paradoxically need more oil to end its reign over society, and it is meaningful to think that the way out of oil is maybe not simply away from it, but *closer* to it, at least temporarily.

One last sculpture ensemble by Ernst Logar, probably the most moving artwork of the show despite its unostentatious aspect, presents an honest picture of where to start this journey. In *The Space Between Us*, white and greenish shapes resembling bleached coral or even miniature glaciers seem to float on a sea of brownish-black crude oil. Set into a glass cube, the strange landscape provides a welcome distancing from the intense proximity displayed by some of the other artworks. More importantly, by zooming out, we get to see oil as part of an ecosystem. Are these shapes, all made of white plaster, except one made of pieces of shredded money, a reference to the coral reefs currently dying because of the rising temperature of the oceans? Or are they melting glaciers surrounded by a massive oil spill? Many interpretations are possible, and each is free to imagine what landscape they see. Over time, the porous materials of the white shapes absorb part of the surrounding crude oil by capillarity. The effect is quite dramatic, and by the end of the exhibition only the green shape made of shredded money has kept its original colors, while all the other white shapes have soaked in the oil and are now brown. The fact that only the money shape remains practically unaltered is quite telling. The nature of these shapes adds a further layer of significance, perhaps a more hopeful one: each of these forms is the molded space between a pair of shaking hands. The artist could easily have just used his own clenched fist to mold these shapes. But the fact that this artwork required different people, from different backgrounds, and with different relationships to oil, to come into close contact to create these shapes resembling natural entities is quite thought-provoking. A poignant metaphor for the impressive and inspiring dialogue held throughout the whole *Reflecting Oil* project between art and science, artists, and scientists, the “space between us” is this contaminated landscape from where to summon a common willingness to tear down the dominant energy consumption regime and the symbolic value system it helps sustain. It reflects how crude oil is composed of a myriad of identities to interact with, to understand, to challenge, and to bid farewell to; nay, to *fight* to be able to *collectively* and *ubiquitously* bid it farewell.

The Space Between Us, 2024
Hand spacings (plaster, shredded money), crude oil, steel tub on steel pedestal, glass cover

1 "We Thought It Was Oil, But It Was Blood" is the title of both a collection of poems published by Nigerian writer and activist Nnimmo Bassey in 2002, and of an online essay. See Nnimmo Bassey, "We Thought It Was Oil, But It Was Blood. Resistance to the Military-Corporate Wedlock in Nigeria and Beyond" (2016). In an interview with journalist Vanessa Baird about environmental activism, Bassey explains: "[...] I found that in the struggle it's essential to take some aspects of performance. [...] and so some of my poems are not just for people to read quietly, but for people to be part of the reading so that there are calls and responses; so, for example, when I say 'we thought it was oil' the audience responds 'but it was blood'." Vanessa Baird, and Nnimmo Bassey, "I've not got a nice one for fracking…" *New Internationalist*, n° 448 (2011), 39–40. I originally saw an excerpt of this interview in Philip Aghoghovwia, "The Poetics and Politics of Transnational Petro-Environmentalism in Nnimmo Bassey's 'We Thought It Was Oil but It Was Blood'," in *English in Africa* 41, n° 2 (2014), 62. Hence, the epigraph to this text is meant to be read with the performative and oral quality that Bassey describes, chanted between poet and crowd.

2 Rosemary Hennessy, *In the Company of Radical Women Writers* (University of Minnesota Press, 2023), 1.

3 Chorus from the lyrics of the song "Everybody Knows" released in 1988, co-written by Leonard Cohen and Sharon Robinson.

4 I would like to heartily thank Amanda Boetzkes for her companionship throughout this project.

5 A term coined by professor of English and Environmental studies Stephanie LeMenager in her book, *Living Oil: Petroleum Culture in the American Century* (Oxford University Press, 2014). For further exploration of this, see Imre Szeman, Jennifer Wenzel, and Patricia Yaeger, eds. *Fueling Culture: 101 Words for Energy and Environment* (Fordham University Press, 2017).

6 See of course Matthew T. Huber, *Lifeblood: Oil, Freedom, and the Forces of Capital* (University of Minnesota Press, 2013); or for an aesthetic approach to oil: Amanda Boetzkes and Andrew Pendakis, "Visions of Eternity: Plastic and the Ontology of Oil," in *eflux* 47 (2013). For other examples of quotes and different valences between petroleum and blood, see Alexander Klose and Benjamin Steininger, *Atlas of Petromodernity* (Punctum Books, 2024), 252.

7 For the relationship between oil and the unconscious, see Oxana Timofeeva, "Ultra-Black: Towards a Materialist Theory of Oil," in *eflux* 84 (2017).

8 Philip Aghoghovwia, "The Poetics and Politics of Transnational Petro-Environmentalism in Nnimmo Bassey's 'We Thought It Was Oil but It Was Blood'," (2016), 61.

9 Each type of crude oil presents at least a thousand different chemical compounds. See Sabine Rode, "Éléments de distillation continue," video, Université Numérique Ingénierie et Technologie, Fondation Maison des Sciences de l'Homme (2021).

10 Amanda Boetzkes and Andrew Pendakis, "Visions of Eternity: Plastic and the Ontology of Oil," in *eflux* 47 (2013),1.

11 Anthony Swift, "Tar Sands Tailings: Alberta's Growing Toxic Legacy," Natural Resources Defense Council of Canada, June 26, 2017, https://www.nrdc.org/bio/anthony-swift/tar-sands-tailings-albertas-growing-toxic-legacy.

12 For more on this and the porphyrin in blood and oil, see Oxana Timofeeva "Ultra-Black: Towards a Materialist Theory of Oil," 7, especially her take on Reza Negarestani's 2008 novel.

13 *Crude Capitalism* is the powerful title of Adam Hanieh's recent book. See Adam Hanieh, *Crude Capitalism: Oil, Corporate Power, and the Making of the World Market* (Verso Books, 2024).

14 The hula hoop exhibited in the show is reminiscent of the installation *Oil in Honey* that the artist presented during the *Reflecting Oil Colloquium* in 2022. Honey was circulated in a big transparent circular tube where crude oil was regularly injected. The artwork was presented during the performance *Spinning Melancholy,* co-created by Kat Válastur, Mia Lietke, Thomas Grill, and Ernst Logar. In the 2024 exhibition, a photograph of the event by Markus Ladstätter is exhibited close to the version of the hula hoop filled with honey and crude oil.

15 The photograph is by Mari Fraga, 2024.

16 Alejandra Rodríguez-Remedi, "Through a Glass, Darkly: Visualisation, Revelation and Reflection in Ernst Logar's *Invisible Oil*," in *Ernst Logar—Invisible Oil*, Ernst Logar, ed. (Springer, 2011), 65.

17 In this regard see Jeff Diamanti, *Climate and Capital in the Age of Petroleum: Locating Terminal Landscapes* (Bloomsbury Publishing, 2021).

18 See Amanda Boetzkes, *Plastic Capitalism. Contemporary Art and the Drive to Waste* (The MIT Press, 2019).

19 More about the creation of economics' and politics' principles based on oil's properties in Timothy Mitchell, *Carbon Democracy: Political Power in the Age of Oil* (Verso Books, 2011) and Diamanti, *Climate and Capital in the Age of Petroleum: Terminal Landscapes* (Bloomsbury Publishing, 2021).

20 Alexander Klose and Benjamin Steininger, *Atlas of Petromodernity* (Punctum Books, 2024), 113–119.

21 For more about the peculiar position of Dubai with respect to oil and climate change, see Aiora Zabala and Emilie Rutledge, "COP28: Inside the United Arab Emirates, the Oil Giant Hosting 2023 Climate Change Summit," in *The Conversation*, (November 27, 2023).

22 Sara Dorow, "Community," in *Fueling Culture: 101 Words for Energy and Environment*, Imre Szeman, Jennifer Wenzel, and Patricia Yaeger, eds. (Fordham University Press, 2017), 91–94.

23 Gavin Bridge, "The Resource Archipelago: Spatial Aesthetics and Resource Ecologies," in *World of Matter*, Inke Arns, ed. (Sternberg Press, Turtleback Books, 2015), 64.

24 See the work of German artist Albert Scopin titled *Dance, baby, dance,* in European Cultural Centre, ed., *Personal Structures—Reflections* (2022), 28–29.

25 For an analysis of the American "way of life" and oil, see Matthew T. Huber, *Lifeblood: Oil, Freedom, and the Forces of Capital* (University of Minnesota Press, 2013), 30.

26 For the complete story of this board game see Wikipedia Foundation, "Game of Life [The]," Wikipedia, https://en.wikipedia.org/wiki/The_Game_of_Life.

27 Andreas Malm, "Long Waves of Fossil Development," in Brent Ryan Bellamy and Jeff Diamanti, eds., *Materialism and the Critique of Energy* (Chicago: MCM', 2018), 183.

28 Jean-Baptiste Fressoz, *More and More and More: An All-Consuming History of Energy* (Allen Lane, 2024), 2.

29 The question of the "sacrifice zones" has most importantly been raised by Venezuelan artist Sattva Giacosa during the panel discussion "Oil, Petroculture and the Transition out of the Oil Age" organized on October 3 2024 as part of the program accompanying the exhibition. For more on the subject, I advise reading Ryan Juskus' article on sacrifice zones, especially for the notion of "counter-sacrifices": Ryan Juskus, "Sacrifice Zones: A Genealogy and Analysis of an Environmental Justice Concept," *Environmental Humanities* 15, n° 1 (2023): 3–24.

30 Carmen Gonzalez G., "The Sacrifice Zones of Carbon Capitalism: Race, Expendability, and Loss and Damage," in *Research Handbook on Climate Change Law and Loss & Damage*, Meinhard Doelle and Sara L, Seck, eds. (Edward Elgar Publishing, 2021), 19.

31 As part of the accompanying program of the exhibition, and held at the Angewandte Interdisciplinary Lab, Vienna, Austria, on October 3, 2024.

Biographies

Karez Abdulhameed is a master's student majoring in Drilling Engineering at the Department Geoenergy Engineering (formerly the Department of Petroleum Engineering) at the University of Leoben. She holds a bachelor's degree in Petroleum Engineering from the University of Kurdistan Hewlêr and is a member of the Society of Petroleum Engineers (SPE). She was vice president of the SPE Leoben in the year 2023/2024. She is currently working on the research project "Hydrogen transportation—compressor station modeling and market cost analysis." The project involves modeling hydrogen compressor stations and analyzing market costs to evaluate and enhance the economic feasibility of hydrogen distribution networks in Europe. Her project aims to aid the smooth transition from natural gas transportation to hydrogen transportation utilizing similar pathways with improvised technology.

Pit Arnold received his PhD in Reservoir Engineering at the University of Leoben. His research interests include the investigation of rock-fluid and fluid-fluid properties under varying conditions, microemulsion formation in the reservoir during Enhanced Oil Recovery (EOR) processes, analysis of microemulsions, and the investigation of displacement processes using CT scanning.

Amanda Boetzkes is Research Leadership Chair and Professor of Contemporary Art History and Theory at the University of Guelph, Canada. Her research focuses on the relationship between perception and representation, theories of consciousness, and ecology. She has analyzed complex human relationships with the environment through the lens of aesthetics, patterns of human waste, and the global energy economy. She is the author of *Plastic Capitalism: Contemporary Art and the Drive to Waste* (MIT Press, 2019), *The Ethics of Earth Art* (University of Minnesota Press, 2010), and a book titled *Ecologicity: Vision and the Planetarity of Art*. Edited books include *Artworks for Jellyfish* (Noxious Sector, 2022), *Heidegger and the Work of Art History* (Routledge, 2014), and a volume on *Art's Realism in the Post-Truth Era* (Edinburgh University Press, 2023). Her current project, At the Moraine, considers modes of visualizing environments, focusing on Indigenous territories of the circumpolar North.

Alexander Damianisch is a passionate educator, researcher, and advocate for art and research, dedicated to nurturing collaborative, innovative, and future-focused perspectives. Known internationally for his expertise in research funding and institutional development, he is dedicated to promoting transformative practices in both artistic and scientific inquiry. As the head of Support Art and Research and an executive board member of AIL (Angewandte Interdisciplinary Lab) at the University of Applied Arts Vienna, along with his role as a representative board member of ELIA (European League of Institutes of the Arts), he plays an essential role in advancing interdisciplinary research. Damianisch founded Zentrum Fokus Forschung (2014–24), co-initiated the Artistic Research PhD program, and was the first manager of Austria's PEEK program, which sets an international standard in arts-based research funding. Additionally, he has made meaningful contributions as a long-time executive board member of the Society for Artistic Research, where he continually champions fresh and innovative approaches to artistic and academic exploration.

Michael Duchêne received his PhD on cartilage collagen from the University of Munich, working at the Max Planck Institute of Biochemistry. He stayed on at the Gene Center Munich working on molecular studies of Pseudomonas aeruginosa membrane proteins. In 1989, he relocated to the Faculty of Medicine at the University of Vienna, that later became the Medical University of Vienna. Duchêne collaborated closely with allergy researchers, but his main focus were studies on the human protist parasite Entamoeba histolytica. He again turned his attention to antigenic structures such as the lipopeptidophosphoglycan (LPPG), a complex surface molecule. Other projects included research on the mode of action of the well-known anti-amoebic compound metronidazole and the search for alternatives. Duchêne's work was always centered around understanding pathogenic microorganisms. He officially retired at the end of 2024.

Mari Fraga is an artist and researcher working in various media, such as sculpture, photography, video, painting, and installations. She is a professor at the School of Fine Arts of the Federal University of Rio de Janeiro. Mari Fraga holds an arts-based PhD in Art and Contemporary Culture, with a visiting PhD at the Konstfack University of Arts, Crafts and Design in Sweden. She founded the journal *Revista Carbono* (www.revistacarbono.com), was a member of the Cooperativa de Mulheres Artistas, and head of the GAE Arte e Ecologias research group. Fraga investigates human agency in nature, the natural–artificial dichotomy, Anthropocene, climate change, fossil fuels, mining, and industrial land use. Her work proposes body–earth analogies, inspired by ecofeminism and from a Latin American perspective.

Michaela Geboltsberger is an art historian and curator specializing in contemporary art, society, and politics. She has managed numerous exhibitions and projects including tranzit.at, was part of the curatorial team of the Kyiv Biennale 2015, and co-curated the exhibition *Stopover—Ways of Temporary Exchange* in Vienna's Museumsquartier. She was also involved in several symposia, including "Things we suspect of each other!" at the Volkskundemuseum in Vienna and "Whose Europe?", an international conference that took place in Yerevan, Armenia, Belarus, Georgia, Ukraine, and the Republic of Moldova. She also led the project "The Empire Strikes Back? A Traveling Academy through the Post-Soviet Urban Landscape." She is a co-founder of several residency projects such as Solidarity Belarus and FOCUS International, which support international cultural practitioners. She was part of the management team of the Kyiv Biennale 2023 in Vienna and is currently managing director of IG Architektur.

Simone Gingrich is Professor in Environmental History at the Institute of Social Ecology, BOKU University, in Vienna, Austria. Trained as an ecologist (master's degree from the University of Vienna), she advanced into interdisciplinary sustainability sciences and environmental history (gaining a doctorate and habilitation in social ecology). Her research explores the historical dynamics of present sustainability challenges from land and resource use, particularly during industrialization processes. This includes, for example, reconstructing the climate impacts of agriculture, forestry, and energy use during the past centuries, by integrating historical statistical sources with environmental accounting and modeling. Increasingly, she also investigates the political dynamics that have shaped these socio-ecological changes. In 2018, she was awarded a European Research Council Starting Grant. She is a member of the Austrian Academy of Sciences' Young Academy.

Patrick Jasek is a PhD candidate in the field of Reservoir Engineering at the University of Leoben (Department Geoenergy), and is dedicated to advancing subsurface engineering, focusing on energy storage, geo-methanogenesis, and geothermal energy recovery. Employing experimental and numerical methodologies, his research focuses on porous media flow phenomena on the pore- and continuum scale. In collaboration with his research team, he pioneers screening methods to discern critical subsurface parameters crucial for ensuring the safe and reliable operation of energy recovery and storage processes in porous reservoirs.

Kinga Kiełczyńska lives and works in Warsaw. She studied Spanish philology at Warsaw University before graduating in fine arts from the Gerrit Rietveld Academy and the Sandberg Institute in Amsterdam. Through her multidisciplinary practice, she reflects on the relationship between humans and the environment. Her mediums include video, text, drawing, and installation. She calls her works "environments" to underline the works and physical extension into their context and modes of production. Kiełczyńska frequently shows her works outside of the gallery setting—at a nudist beach, a nightclub, a forest. She has created several pieces centered around the Białowieża primeval forest, a UNESCO World Heritage Site in Poland. Her work has been shown at Exile Gallery, Berlin and Vienna; Manifesta 12, Palermo; MoCAB, Belgrade; WWB/MOMA, Warsaw; Mediamatic, Amsterdam; Aether, Sofia; SAVVY, Berlin; FOAM, Amsterdam; and De Appel, Amsterdam, among others.

Jordan B. Kinder is assistant professor in the Department of Communication Studies at Wilfrid Laurier University where he studies and teaches on the cultural politics of energy, media, infrastructure, and environment. He previously held postdoctoral fellowships at McGill and Harvard universities. He is a citizen of the Métis Nation of Alberta.

Ernst Logar (*1965 in Klagenfurt, Austria) is an artist and cultural worker, active in the fields of photography, film, video, sound, sculpture, and installation. In addition to international exhibition activities and interdisciplinary collaborations with various experts and institutions, Logar realizes projects in public spaces and site-specific works that tackle prevailing power relations as well as contemporary historical, sociocultural, ecological, and socio-political phenomena. His works have been presented in the Austrian Parliament, at the scenes of Nazi crimes, and other locations relevant to his artistic engagement. Logar is active in local cultural politics and is currently a research assistant and lecturer at the University of Applied Arts Vienna.

David Misch holds a doctoral degree from the University of Leoben, where he also obtained his habilitation in geology. He worked as an invited postdoctoral fellow at RWTH Aachen University and was awarded the Walther E. Petraschek and Hans Höfer von Heimhalt prizes of the Austrian Academy of Sciences (ÖAW) and Austrian Geographical Society (ÖGG), respectively, for his early career research in sedimentology. He was appointed Professor of Energy Geosciences at the University of Leoben in 2023 and currently heads the Chair of Energy Geosciences as well as the Department of Applied Geosciences and Geophysics.

Andrei Molodkin was born in Boui, Moscow, in 1966. His artistic practice is recognized as a leading example of Political Minimalism, due to the formal approach that he takes to material, working almost exclusively with human blood, crude oil, steel, and biro. Molodkin's projects have been censored throughout his career, from the Venice Biennale in 2009, where he represented his country in the Russian Pavilion, to his 2021 piece *White House Filled with the Blood of US Citizens* that was deemed too dangerous to show and was pulled from its intended location due to political tensions in the lead up to the insurrection in Washington D.C. Recently, he made international headlines with *Dead Man's Switch* which saw him hold over $45m worth of artworks hostage in exchange for the life of Julian Assange. His large-scale installations are held in distinguished museum collections with *Liquid Modernity*, 2009, entering the Tate Collection, UK, in 2012. Molodkin has exhibited world-wide.

Arianna Mondin is an architect and PhD candidate, her research and production focuses on the relationship between oil, architecture, and power. She is currently in charge of educational projects and spaces at The Foundry art institution in France. Mondin has lectured in universities and institutions and curated workshops for university and PhD students. She participated in research groups including the PRIN (Research Projects of National Interest) and SYLVA—Rethink *selva:* Towards a new alliance between biology and artificiality, nature and society, wilderness and humanity, in the research unit of the University of Genova. Mondin was a member of the editorial staff of *Vesper. Rivista di Architettura, Arti e Teoria | Journal of Architecture, Arts and Theory* at the Iuav University of Venice. She has participated in international conferences and published articles and book contributions.

Johannes Novak received his PhD in medicinal and aromatic plants after studying agricultural sciences at the University of Natural Resources and Life Science, (BOKU) Vienna. He has been employed at the University of Veterinary Medicine since receiving his PhD, where he leads the Functional Plant Compound working group. His scientific work has always placed a particular emphasis on the chemicals that give fragrant herbs their distinct scents.

Raphaelle Occhietti is an art historian. She is currently a postdoctoral fellow at the University of Guelph, Canada, and was a guest researcher in 2023–24 at the Amsterdam School for Cultural Analysis (ASCA) at the University of Amsterdam, the Netherlands. Her postdoctoral research has been funded by the Fonds de Recherche du Québec—Société et Culture, and is now funded by the Social Sciences and Humanities Research Council of Canada. She recently co-edited a special issue of *La Furia Umana—International Journal of the History and Theory of Cinema* on Donna Haraway's *Staying with the Trouble: Making Kin in the Chthulucene*. Her recent writing has appeared in *Espace Art Actuel*, *Senza Cornice*, and *Afterimage: Journal of Media Arts and Cultural Criticism*. Her current book project explores contemporary art's ability to represent and confront the capitalist socio-ecological system.

George Osodi is a Nigerian photographer from Ogwashi-Uku, Delta State. He studied business administration at the Yaba College of Technology, Lagos. He worked as a photojournalist with *Comet Newspaper* in Lagos from 1999 to 2001 before joining the Associated Press News Agency in Lagos from 2001 to 2008. His photographs range between photojournalism and artistic documentary, covering topics from contemporary Nigerian monarchs to injustices in the Niger Delta over its natural resources. George Osodi was awarded first prize at the Fuji Africa Photojournalist of the Year Award in 2004 and was shortlisted for the Sony World Photography Award in 2009. He has exhibited at Newark Museum, New Jersey, in 2015; The Photographers' Gallery, London, in 2012; the Stedelijk Museum, Amsterdam, in 2010; National Museum of Contemporary Art, Oslo, in 2009; and Documenta 12, Kassel, in 2007.

Olaf Osten is a German artist and graphic designer. His work deals with issues of nature, identity, and movement based on drawing and has been presented in numerous international exhibitions. His works are part of collections such as the International Peace Institute, New York/Manama; Wien Museum, Vienna; Complexity Science Hub, Vienna; and the Austrian Chamber of Labor. He studied graphic design at the University of Applied Sciences and Arts, Hildesheim, and the Institute of Art, Design and Technology, Dublin. Olaf Osten has carried out many interdisciplinary projects in culture and science with Viennese partners such as the Impulstanz Festival, Wiener Festwochen, and Mumok.

Holger Ott studied physics in Stuttgart and Berlin and received his PhD in 2004 from the Free University of Berlin with a focus on solid state physics. Before joining the Exploration and Production (E&P) industry in 2006, he was a fellow and postdoctoral researcher at the University of Tokyo, Japan, in 2002, and the University of Cologne, Germany, in 2004–06. From 2006, Holger Ott worked as a Senior Scientist and Project Manager at Shell Global Solutions International B.V. in the Netherlands, including as scientific lead in the field of geological CO2 storage. During this time, Holger Ott taught as an honorary reader at Imperial College London and completed his habilitation in applied geosciences at RWTH Aachen University in Germany in 2015. In 2016, Holger Ott was appointed to the University of Leoben. He holds the Chair of Reservoir Engineering and is currently head of the Department Geoenergy. His main research interests are decarbonization of fossil fuels, negative emission technologies, and geological energy storage.

Ulrike Payerhofer studied art history and cultural management in Vienna. After heading a contemporary art gallery for seven years, she joined the University of Applied Arts Vienna as a curator and senior artist on the interdisciplinary project UniNEtZ (Universities and Sustainable Development Goals). The focus of her curatorial practice and research is on multidisciplinary collaborations and participatory methods at the intersection of arts, science, and society. Payerhofer is currently establishing the platform Projektwerkstatt (2022–24) for transdisciplinary collaborations on sustainability, which she will head from a curatorial perspective.

Cleo Reece is Cree and a Fort McMurray #468 First Nation member. She received a Bachelor of General Studies: Education and Environmental Studies from Simon Fraser University, Vancouver. Reece has worked as an adult educator for Keyano College and Northland School Division, Fort McMurray, and has been involved in Cree language revitalization and oral history. In 2011, she was elected as a councilor for the Fort McMurray First Nation and served for three years. She has been on the Traditional Knowledge Steering Committee for the Mackenzie River Basin Board as the Indigenous member for Alberta from 2013 to 2017. As the founding director of the Keepers of the Athabasca Watershed Society (today Keepers of the Water), she is currently the co-chair and involved in their many activities. In addition, she is an elder advisor on the Aramat project which brings together a team on a six-year project with focus on global biodiversity and the health and well-being of Indigenous people led by the University of Alberta and Indigenous partners.

Alejandra Rodríguez-Remedi obtained a Masters of Education at the University of Concepción, Chile, where she gained experience of holistic methodological approaches on several educational research projects. Relocating to the UK, she completed the funded doctoral project "The arts as means of cultural integration: A Chilean case study" at Gray's School of Art in Scotland. She collaborated with Ernst Logar in 2008, when he was researching the Scottish oil industry, and she has contributed to *Reflecting Oil* as a proposal writer and researcher since 2017. She is a lecturer in Film and Visual Culture at the University of Aberdeen and her research focuses on arts-based approaches to petroculture and the poetics of filmmaker Raúl Ruiz. In 2024, she designed an honors degree course entitled Art and Oil: Crude in Film and Visual Culture and ran an interdisciplinary workshop called Creative Approaches to the Energy Crisis that brought together diverse stakeholders in imaginative discussions about Aberdeen, Europe's "energy capital."

Johannes Schmidt is an associate professor in energy and resource economics at BOKU University in Vienna. He develops integrated models of energy systems with high shares of renewables focusing in particular on integrating climate and land-use perspectives into his work. Using this approach, he aims at understanding the techno-economic robustness of renewable energy systems considering climate variability, but he is also interested in land-use conflicts that are emerging due to the expansion of renewables. Geographically, he focuses on Europe and Brazil to explore the different perspectives on the renewable energy transition in the Global North and the Global South, in particular related to conflicts over land.

Iris Stappen has been an assistant professor at the Department of Pharmaceutical Sciences at the University of Vienna (Faculty of Life Sciences) since 2009. She studied pharmacy at the University of Vienna and, after qualifying as a registered pharmacist in Vienna, did her doctorate in Pharmaceutical Chemistry in 1997 followed by a postdoctoral stay at Stanford University, California, USA, in the Department of Psychology, Cognitive and Affective Neuroscience. She is currently a member of the Clinical Pharmacy Group in the Division of Pharmaceutical Chemistry. Her research interests include the biological activity of essential oils and single oil components; psychophysiological and behavioral studies in humans; gender-aspect in aromatherapy/olfaction; ADME of mono- and sesquiterpenes; and GC/MS analyses of human blood and urine samples. She has been a board member of the Austrian Society for Scientific Aromatherapy and Aroma Care (ÖGwA) since 2010 and a member of the editorial board of the Journal of Essential Oil Research since 2023.

Herwig Steiner (HST) is a video and media artist and musician. The artist HST lives and works in Vienna, Lower Austria, and Carinthia, splitting his time equally between them. He develops, designs, and realizes projects at the interfaces of non-specific media. Steiner studied visual media design at the University of Applied Arts Vienna under the guidance of professors Peter Weibel, Thomas Fürstner, and Karel Dudesek and was later a longstanding assistant at the same school after graduating. HST operates from a studio and atelier located in a monastery in Lower Austria. Previously, he was a guest artist at the Haus der künstlerischen Begegnung (House of Artistic Encounters) in Villach St. Martin. A professional media worker, HST has been part of countless international collaborative projects as well as music and video productions featured in the music charts. In 2023, HST founded the artist duo yell:0 with his alter ego Martin Dueller.

Benjamin Steininger is a cultural and media theorist, historian of science, and curator. He works as a postdoctoral researcher at the UniSysCat Cluster of Excellence at the Technical University Berlin and the Max Planck Institute for Geoanthropology, Jena. From 2012 to 2016, Benjamin Steininger headed a research and collection project on 100 years of oil and gas in the Vienna Basin. In 2016, he co-founded the research collective Beauty of Oil (beauty-of-oil.org) with Alexander Klose. They write the book *Erdöl. Ein Atlas der Petromoderne* (Oil. An Atlas of Petromodernity) (Berlin, 2020) and curated the exhibition *Oil. Beauty and Horror in the Petrol Age* at the Kunstmuseum Wolfsburg (2021–22, German/English book with the same title edited with Andreas Beitin in 2021). In 2022, *Petro-Melancholie. Das Erdölzeitalter im Spiegel der Kunst* (Petro-Melancholia. The petroleum age in the mirror of art), a film by Matthias Frick about their project, was broadcast on Arte. In 2024, *Atlas of Petromodernity* (Santa Barbara, 2024) was published, the updated and enlarged American version of their book with an introduction by Stephanie LeMenager.

Janet Stewart is currently Executive Dean of the Faculty of Arts and Humanities at Durham University. She joined Durham in 2014 from the University of Aberdeen as Professor of German and Visual Culture. She was the founding director of the Centre for Visual Arts and Culture and part of the team that successfully bid to establish a Leverhulme Doctoral Training Centre for Visual Culture in Durham. She also served as head of the School of Modern Languages and Cultures from 2015 to 2018. She holds an MA and a PhD from the University of Glasgow. Stewart is the author of two monographs, *Fashioning Vienna* and *Public Speaking in the City*. Her current research project develops her interests in modernity and visual culture in relation to energy, oil, memory, and sight.

Imre Szeman is the Director of the Institute for Environment, Conservation and Sustainability and Professor of Human Geography at the University of Toronto Scarborough. He is co-founder of the Petrocultures Research Group, which explores the socio-cultural dimensions of energy use and its implications for energy transition and climate change, and the founder of the After Oil Collective. Szeman is author (most recently) of *On Petrocultures: Globalization, Culture, and Energy* (West Virginia University Press, 2019) and *Futures of the Sun: The Struggle Over Renewable Life* (University of Minnesota Press, 2024). *Keywords for a New Politics of Energy* (co-edited with Jennifer Wenzel) will be published in 2025. He is a Fellow of the Royal Society of Canada.

Herwig Turk's projects probe the interconnectivity of the fields of art, technology, and science. Since 2016 he has been conducting artistic research on the Tagliamento River in Northern Italy and other river systems, like the Danube or the rivers close to Bolzano, cooperating with artists and scientists. For many years, a central topic in his work has been the landscape as an anthropocentric laboratory and as a mirror of the Western economy, technology, and culture. In the last years, his work has been shown at venues such as the MAK, Vienna; LENTOS, Linz; MMKK, Klagenfurt; Seoul Museum of Art; Neues Museum Weserburg in Bremen; Museum Sinclair Haus in Bad Homburg; Lungomare in Bolzano; Listasafn Árnesinga (LÁ Art Museum), Iceland; gallery rauminhalt_harald bichler in Vienna; Gallery Georg Kargl in Vienna; and Transmediale in Berlin, among others. From 2014–22 he worked as Senior Artist at the Department of Social Design at the University of Applied Arts, Vienna.

Imprint

Ernst Logar (ed.)

This publication is a result of the FWF—PEEK project *Reflecting Oil: Arts-Based Research on Oil Transitionings* (2019–2024), led by Ernst Logar.

The following events were organized as part of the project's research activities: *Reflecting Oil Colloquium* at the University of Applied Arts Vienna (June 9–12, 2022) and the *Reflecting Oil—Petroculture in Transformation* exhibition at the Angewandte Interdisciplinary Lab (AIL), A-Vienna (October 3–November 15, 2024).
www.reflectingoil.info

This research was funded in whole by the Austrian Science Fund (FWF) [10.55776/AR547]. For open access purposes, the author has applied a CC BY public copyright license to any author accepted manuscript version arising from this submission.

Printed with kind support of Divison IV—Arts and Cultures of the Republic of Austria's Federal Ministry of the Arts, Culture, the Civil Service and Sport; as well as Bildrecht; City of Vienna Department of Cultural Affairs (MA7); Land Kärnten Kunst und Kultur, and the Otto Mauer Fonds.

Project Management
Roswitha Janowski-Fritsch—"Edition Angewandte" on behalf of the University of Applied Arts Vienna
Publication assistance
Iseult Grandjean

Translation
Christine Schöffler & Peter Blankeney
Copyediting/proofreading
Charlotte Maconochie
Graphic design
Leopold Šikoronja
Cover
Ernst Logar, *Oil Soaked Dubai*, 2021
Introduction photography
Ernst Logar, *Oil and Honey*, 2024, 1.
Ernst Logar, *Oil and Blood*, 2024, 2.
Photography
Holger Ott 19, 20.
Ernst Logar, digital photography lab—University of Applied Arts Vienna 17, 123, 133, 135, 138, 139, 140-141, 143, 144, 145.
Markus Ladstätter 60, 61.
Johannes Puch 87.
Andrea Siegl 79, 103, 118-119.
All other photographs by Ernst Logar.
Printing
Gerin Druck GmbH, Wolkersdorf

Library of Congress Control Number
2025935156
Bibliographic information published by the German National Library
The German National Library lists this publication in the Deutsche Nationalbibliografie; detailed bibliographic data are available on the Internet at http://dnb.dnb.de.

ISSN 1866-248X
ISBN 978-3-68924-253-4
e-ISBN (PDF) 978-3-68924-046-2 Open Access
DOI: https://doi.org/10.1515/9783689240462

published by Walter de Gruyter GmbH, Berlin/Boston, Genthiner Straße 13, 10785 Berlin.

www.degruyter.com
Questions about General Product Safety Regulation productsafety@degruyterbrill.com

The book is published open access at www.degruyter.com.

FWF Österreichischer Wissenschaftsfonds
LAND KÄRNTEN Kultur
di:'ʌngewʌndtə
dge DEPARTMENT GEO ENERGY
Bildrecht
Federal Ministry Republic of Austria Arts, Culture, Civil Service and Sport
Stadt Wien Kultur
Otto Mauer Fonds
PETRO CULTURES
FSC www.fsc.org MIX Papier | Fördert gute Waldnutzung FSC® C108696